The Manufacture of Scottish History

Edited by Ian Donnachie
and Christopher Whatley

Polygon
EDINBURGH

© Polygon 1992

Published by Polygon
22 George Square
Edinburgh

Set in Linotron Sabon by
Koinonia, Bury and printed
and bound in Great Britain by
Redwood Press Limited,
Melksham, Wiltshire

British Library Cataloguing In Publication Data
The Manufacture of Scottish History – (Determinations)
    I. Donnachie, Ian, 1944 –   II. Whatley, Christopher A.
    III. Series
    941.1

ISBN 0 7486 6120 4

The Publisher acknowledges subsidy from the
Scottish Arts Council towards the publication
of this volume.

Contents

Series Preface

CAIRNS CRAIG

Scotland's history is often presented as punctuated by disasters which overwhelm the nation, break its continuity and produce a fragmented culture. Many felt that 1979 and the failure of the Devolution Referendum represented such a disaster: that the energetic culture of the 1960s and 1970s would wither into the silence of a political wasteland in which Scotland would be no more than a barely distinguishable province of the United Kingdom.

Instead the 1980s proved to be one of the most productive and creative decades in Scotland this century – as though the energy that had failed to be harnessed by the politicians flowed into other channels. In literature, in thought, in history, creative and scholarly work went hand in hand to redraw the map of Scotland's past and realign the perspectives of its future.

In place of the few standard conceptions of Scotland's identity that had often been in the past the tokens of thought about the country's culture, a new and vigorous debate was opened up about the nature of Scottish experience, about the real social and economic structures of the nation, and about the ways in which the Scottish situation related to that of other similar cultures throughout the world.

It is from our determination to maintain a continuous forum for such debate that *Determinations* takes its title. The series will provide a context for sustained dialogue about culture and politics in Scotland, and about those international issues which directly affect Scottish experience.

Too often, in Scotland, a particular way of seeing our culture, of representing ourselves, has come to dominate our perceptions because it has gone unchallenged – worse, unexamined. The vitality of the culture should be measured by the intensity of debate which it generates rather than the security of ideas on which it rests, and should be measured by the extent to which creative, philosophical, theologicial, critical and political ideas confront each other.

If the determinations which shape our experience are to come from within rather than from without, they have to be explored and evaluated and acted upon. Each volume in this series will seek to be a contribution to that *self*-determination; and each volume, we trust, will require a response, contributing in turn to the on-going dynamic that is Scotland's culture.

Acknowledgements

The editors would like to thank Cairns Craig for encouraging this enterprise, the contributors for their respective chapters, and Marion Sinclair and Kathryn MacLean of Polygon for their assistance.

They express their gratitude to Anne Grieve of the Open University in Scotland for her efforts in typing and recasting much of the manuscript and to Mr H. A. Whatley for kindly preparing the index.

1

Introduction

THE EDITORS

Scotland's history is important. It gives us as individuals and as members of Scottish society a vital sense of where we are and how we got here. History could be said to set the context for a clearer understanding of the present, helping explain the contemporary scene – political, social, economic, and cultural. Such a fundamental justification for the study of Scotland's history – or that of any other nation – can stand on its own merits. But historical study (either learning or simply reading) brings more than understanding, for it develops a whole range of critical skills in the analysis of sources, complex problem solving, and communication. History is no longer the dry, dusty subject it all too often was. Interdisciplinary approaches of the kind developed by The Open University are increasingly common. New questions are being asked, and new methods call for the latest in information technology – in addition to the subject's longstanding reliance on the resources of archives and libraries.

It is certainly the case that the scholarship of the past three decades has done much to modify our views of Scotland's past, if not rewrite much of its previous history. Many of the myths surrounding Scotland's past have been revisited and in some instances utterly debunked. The prime objective of this symposium is to examine how Scotland's history has been treated, how some of the myths and received wisdom have evolved, and to show how Scottish history is now being largely rewritten.

Our task in this introduction is three-fold. Firstly, we hope to convey to the reader something of the excitement of the subject today, second, we look briefly at the development of Scottish history and historiography and attempt to explain how they evolved before the recent renaissance in Scottish historical studies, and third, we will aim to set the context for the essays that follow, bearing in mind that the contributors were asked to address themselves to specific questions.

In the past, Scottish history was often perceived (not without justification) as being rather dull and parochial, and in the schools as not being respectable or challenging enough for serious study. Scotland's universities in the nineteenth century taught history ineffectively, and it has been argued that any Scottish tradition of historical writing disappeared in 1793 with the death of Principal William Robertson at Edinburgh. By the end of the Victorian era a clear 'agenda' in Scottish history – usually heavily political in thrust – had been set and was followed by a stream of impressive, but to modern eyes, somewhat uninspiring textbooks. Fairly typical of the genre was P. Hume Brown's *History of Scotland* (1911), later shortened and in print until the 1960s, with chapters embracing such topics as 'William & Mary', 'Scotland on the Eve of Union', 'Anne 1702–14', 'The Rising of 1715', 'The Argathelians', 'The Squadrone 1719–45', 'Religion and Social Progress', 'George III', and 'The Disruption of 1843'. Although the quality of scholarship was high, and the book is still well worth reading, the tone throughout was assured, whiggish, patronizing, and principally concerned with high politics, Jacobitism and church history. Social history degenerated into a series of scrapings from the kailyard, as in Dean Ramsay's *Reminiscences of Scottish Life and Character*, of which the first of many editions appeared in 1857. History became gossip for Ramsay, who believed that the characteristic peculiarities of our Scottish people are indicated in a very marked manner by our Scottish anecdotes.

Criticism, however, must be tempered by the fact that historians operate within the intellectual climate of their own times. An example is to be seen in Michael Fry's essay in this collection, which identifies the ideological forces that caused Scottish history to end either with The '45 or the Disruption. Earlier practitioners did not always have access to primary sources which are readily available to the present generation. Potentially rich resources were often widely dispersed in baronial halls, or lawyers' chambers, or otherwise neglected. Although they could readily have access to material published by societies like the Bannatyne and Maitland Clubs, previous generations were drawing on a more restricted range of sources which are now commonplace. Nevertheless, far too few historians in the past seemed aware that 'All perception is selection', as A. J. Youngson observed in *The Prince and the Pretender: A Study in The Writing of History* (1985). The tone of much older Scottish history (as well as some of the new) is uncomfortably certain and too assured to be true.

Youngson brilliantly reminds us that even the producers of the raw evidence upon which all history is ultimately based – the letter writers, diarists, social observers, and so on – selected what they chose to see and record. But in addition, says Youngson, 'in the manufacture of history a second process of selection takes place... this time in the mind of the historian.' In a book which professional historians and their readers would do well to keep by their elbow, Youngson stresses the part played by the historian's subjectivity. The historian selects, and prefers one interpretation of the evidence to another. He selects and prefers, 'so as to produce a version of events which he himself finds believable and agreeable in the sense that it accords with his view of human nature and of how things are apt to happen.' Readers should know their historian. Significantly, Scottish history until the 1950s or 60s was generally, but not exclusively, the province of (mainly) men who if not upper class in background were upper class in outlook.

This book reveals how much approaches have changed in the relatively recent past – mainly but not exclusively since the 1950s. The contributors attempt to show that the subject is alive, as new evidence is examined and new, often imported, concepts and methods are applied. There was some resistance from historians at first however, and in 1968 one senior Scottish historian proudly proclaimed that his work was free from 'apocalyptic "models" or sweeping sociological generalizations.' Few others have been as uncompromising in their attitude to methodological change. Scottish history has emerged from its parochial rut and is trickling into the mainstream of historiographical development elsewhere. Comparative studies, seen for example in the work of T. M. Devine, R. A. Houston and I. D. Whyte, are beginning to set Scotland in a wider European context. Houston's own work on literacy (1985), although not universally acclaimed, has at least punctured the long standing and unqualified assumption that Scots of all ranks were better educated than their English neighbours. Quite properly though, the best of those Scottish historians who have adopted explicitly theoretical approaches and other new analytic tools, have done so cautiously, reluctant to abandon their firm foothold within the empirical historical tradition.

One big problem which faces those presently in the engine room of the manufacture of Scottish history is that while much new work has been done, especially in the universities, little of this has percolated through to the wider public. New findings in learned journals, disparate collections of essays, and expensive monographs often go unnoticed and are, in effect, inaccessible. In spite of the efforts of the Sunday Mail and its attractively produced *Story of Scotland* (1988) too little of the great output of Scottish historians in recent years has been widely disseminated. Listening to the speeches of Scottish politicians, reading the columns of respected journalists, and letters to the editors of newspapers, or in conversation, it is clear that there is little recognition that Scottish history is in the process of being remade. Until recently, one of the Scottish political parties was still claiming that James Watt invented the steam engine. Necessarily selectively, this volume tries to show how a range of aspects of Scottish history have been interpreted, and in what ways views have changed over time.

Treatment of the Union of 1707 is a case in point. Victorian historians were confident of its causes and consequences. As far as the Scots were concerned, it was primarily economic, and beneficial; indeed it transformed Scotland. It was also judged to have been an act of great political wisdom and foresight. This is how it was viewed as recently as 1963 by G. S. Pryde, Professor of Scottish History at Glasgow University, who wrote, 'for its own day, grounded on common sense and reached through fair and open bargaining, [it] was one of the most statesmanlike transactions recorded in our history.'

During the later 1960s older certainties were swept away by the critical and radical revision of W. Ferguson (1977), who also dismissed T. C. Smout's then freshly substantiated claims (1963) that the Union was in large part economically inspired. Since then various writers have entered the fray, but all have veered towards the political-corruption interpretation. Some have even denied economic influence, I. B. Cowan (1981b) being one such writer. The economy is now back on the agenda, but from a different perspective, illustrating the importance of new perceptions of old evidence. Private economic interests, often in the guise of national interests, were carefully looked after, as C. A. Whatley (1989) has shown. Today the whole thing looks very unstatesmanlike and its direct beneficial effects appear much less certain. Scots who nowadays search for the legitimacy of their cause by referring back to 1707, and certainly if they are of a unionist persuasion, are skating on rapidly melting ice.

As the case of the Union shows, economic (and social) history is playing an increasingly important part in the process of the manufacture of Scottish history. The evolution of economic and social history in Scotland, however, is much longer term than might be imagined given the volume of work which has appeared since the 1960s. Among the much quoted pioneers were some distinguished historians, including Dr. Isabel F. Grant, one of the few women; Henry Hamilton, Professor of Political Economy at Aberdeen University; and the redoubtable W. H. Marwick of Edinburgh University.

Grant wrote about the social history of the Highlands and also produced a pioneering and much-read social and economic history of Scotland. Hamilton was the first to look at the impact of industrialization on Scotland and he followed this many years later with an important and influential study of Scottish economic history in the eighteenth century, which considered agriculture as a prime mover of change. By contrast, Marwick's early work focused on economic developments in Victorian Scotland and following a more general survey of Scottish industry and enterprise since the nineteenth century he concentrated on his principal interest, the history of labour. All three were exceptional for they looked at the world of ordinary people. In their different ways, they inspired the next generation that emerged from the expansion of economic and social history in the 1960s.

Our knowledge of Scottish economic and social change has been greatly enhanced by such eminent historians as S. G. E. Lythe, John Butt, R. H. Campbell, A. Slaven, B. Lenman, Rosalind Mitchison, and T. C. Smout, who have written invaluable survey volumes. These and an array of monographs show that modernization began earlier, industrialization was much more rapid, and social change more dramatic and dislocating than was previously supposed. Scotland's economic and social problems in the twentieth century were seen to have origins of a longer-term due to the over-concentration on heavy industries and old-fashioned technology, management and labour practices which Ian Donnachie touches on in his chapter. The work of economic historians was important in the sixties and seventies but the impetus has since shifted to social history – revealing in the process many remarkable new findings, some of which are reported in this volume.

The influence of English Marxists and those of leftist-inclination on Scottish history should also be noted. While the work of historians such as E. J. Hobsbawm, E. P. Thompson, and G. Rudé touch only tangentially on Scotland (their main concern being England, and in the last case France) they address universal issues about social and political evolution in the Age of Revolutions. Whether a Scottish working class on Thompsonian lines was created during the Industrial Revolution is a question which still remains to be resolved, though this and other controversies are beginning to be tackled north of the Border. Those brave enough to pick up this and other hot potatoes include J. D. Young, whose work is nothing if not thought-provoking, and W. H. Fraser, who has written extensively on the history of organized labour and labour relations in Scotland. As is clear in Chris Whatley's contribution some questionable assumptions have been made about labour and social relations in eighteenth- and early nineteenth-century Scotland, amongst them the apparent docility of the Scottish people both in the workplace and beyond and the significance of the 'Radical War' in 1820. This essay also shows how the ideas of Thompson and others can usefully be applied to re-interpret Scottish society.

In fact, it fell to an Englishman, T. C. Smout, first at Edinburgh then St Andrews, to provide the most successful overview of Scottish social evolution since the Reformation. His work is erudite and wide-ranging and he has more recently been able to draw on a vast corpus of modern research and archival material that has never before been seriously investigated. The road he took is not without interest itself. An early concern of his was Scottish trade and industry before the Union. He later moved on in time to investigate eighteenth-century Scottish society, including demography, religion, and the role of landowners in economic development. He then took the story further into the nineteenth century, examining among other issues, standards of living and popular protest during the Industrial Revolution, and the plight of the poor as revealed by government enquiries in the 1840s. Both *The History of the Scottish People* (1969) and its sequel, *A Century of the Scottish People* (1986) are seminal works which have become best-sellers.

John Prebble's writings have also been highly successful in commercial terms and are widely read. He deliberately focuses on controversial issues, such as the Massacre of Glencoe, the events surrounding the Battle of Culloden and the later Highland Clearances. Although much criticized for his journalistic approach by professional historians – perhaps jealous of his success – Prebble's work has been highly influential for more than a generation. Many of the issues about Scottish history which he raised in these and other works (including his less familiar *The Darien Disaster*) have subsequently been investigated in detail by academic historians – such as T. M. Devine, J. Hunter, E. Richards, and C. W. J. Withers – and some major reinterpretations have emerged.

If this survey gives the reader the impression that economic and social history has held the centre stage in recent times, this is certainly not meant to be dismissive of major revisions which have taken place in the field of political history. Indeed the traditional concerns of Scottish history have been political, and numerous studies of the major personalities have appeared, arguably too many in the cases of Mary, Queen of Scots and Charles Edward Stuart. Yet major revisionist work has been done, notably on Jacobitism by Bruce Lenman, and some old characterizations have been recast, as, for example, in Norman Macdougall's biographies of James III and James IV. Unfortunately, space has not allowed us to do full justice to the important new findings of scholars in the pre-Reformation era. However, some key issues of sixteenth- and seventeenth-century political history are surveyed here by George Hewitt. The dividing line between political history and economic and social history can be too sharply drawn. One of the most interesting developments in the manufacture of Scottish history in the last three decades has been the appearance of several general histories of modern Scotland. Not all that long ago, Scotland's history was thought to have evaporated, along with its parliament, in 1707. Indeed it was as late as 1941 that Agnes Mure Mackenzie could claim to be breaking new ground in writing a rounded history of the period 'of which most Scots know least...the last two hundred years.' Two series, 'The Edinburgh History of Scotland' and Edward Arnold's 'New History of Scotland', although dealing first with the pre-Union period, also takes the story of Scotland up to the present day covering political as well as economic and social themes. While the politics of eighteenth-century Scotland are now much better understood following the publication of books by Murdoch (1980) and Shaw (1983), there are still major gaps in our knowledge of the nineteenth and twentieth centuries. But the work of C. Harvie (1977 and 1981), I. G. C. Hutchison (1986) and M. Fry (1987) has done much to remedy this and highly controversial topics such as Red Clydeside (looked at by John Foster in this volume) and religious sectarianism have been subject to serious historical investigation.

Elite and learned culture, and shifting perceptions of Scotland's worth in this regard, as Angus Calder indicates, has been a critical ingredient in the process of manufacturing Scotland's history. Literature, especially the novel, has done much to shape and reinforce popular notions about Scotland's past. The works of Sir Walter Scott and later writers like Robert Louis Stevenson have been of profound importance in creating couthy images of bygone Scotland. The genre, maintained by kailyard authors like S. R. Crockett, found its setting in pre-nineteenth-century Lowland or Highland idylls and generally rejected the realities of modernization accompanying the Industrial Revolution. The literary heroes were often real historical characters, Rob Roy for example, but the story-lines were essentially fictional. Much the same approach is seen in the hugely popular novels of Nigel Tranter, arguably as powerful an influence today as the works of Scott on earlier generations. Also at the popular level the ballad-embraced myths and legends rooted in Scotland's past and these are still powerfully articulated in modern renderings of folk songs. There is also a natural link between history and theatre through productions of plays based on episodes from the past by 7:84 and other companies. John McGrath's *The Che-viot, the Stag and the Black, Black Oil* and Billy Kay's *They Fairly Mak' You Work* undoubtedly present dramatic images. On the other hand if social history is purveyed as entertainment there is a danger that new myths will be created, not least because historical truth can often be too complex for presentation on stage or screen – media which prefer to work in the bright colours of black and white rather than hodden gray. Whatever the issue in history there is probably a truth somewhere, as John Foster says in his essay, but the problem is finding and presenting it.

So far our main concern has been the manufacture of Scottish history by professional historians. But the teaching of the subject in schools has exercised considerable influence on the public's perception of the nature and, especially, the significance of Scot-land's past. As we suggested earlier, Scottish history was for generations largely neglected in schools, the exceptions being some primary schools where stories from Scottish history might be told, or in the teaching of Higher Grades where personalities or events might be touched upon in the traditional British (i.e. English) history syllabus. Anglicization played a big part in this process of marginalizing the significance of Scotland's past, and what Aus-tralians call the 'cultural cringe' was all too evident in the curricula devised for the Leaving Certificates in 1888 by the Scotch [sic] Education Department. Like geography, history for a while was part of the paper in English. However, criticisms of neglect and anglicization need to take account of a prevailing ethos which saw schools providing a basic education for the bulk of the population, so only the academically able were ever exposed to much history – Scottish or otherwise. Even with the post-1945 expansion of secondary education the Scottish Leaving Certificate History sylla-bus remained very traditional. It was not until the introduction of the Scottish Certificate of Education in 1961 that a more sympa-thetic approach was adopted. Study of Scottish themes was further encouraged in Alternative Syllabuses and in new certificates for Economic History. Even so, the current Revised Higher and Sixth Year Studies curricula could still place more emphasis on the Scottish dimension, especially in the largely neglected modern period. Several specifically Scottish options are available however, although how many pupils are able to study one of the more imaginatively conceived Higher Special Topics, 'Patterns of Mi-gration in Scotland' will depend to a large extent on how many teachers can be persuaded to abandon the teaching of much more familiar non-Scottish topics such as 'Appeasement and the Road to War'.

In primary schools more attention than before has been given to Scottish history. A recent survey of history teaching in schools throughout south-west Scotland highlighted the enthusiasm of the head teacher as the prime mover in deciding what pupils learned about local or national history. In most of the schools surveyed, pupils were exposed to an interesting range of historical studies, mainly through topic work and Environmental Studies with a local flavour. Middle Primary classes addressed such topics as 'Vikings', 'Medieval Scotland', 'Local History', and 'Mary, Queen of Scots'; while in Upper Primary 'Tudors and Stuarts' had the edge on both 'Robert Burns' and 'Highland Clearances'. Historic sites, such as castles and abbeys, museums, and heritage centres were much visited as part of these programmes. Unfortunately there seemed to be little progression or consolidation of historical skills at later stages, though the development of Standard Grade has gone some way to remedying the situation. Pupils have the opportunity to discover their heritage, to study people in different situations from their own and to become familiar with the forces of change which have shaped the world. They learn to weigh up evidence of various sorts, and to consider issues on which opinions differ. Skills of investigating and explaining are needed, and these encourage students to think in an organized way. Skills rather than facts also underpin several SCOTVEC modules devised to embrace topics like 'Local Investigations' and 'People and the Past: Scottish Society'. However there are problems for Scottish history in the non-university sector. George Hewitt refers to these in his essay.

At the universities, where chairs in the subject date back to the 'Scots Renascence' at the end of last century, Scottish history teaching was relatively small in scale, and uncertain about its direction until the 1960s when it began to share in the general expansion of higher education. As Bruce Lenman showed in a survey conducted in the early 1970s, it was proving attractive both to undergraduates and to a healthy cohort of postgraduates and new research findings enhanced knowledge of previously neglected topics across a broad chronological spectrum. More attention was devoted to the modern era and to economic and social issues, thus contributing further to the reassessment of Scotland's past and the re-creation of its history. The teachings of Scottish history in universities currently presents some paradoxes, for while there has been a decline at Aberdeen, Dundee, and Heriot-Watt (where it had only a token presence), there has been notable expansion at St Andrews. The arrival there of T. C. Smout in 1980 heralded the development of what is now a healthy department. Despite cuts in some areas, 'rationalization', and only a modest rise in the level of university funding since 1979, vigorous Scottish history teaching and research is also being conducted at the University of Strathclyde, as well as Glasgow, Edinburgh and Stirling.

In the wider world beyond school and university local history in Scotland appears to be flourishing, although it continues to maintain a strong uncompromising empirical tradition. As yet there is little sign that the French Annales school, with its emphasis on the community, has had any impact on Scottish local studies. Some local historical and antiquarian societies date back to Victorian times and have sustained a scholarly, if largely parochial, output in their proceedings and publications. There has also been a recent substantial growth in what might be described as 'grass-roots' history, partly assisted by the revived Scottish Local History Forum. While some of the output verges on the antiquarian, much useful work – often drawing on archaeology or oral sources – has been produced on local themes. We desperately need to know more about local and regional history, for the sum of such studies helps to reconstruct the national picture. This is a prime objective of the Centre for Scottish Studies at Aberdeen University; and the establishment of the Centre for Tayside and Fife Studies, a joint venture by St Andrews and Dundee universities, should go some way toward satisfying this need further south.

What has just been said about the locality, might also be said of family history, for the sum of individual family histories often add up to the history of a community. Family history too is dominated by legend, and putting this to rights can be a tedious but rewarding business. Scots are fiercely proud of their roots, and partly thanks to the increasing accessibility of archives at regional as well as national level, ancestry research has become a major growth industry. Clan societies – at home and overseas – are immensely popular, despite the fact that the origins and history of many of the clans are lost in the mists of time and are likely to remain so.

Time too needs to be taken to digest the flurry of publications which have appeared in the last two decades. Such are the pressures in the university sector to publish that it is an extremely risky business to have one's name disappear from the annual list of staff publications for the two or three years which it would take to produce any worthwhile synthesis. Yet despite the Arnold series mentioned earlier, there is still a need for a good history of Scotland during the crucial eighteenth and early nineteenth centuries. More specifically, but equally important, while Scottish agriculture has been served well in the sixteenth and seventeenth centuries by M. H. B. Sanderson (1982) and I. D. Whyte (1979) respectively, we do not have a modern account of the era of the traditional 'agricultural revolution', and know little about farming and rural life in Scotland from the later nineteenth century to the present day. Other topics have hardly been touched. One example is popular culture and leisure – although the social history of sport is attracting growing attention. There are many others. It is regrettable that the links between Scottish history and other disciplines such as literary studies, art history, and philosophy have not generally become closer outside of The Open University (which, sadly, has not yet developed an interdisciplinary course on a Scottish theme), for there is no doubt that their interests overlap even though their adherents sometimes appear to speak different – and not infrequently incoherent – languages. Nevertheless there are signs that genuinely interdisciplinary programmes of Scottish cultural studies are being made available to students, most recently at the universities of Strathclyde and Edinburgh.

While we will be gratified if fellow professionals find some merit in this volume it is primarily intended to communicate to a wider audience. With this in mind, we decided not to draw all the contributors from the ranks of Scotland's professional historians. We thought it might be useful and perhaps instructive to have others examine and attempt to assess the work of the professional historians. Sadly, the Englishman we asked to write a chapter on how he thought the Scots portrayed their history had to withdraw owing to illness. Joy Hendry, a well-known writer, journalist, and broadcaster on Scottish literary and cultural matters, and George Rosie, freelance journalist and writer, who nevertheless has more than a passing interest in Scottish history, fit this bill admirably. The former examines the treatment of Scotland's women by historians. George Rosie was asked to write about the 'heritage industry' and how those responsible for selling Scotland were using and abusing Scottish history in the marketplace.

Although the rest of the contributors have all written serious history, only three are employed in the university sector, one at St Andrews University, the other two at The Open University. George Hewitt is in further education. Balancing Professor John Foster's Marxist perspective is Michael Fry, also a respected historian and newspaper columnist who veers to the right of the Scottish political spectrum.

In selecting the topics which were to form the basis of the chapters of the book, the editors were faced with a formidable problem. Early on we concluded that it would be impossible to provide a comprehensive survey and therefore selected what we judged to be a representative range of subjects which would demonstrate effectively how Scottish history is in the process of being remade. George Hewitt's is a solidly-based survey of the changing perceptions of historians of the sixteenth and seventeenth centuries, key events in which were, first, the Reformation, and second, the Scottish Revolution.

The eighteenth century is tackled on two fronts. The first deals with the Enlightenment in Scotland, the roots of which recent historiography reveals can be traced back to the 1600s, if not earlier. Angus Calder's vigorous essay sets out not only to ascertain what was distinctive about the 'Scottish' Enlightenment, but also to ask why it flourished in a society which not so long ago could be described by one senior English historian – without serious challenge – as a 'byword for backwardness'.

Chris Whatley's essay, also concerned mainly with the eighteenth century, but with the masses rather than the élite, examines the question of the apparent passivity of the Lowland Scot, a characteristic which it has been argued goes a long way towards explaining the quiescence of Scottish society in the eighteenth and early nineteenth centuries. Although constraints of space have made it impossible to deal with Radicalism in the 1790s and the impact of the French Revolution (currently being reassessed by John Brims), attention has been paid to recent developments in labour history in the later eighteenth century, as well as the 'Radical War' of 1819–20.

Although adopting a very different perspective – he disapproves of the current 'fashion' of 'dredging the lower depths of history from below' – there is a sense in which Michael Fry's essay complements this by accounting not only for the absence until recently of serious modern Scottish political history but also for the tendency of earlier Scottish historians to focus their attention on the kailyard, allegedly, as has been seen, the locus of the 'inner life' of Scotland.

In a provocative finale, Fry condemns the growing tendency amongst some professional historians, armed with 'the standard techniques of social science', to use Scottish data as a laboratory experiment, in which Scottish experience simply becomes a 'mere variant' of that of England, or as a means of resolving or at least better understanding some other, non-Scottish, historical problem. While the editors would not wish to decry the use of the methods and concepts of the social sciences – on the contrary they take the view that the application of these has enriched Scottish historical studies – they share with him the concern that sight should not be lost of the search for what makes Scotland unique. De-mythifying and removing some of the worst romantic excesses from Scottish history is not, or should not be, the same thing as denying the distinctive features of Scottish society, or more important the much less tangible fact of Scottish nationhood. While there are undoubtedly large areas of life – work experience and leisure patterns for instance – where it is virtually impossible to distinguish differences between the south of Scotland and the north of England, the border, both historically and today, matters for most Scots. Yet potentially influential claims that it does not, and that Scotland should not be studied for itself – a revived Victorianism – are to be found re-emerging in late twentieth-century guise from the gloomy corners of at least two of the country's oldest, Anglophile, universities.

There is the perfectly legitimate and hugely illuminating task of understanding Scotland within the comparative context of the British Isles, Europe, and the wider world. The immensely important recent work done by Professors T. C. Smout, Rosalind Mitchison, and T. M. Devine and others on Scotland and Ireland (and in Smout's case Scandinavia) is a case in point.

One topic which has benefited greatly from comparative analysis, with Ireland in particular, as well as a 'British' approach to Scottish history, is Victorian Scotland's 'economic miracle'. Many explanations for this spectacular – and too short-lived – achievement have been advanced, from the role of Calvinist religion, through the fortuitous geological facts of vast reserves of coal and blackband ironstone, to long standing favourable aspects of Scottish economic and social structure. Another major contributory factor has been said to have been the 'Enterprising Scot', the great men of business such as David Dale, the Bairds of Gartsherrie and the Cox and Baxter families in Dundee. Yet how typical were they? In his essay Ian Donnachie examines and assesses the proposition that the Scots were exceptionally able businessmen as well as the allegation that Scotland's entrepreneurs 'failed' in the later nineteenth century.

As the cavalry charge of Scottish heavy industrial success slowed in the late Victorian and Edwardian eras, the apparent calm which had marked social relations in Scotland from the 1840s disappeared. How deeply the fissures of discontent had penetrated Scottish society by the time of the First World War and its aftermath is examined by Professor John Foster in a compelling essay which looks at the way events leading to the creation of the image of Red Clydeside have been portrayed and recreated from a variety of points of view over the past seventy years. Foster concludes that it is the contemporary evidence which is most telling in its effect, and that this provides undiluted support for the view that a revolutionary situation existed on Clydeside in 1919.

In both essays by Whatley and Foster attention is drawn – at least in passing – to the significance of the role of women, in riots in the first instance, and in reconstructing the political agenda and reshaping political consciousness on Clydeside during the 1914–18 war in the second. Until the 1980s however women were virtually absent as actors on the Scottish historiographical stage. In this they were not alone, although without a Scottish Alice Clark or Ivy Pinchbeck to call upon, when Scottish historians began to 'discover' the female gender, they were not even at the starting line when modern women's history elsewhere first began to make an appearance during the 1960s. The assumption of most Scottish historians has been that the realities of women's lives are of lesser national importance, and there was until very recently almost no awareness that women's values and priorities might have deeper significance in themselves. Nevertheless, while Scotland's historians still have a long way to go before they catch up with the sophisticated investigations into the lives and experience of women in France, the USA, and England, Joy Hendry shows that a start has been made.

The final two essays in the collection address issues which are of crucial significance as far as the modern image of Scotland and its history are concerned. Rightly, the Highlands have been the subject of serious study in the past two decades, and books of major importance have appeared, most notably by James Hunter (1976), Eric Richards (1982), and T. M. Devine (1988). Yet, as Charles Withers points out in an essay which reflects the way in which theory and the exploration of ideology have now become part of the historian's craft, mythical images of the Highlands and of the nature of Highland society have been immensely powerful, and hard to dispel, as in part they have had a toehold in historical reality. Withers traces the origins of 'Highlandism' back to the late eighteenth and early nineteenth centuries, but interestingly, demonstrates that the phenomenon was part of a Europe-wide cultural process. And he reminds us that however fictional much of the Highland legend is, it forms an important part of Scottish national identity: damn the facts, what seems to matter not only to outsiders but also to too many Scots are the myths about clans, heather and bonnets which have been created, often within Scotland itself, but by comfortable Lowlanders rather than hard-pressed Highland dwellers.

Relatively few people discover Scotland's history in scholarly tomes or the publications of learned societies. For many inhabitants and visitors alike contact with the past is made in museums, and increasingly nowadays, heritage centres. George Rosie's essay, 'Museumry and the Heritage Industry', looks at the way Scots wish to be seen and if the growing number of museums are any guide, they wish to be seen as monarch– and (Jacobite) aristocrat-loving gun and sword-toting guardians of the land of Burns. There are of course museums both large and (generally) small, which try honestly to capture aspects of Scottish life as it once was, but strikingly in a country whose history has been seared by religion, Rosie reveals that 'God is hardly to be found in the Scottish museums'. What is to be found in plenty are cash-registers. Increasingly it is the commercial men, who defend their decisions on the basis of assumed demand for a heavily sanitized past who are recreating the popular image of Scotland's history. The danger is that only the spectacular and saleable aspects of it – whisky, tea towels and key rings, along a whisky trail for example – will be available to the non-specialist public. The seamy, awkward and mundane parts of Scotland's past are in danger of being forgotten or confined, if they are seen at all, to the less fashionable museums.

Serious historical scholarship too is in danger of being overlooked if its practitioners fail to communicate their findings more widely and in an accessible form. Scottish history, we asserted at the outset, matters, and there is clearly a demand for it. Yet it matters too that potential readers, listeners, or viewers have access to ideas about Scottish history as it is now and not as it was thirty or more years ago. A new past provides an opportunity for fresh thinking about the present and the future. The essays in this book show how that past is being remade.

2

Reformation to Revolution

GEORGE HEWITT

What, it might be asked, would someone living a century ago and interested in Scottish history have been likely to consult? There were certainly the multi-volumed works of John Hill Burton and Patrick Fraser Tytler, although the latter, unfortunately, ended his account of events in 1603. It was his intention to carry on to the Treaty of Union but because of 'the voluminous and important nature of the documents to be arranged and consulted he found himself unable to enter on this Herculean task' (Tytler, 1864, IV, xxiii). Although primarily narrative histories, Burton and Tytler were based on extensive research. Tytler, for example, relied heavily on primary sources such as David Calderwood's *History of the Kirk of Scotland*, John Knox's *History of the Reformation in Scotland*, John Spottiswoode's *History of the Church of Scotland* and the relevant *Calendars of State Papers*. The regular appearance of the *Calendars* in printed form during the second half of the nineteenth century as well as the publication of *The Register of the Great Seal* and *The Register of the Privy Council* must have benefited anyone at this time interested in furthering their knowledge and understanding of Scotland's history. So too must the publications of the various historical clubs and societies despite the ominous demise of some. Both the Bannatyne and Maitland Clubs had gone out of business by the 1890s while the Spalding club had required resuscitation. However from 1887 volumes of original documents were produced by the Scottish History Society, followed in 1903, less than twenty years after its English counterpart, by the first issue of the *Scottish Historical Review*. Shortly afterwards, in 1911, in what has been described as 'one of the notable efforts to bring Scotland into the twentieth century' (Burns, 1985, 47), Brown's *History of Scotland* was published. Then came the Great War.

If the sterility of the inter-war period is anything to go by, the manufacture of Scottish history as an academic discipline does seem to have been adversely affected by the First World War. Thus, not only did the *Scottish Historical Review* cease publication in 1928, leaving the nation with no scholarly historical periodical, but as has been aptly stated 'neither in monography nor in works of synthesis, neither in established nor in the newer kinds of history was an adequate harvest of scholarship being garnered' (*ibid.*, 47). In short, during these years Scottish historical studies, if not quite dead, were moribund.

However, the aftermath of the Second World War saw a revival. In 1947 the *Scottish Historical Review* reappeared, to be followed in 1950, under the auspices of Catholic historians, by the *Innes Review*. Meanwhile the Scottish History Society continued its series of publications as did the Scottish Record Society which had been printing indexes and abstracts of Scottish records since 1898. Furthermore, by the 1960s in both secondary schools and universities there were signs of increasing interest in Scottish history, and this was especially so after the publication of the Robbins report in 1963 with its ambitious programme for widespread expansion in higher education. At the same time there occurred what is sometimes referred to as a 'renaissance' in Scottish historical scholarship. Whether such a description is really justified is immaterial since unquestionably there was a tremendous upsurge in historical output – as a glance at certain publisher's catalogues will confirm.

The first major publishing event was the *New History of Scotland* written in two volumes by W. C. Dickinson and G. S. Pryde. These appeared in 1961 and 1962 with a revised version of the first volume, *Scotland from the Earliest Times to 1603*, in 1965, followed by another more extensive revision by A. A. M. Duncan in 1977. Then appeared the four volume Edinburgh History of Scotland (1965–75) a magnificent undertaking comprising Duncan's *The Making of the Kingdom*, Nicolson's *The Later Middle Ages*, Donaldson's *James V – James VII* and Ferguson's *1689 to the Present*. This whole enterprise ran to a total of over 2300 pages with each volume accompanied by an invaluable critical biography. The Edinburgh History of Scotland has been described, and rightly so, as 'the clearest evidence so far that Scottish history has "arrived"' (Burns, 1985, 49), but there was more to come. T. C. Smout's brilliant survey of Scottish society, *A History of the Scottish People, 1560–1830* was published in 1969 while the following year Rosalind Mitchison produced her single volume *History of Scotland*. Finally, to complete this list of general histories, the first of eight volumes under the editorship of Jenny Wormald in the New History of Scotland series was published in 1981. The avowed objectives of this project were to provide a blend of synthesis and fresh interpretation 'to act as a bridge over the gap between the general and the more detailed treatments', and lastly, to serve as a means of 'inexpensive access to some of the best current thinking in the field of Scottish history' (quoted in Burns, 1985, 50). When these and a veritable flood of specialist studies, monographs, biographies, and learned articles which accompanied them are taken into account there seems little justification any longer for Richard Cobb's mischievous comment, erstwhile, that Scottish history was merely a 'harking back to the somewhat dubious glories of an uncertain past' (quoted in *SHR*, 1983, 95).

Not surprisingly, considering its historical importance, the Reformation and the subsequent struggle between the kirk and state which only ended with the 'Glorious Revolution' of 1689–90, have featured prominently in the post-war boom in the manufacture of Scottish history. For a comprehensive modern account of the Reformation the starting point must be the relevant chapters in Gordon Donaldson's *James V – James VII* and Jenny Wormald's *Court, King and Community* in the New History of Scotland series. These discuss both the antecedents of the great religious upheaval as well as the distinctly limited nature of the settlement reached in 1560. Moreover, Donaldson and Wormald make it clear that the events of these years were not simply the outcome of the admittedly serious shortcomings within the church plus the activities of Knox and his supporters. Wormald went as far as to declare that 'considerations that had prompted people to throw in their lot with the leading Protestants in the years between 1557 and 1560 can not now be determined. Motives sacred and profane were inextricably linked' (Wormald, 1981, 117–18).

Both argued that careful notice needed to be taken of the complex political situation which existed at that time. Thus, apart from the widespread antagonism towards French influence in Scotland, attention should also be focused on the impact of the accession of the Protestant Elizabeth in November 1558 and the significance of the Treaty of Cateau-Cambresis, in March 1559, between France and Spain. It was these latter developments, both contend, which seriously altered the attitude of Mary of Guise, the Scottish regent, towards the reformers, and provoked the crisis of 1559–60. Again, the motives behind Elizabeth's reluctant intervention in Scottish affairs are shown to be essentially political rather than an indication of any sympathy for Knox's religious proclivities. In addition, much greater stress than formerly is given to social and economic causes. Accordingly, there is increased emphasis on the desire of the lairds and burgesses to have more influence in national affairs, or as Donaldson puts it, 'attaining a new self-esteem' (Donaldson, 1965,

137), the dissatisfaction of the rank and file of the population at the irksome financial demands of the church, and the desperate plight of the impoverished, who were prepared to support any movement which attacked the wealth of the church hierarchy. Likewise, when dealing with the Reformation parliament, Donaldson and Wormald both underline the glaring defects in the arrangements drawn up at Edinburgh in 1560. Consequently, although Protestantism had been arguably established by parliament nothing had been done about the endowment of the kirk, or, for that matter, the system of government which was to prevail within it. As Wormald states 'The squalid argument about money, the row between church and state over rights of political and religious interference' (Wormald, 1981, 121) were to continue for many years thereafter.

For more detailed coverage of specific aspects of the Reformation we need to examine the *Essays on the Scottish Reformation* edited by D. McRoberts, C. H. Haws *Scottish Parish Clergy at the Reformation* and above all, the numerous contributions of Gordon Donaldson. Particularly useful, especially if read in conjunction with *James V - James VII*, are the extracts and commentaries in *A Source Book of Scottish History II & III* written in partnership with W .C. Dickinson (in the case of volume II joined by Isabel Milne), and scandalously out of print for many years. Also of considerable value is Donaldson's highly informative introduction to *The Accounts of the Collectors of Thirds of Benefices*; but pride of place must be awarded to *The Scottish Reformation* – a magisterial work which skilfully delineates the causes and consequences of the changes in religion. 'The history of the Reformation will never be quite the same again' stated *The Scotsman* in its review and for a number of years that was undoubtedly so. However, in what has been termed 'the post-Donaldson era' (Wormald, 1981, 200), a few historians have been prepared to challenge, or at least suggest, modifications and amendments to some of Donaldson's arguments. Into this revisionary category, fall Michael Lynch, James Kirk and Ian Cowan among others.

In *Edinburgh and the Reformation* Lynch has provided the first detailed account of the impact of religious change on a Scottish town. He queries the significance of Knox's role after 1560, pointing to his frequent absences from the capital and, generally, how the famous reformer was conspicuous by being missing from the centre of the political stage in these years. Accordingly, in Lynch's opinion, 'his contribution to Edinburgh's reformation ... was probably a good deal more limited than historians have allowed' (Lynch, 1981, 220). At the same time, while advocating that greater prominence should be given to some of the lesser participants, such as Adam

Fullerton, spokesman for the Congregation in 1559, or Alexander
Guthrie, the long serving town clerk, Lynch is at pains to stress the
limited progress of the Reformation within the town. 'There were
two things', he comments, 'most dear to an Edinburgh Burgess, ...
his privileges and the money which those privileges allowed him to
make. Both seemed to be threatened by the new religion' (ibid, 221).
In other words, as Lynch convincingly demonstrates, the Protestant
reformers in the 1560s had to modify their ambitious religious
programme to suit the materialistic attitudes of the Edinburgh
citizenry. To do otherwise was to court disaster.

While Lynch has queried previous assumptions about Knox and
the development of the Reformation within Edinburgh, one of the
main contributions of Kirk to the historical debate has been to
challenge the virtually universal belief that Andrew Melville's return
from the continent in 1574 marked the beginning of a new radicalism within the Scottish clergy. By taking such a stance Kirk brought
himself directly into conflict with Donaldson's views. The latter
categorically states in James V – James VII that 'Melville's new
concepts initiate a period of controversy within the church of
Scotland' (Donaldson, 1965, 150), and that the reformer and his
followers only got off the ground as a radical group within the kirk
following his return. Moreover, in Donaldson's opinion 'The
presbyterian programme was formulated in England before it was
heard of in Scotland ... in no sense (was it) an indigenous Scottish
movement' (Donaldson, 1960, 71).

Kirk, on the other hand, in a lengthy introduction to The Second
Book of Discipline and an important article 'The Polities of the Best
Reformed Kirks', argues that Melville 'was no ayatollah who engineered and master minded a revolution in the Church' (Kirk, 1980,
42). Besides, Kirk would contend, most of the ecclesiastical changes
sought by the English presbyterians in the 1570s had already been
introduced in Scotland some time before Melville's return. Therefore, the real importance of the latter was to act as a leader on behalf
of the church against the erastian tendencies of the regent Morton.
Nor, according to Kirk, was Melville so extensively influenced by
the theories of Theodore Beza, Calvin's successor at Geneva, as has
been previously asserted. Accordingly, Melville's reform programme was as much 'a practical reappraisal of Scottish circumstances' as one dominated by 'any dogmatic beliefs emanating from
Geneva' (ibid., 77). Consequently it is Kirk's contention that the
Second Book of Discipline rather than representing the 'novel
ideals' of Melville, as Donaldson and others would claim, was more
'a restatement of earlier ideals and priorities espoused by the reformer' (ibid., 77).

If the works of Lynch and Kirk exemplify some of the revisionist views which have emerged in recent years, Ian Cowan's *The Scottish Reformation* is by contrast a major re-assessment of the whole Reformation period. Particularly invaluable are the close re-examination of the condition of the pre-Reformation church and a detailed analysis of the spread of Protestantism within individual regions. One of Cowan's most significant assertions concerns the state of the monasteries before 1560. 'Monasticism', Cowan writes 'was in a better shape than sometimes allowed'. He then shows that 'in a considerable number of larger houses monks and canons were still engaged in their traditional devotions and pursuits ... reforms were being contemplated and in some cases fulfilled'. Thus, as Cowan persuasively argues, if it had not been for the upheaval of 1559–60, 'Reformed monasteries bereft of many of their former endowments but spiritually more alive might have emerged' (Cowan, 1981a, 43–44). Another significant aspect of this study is that it queries the inevitability of the Protestant victory in 1560 and the years thereafter. 'For over a decade' Cowan states, 'religious issues hung in the balance and recusancy remained a problem until the end of the century' (*ibid.*, 159). Then, following a review of the progress of the Reformation at a local level, he concludes that 'the committed Protestant believers remained for a long time in a decided minority. Time and changing political circumstances', he avers, 'allowed that minority to win increasing support by a mixture of persecution and admonition (assisted by the increasing pressures of social conformity)' (*ibid.*, 186).

Reference to some of Cowan's arguments and those of others is also made in a collection of essays edited by Norman Macdougall entitled *Church, Politics and Society, Scotland 1408-1929*. Wormald's article on 'Princes and the Regions in the Scottish Reformation' casts serious doubts on the idea that there was universal support for the Protestant cause in 1559-60; Macfarlane in 'Was the Scottish Church Reformable in 1513?' presents a strong case for contending that the church could have been cleansed internally; while Lynch, in 'From Privy Church to Burgh Church: an alternative view of the process of Protestantism' elaborates further on the subject of the impact of the Reformation on Edinburgh.

Melville's appearance on the scene and the drafting of the *Second Book of Discipline* marks the beginning of another stage in the relations between kirk and state, which fall into two distinct phases. First came the period before the Union of the Crowns when James VI and his governments were locked in a protracted struggle with the Melvillians. Then followed the era after 1603 when the king overcame his religious adversaries and episcopacy triumphed over

Presbyterianism. Chapter XI of Gordon Donaldson's *James V –
James VII* provides the best outline of the contest between James VI
and the kirk. Donaldson examines in some detail the *Second Book
of Discipline* and its aftermath, attempts to unravel the tortuous
ecclesiastical policy of the crown over the next two decades and
gives a description of the king's ultimate victory over the
Melvillians. Brief coverage of James VI's handling of the church
after 1603 can also be found in Mitchison's *Lordship to Patronage*
while Donaldson's *A Source Book of Scottish History III* is again
indispensable. There is also a very useful chapter by Donaldson,
'The Scottish Church 1567–1625', in *The Reign of James VI and I*.
edited by A. G. R. Smith. Donaldson looks favourably on James's
performance over his long reign, his concluding comment that 'the
days were to come when men would look back with regret to the
'great wisdom' of 'Blessed King James'" (Smith, 1973, 56) echoing the
sentiments of the nineteenth-century church historian John Row.

For specific aspects of the religious struggle in these years there is,
as already mentioned, Kirk's introduction to the *Second Book of
Discipline* and further treatment of the early clashes with Melville is
provided in *Scotland under Morton*, my own political study of
James's most effective regent. Regarding the vexed question of the
Melvillians and their campaign for further change in the church it is
the present writer's opinion that Morton's policy was essentially the
same as the king himself would subsequently adopt. Thus, the
regent while 'he clearly endeavoured to establish a polity favourably
inclined towards episcopacy' was forced by circumstances, especially the challenge to his authority from rival magnates, to pursue
tactics wherein 'the strength and weakness of his own position
determined his approach to ecclesiastical affairs' (Hewitt, 1982,
107, 116). I have also taken the view that under Morton 'the kirk
undoubtedly still continued to receive less than it might have done'
(*ibid.*, 99), but for the whole question of endowment in the post-
Reformation era there is J. Kirk's 'Royal and Lay Patronage in the
Jacobean Kirk, 1562–1600', another essay from *Church, Politics
and Society, Scotland 1408–1929*. In Kirk's opinion the difficulties
faced by both the crown and the kirk in recovering what they had
lost were primarily a result of the alterations in ownership of the
previous ecclesiastical properties. What the clergy were actually in
receipt of by the early seventeenth century is detailed in W. R.
Foster's 'A Constant Platt achieved: Provision for the Ministry,
1600-38', one of the essays in *Reformation and Revolution* edited
by Duncan Shaw. One of Foster's more interesting revelations is
that by that date the stipends of Edinburgh ministers made them
financially better off than the Scottish bishops. In the same collec-

tion Cowan addresses the 'Five Articles of Perth', wherein the liturgical innovations forced upon the kirk, particularly the unpopular insistence on kneeling at communion, are dealt with at some length. Finally, the meeting of the General Assembly in 1618 was to be the last of James VI's reign, but the earlier history of the Assembly and details of its relations with the king are described in Shaw's *The General Assemblies of the Church of Scotland, 1560–1600*.

Whether James VI deserves the generally sympathetic 'press' he has received over the years is debatable and even if in his handling of religious matters he was much more astute than his son, Charles I, a revisionary account of the reign of 'God's silly vassal' does seem overdue. Maurice Lee, whose *Government by Pen* also takes a favourable view of James's performance, makes the interesting suggestion in an essay entitled 'King James's Popish Chancellor', that 'religious animosities may have run less deeply than supposed' (in Cowan & Shaw, 1983, 182). Perhaps they did, if the attitude of the Presbyterian party to the Catholic earl of Dunfermline, the subject of Lee's article, is anything to go by. Nonetheless, religious controversy could be all too easily stirred up, with disastrous consequences, as Charles I discovered.

There is a broad outline of the causes of the revolution against the crown and the events which followed in Donaldson's *James V – James VII* and Mitchison's *Lordship to Patronage*. Both identify the main reasons for the growing hostility towards Charles stemming from three interacting factors. First, was the ill-advised Act of Revocation by which the king revoked all grants made since 1540, not least the erection of church properties as temporal lordships. Admittedly there were some good intentions behind this legislation (the clergy for example would receive adequate stipends) but it was presented to the magnates and others in a maladroit fashion causing serious dissension between the government and the most influential section of Scottish society. Second, was the crown's financial policy by which Charles continued his father's highly unpopular practice of relying on what amounted to a system of regular taxation. In addition many Edinburgh citizens were also aggrieved at having to bear the pecuniary burden of the royal coronation in 1633 and the cost of the new parliament building. Third, as Donaldson states, 'ecclesiastical grievances arose alongside the financial and constitutional grievances' (Donaldson, 1965, 305). In other words, the Code of Canons and the Prayer Book were imposed on the populace, and it was these religious innovations which effectively united most of the nation against the crown. The subsequent outcome was the signing of the National Covenant, the Bishops' Wars, and the eventual defeat of the king by the Covenanters.

Bridging the gap between the basic outline of events and more specialist accounts of these years the reader can once more consult *A Source Book of Scottish History, III*. Details of the organization of the Jacobean church can be found in W. R. Foster's *The Church before the Covenants*, not to be confused with *The Church of the Covenant* by W. R. Makey which explores, among other factors, the social origins of the various ministers and elders involved. 'It is clear' says Makey 'that only a small proportion of the ministers came from a wealthy or a powerful background and that a much larger proportion emerged from the ranks of the ministry itself'. As for the elders, 'they tended to be tenant farmers or feuars. They were seldom cottars and never servants, some were small landowners but few were magnates' (Makey, 1979, 101, 152). Makey also stresses what he calls the 'silent revolution', that is, the growing resentment of the lower orders against the upper classes and how events in mid-century 'were the final episode of a social revolution deeply rooted in a long feudal past' (*ibid.*, 1).

However in his opinion, this discontent merely simmered under the surface between 1637 and 1641 since the great landowners and their allies remained firmly in political control. Full details of the activities of Argyll, Montrose and their covenanting colleagues are given by David Stevenson in *The Scottish Revolution 1637-44*, the best narrative account of events. When writing about the earlier years of Charles I's reign, Mitchison observed that there was 'a gap in confidence between the king and the Scottish administration' (Mitchison, 1981, 29). This whole question was extensively discussed at a conference at Edinburgh University in September 1988 to commemorate the 300th anniversary of the signing of the Covenant. One of the main speakers, E. J. Cowan, convincingly argued that it was the Union of the Crowns and with it the royal departure to London which had begun the process of straining relations between the king and his leading subjects. By the 1630s, according to Cowan, the Scottish covenanting leadership, influenced both by the political theories of certain Dutch writers and the example of the revolt of the Netherlands, perceived the distinct advantages to be achieved by harnessing Presbyterianism to their own political ends. Meanwhile, the main thrust of Alan MacInnes, another speaker, was the view that the Covenanters formed part of a 'radical mainstream' existing in both Scotland and England. In both countries they sought to challenge and place permanent restrictions on royal absolutism. Hence, in MacInnes's opinion, the important constitutional changes conceded by Charles, when he forfeited the right to choose his own ministers and officials, agreed to the abolition of the Lords of Articles and consented to triennial parliaments.

While these developments may have provoked the 'first signs of the disruption of the unity of the covenanting movement' (Donaldson, 1965, 326), with the detachment of Montrose from their ranks, the other leading covenanters, well aware that a royalist victory south of the border would have disastrous consequences for them as well, signed the Solemn League and Covenant in 1643. This alliance certainly contributed towards the king's defeat at Marston Moor the following year, but the failure of the parliamentarians to honour all their pledges eventually resulted in the covenanting leaders in December 1647 signing an agreement with Charles known as The Engagement. Under its terms Covenanters such as Hamilton and Lauderdale committed the king, in return for their support, to introduce Presbyterianism in England for a trial period of three years. But the 'Engagers' were easily routed by Cromwell's forces at Preston in 1648 and there followed the brief interlude when the more fanatical covenanters or 'Anti-Engagers' took over the reins of government. Undoubtedly it was their uncompromising behaviour which was instrumental in Scotland's subsequent forfeit of her independence.

The union with England began to be enforced towards the end of 1650. In September, the covenanters were beaten at Dunbar and the systematic occupation of the country by English forces soon followed. As far as religion was concerned during these years the bitter controversies between the two religious factions, the Protestors and the Resolutioners, continued unabated. Cromwell's administration initially tried to reach a modus vivendi with the Protestors, who at least were anti-royalist, but their unremitting intransigence forced them to turn to the Resolutioners. By 1655 it was their clergy who were prepared to cease offering prayers for the exiled Charles II and give guarantees of their allegiance to the regime.

For useful surveys of events in the 1640s and 50s the reader can turn to Donaldson's *James V – James VII* and Mitchison's *Lordship to Patronage* as well as the ubiquitous *Source Book of Scottish History III*. In addition William Ferguson's *Scotland's Relations with England* makes some interesting points about Scotland and the English Civil War. 'The Solemn League and Covenant', Ferguson observes, is often dismissed 'as a monumental piece of bigoted folly the entire blame for which is usually cast at the fanatical Scottish covenanters'. Not so, insists Ferguson, for two reasons. Firstly it is a serious miscalculation 'to ignore the diplomatic side of the League and to over-concentrate on its religious aspects'. Secondly, he argues, the Presbyterian leader Alexander Henderson was not a fanatical zealot obsessed with installing the Scottish brand of Presbyterianism in England. On the contrary, says Ferguson, Henderson envisaged 'the elaboration of a new system agreeable to both parties. Hardly, he concludes, 'the action of people with closed minds' (Ferguson, 1977, 125).

This period has also yielded its quota of detailed studies and, here, David Stevenson has undoubtedly been one of the foremost contributors. His *Revolution and Counter-Revolution in Scotland, 1644–51* examines, in great depth, the complex political and religious manoeuverings of the period, while his *Scottish Covenanters and Irish Confederates* compares developments in Ireland with those in Scotland. Then, in a very useful introduction to *The Government of Scotland under the Covenanters* he provides an invaluable summary of the workings of the administrative system which operated under the direction of Argyll and his associates. Stevenson commences by quoting a piece of royalist doggerel written in 1662:

'From covenanters with uplifted hands,
From Remonstrators with associate bands,
From such committees as governed this nation,
From kirk commissions and their protestation,
Good Lord delivers.'

He concludes his introductory remarks by aptly observing that 'The high hopes of replacing royal absentee absolutism with representative and consultative government had long ago ended in bitter disillusionment' (Stevenson, 1982, IX, L.).

On the other hand, Makey in the *Church of the Covenant, 1637–51*, takes the view that it was only in 1648–50 that the radical elements in the kirk became really 'noisy' and seriously made their presence felt. Thus the Whiggamore Raid of 1648, when the more fanatical Covenanters of south-west Scotland seized power, was, in Makey's opinion, a victory for 'the red guards of the Scottish Revolution. They consistently reminded it of its origins, they were its conscience' (Makey, 1979, 178).

Finally, the Cromwellian Union has remained a comparatively neglected interlude and the only recent study has been Frances Dow's *Cromwellian Scotland, 1651-60*. While primarily an account of the military occupation of the country, it also addresses the difficulties facing English administrators such as Colonel Lilburne, in reaching some kind of understanding with either of the two religious factions, the Protestors and the Resolutioners. Thus, as Dow shows, Lilburne's belief, that if he obtained the support of Patrick Gillespie, a prominent Protestor, he would win over the rest of his followers proved to be illusory and it was the more pragmatic approach of his successor Lord Broghill towards the Resolutioners which provided some sort of working agreement. This situation continued until the collapse of the Protectorate and the return of the Stewarts to the thrones of both kingdoms.

The Restoration Settlement, the political and religious legislation which accompanied the return of Charles II, not only resulted in the revival of episcopacy but also saw the various limitations on the royal prerogative rescinded. Moreover, despite the fact that a majority of the population welcomed the Restoration and with it an end to political instability, as well as some of the economic problems which had characterized the Cromwellian Union, the ecclesiastical settlement fuelled the fires of further religious controversy. Aside from the unpopularity of the restored bishops, the key issue here was the imposition of lay patronage on the kirk. Ministers had to obtain both presentation from a patron and collation from their bishop. Therein lay the roots of the subsequent split within the church between the majority who, albeit reluctantly, conformed with these instructions and the minority who refused to do so. The inevitable outcome was the prolonged and bitter conflict between the latter, the Covenanters, and the upholders of the episcopal system, the administrations of Charles II and James VII. This struggle was only finally resolved by the 'Glorious Revolution' and the Revolution Settlement which followed it in 1689–90. Under its terms episcopacy was ended, lay patronage was abolished, the General Assembly was restored, the Presbyterian system was revived, and the surviving 'outed' ministers were reinstated. In short, the foundations of the modern Church of Scotland were securely established. An outline of the final stages in the contest between the kirk and the state is provided by Donaldson's *James V – James VII* and, since this closed with the abdication of James VII, the first chapter of Ferguson's *1689 to the Present* can also be usefully consulted. Additionally, Mitchison's *Lordship to Patronage* and *A Source Book of Scottish History, III* add to the picture of events.

The consequences of the Revolution Settlement and ecclesiastical developments thereafter are dealt with in some detail by A. C. Drummond and J. Bulloch's *The Scottish Church, 1688-1843*. For the Restoration period there is W. R. Foster's *Bishop and Presbytery* and more recently, Julia Buckroyd, concerned, as she states, that 'ecclesiastical history was felt to be an outmoded study' offers a fresh analysis of the policies of such leading figures as Archbishop Sharp and the duke of Lauderdale. The latter, she contends, 'was gradually pressured by considerations primarily political into abandoning the presbyterian sympathies of his youth and acquiescing in the imposition of an erastian episcopacy'. Indeed, she argues, by 1675 the duke was adopting expedients designed 'simultaneously to preserve his alliance with Sharp, Burnet, and the English High

Church Party, to subdue dissent in Scotland and to destroy Hamilton and his party'. In other words, Buckroyd concludes, 'ecclesiastical policy had relatively little to do with religion and was simply another factor in political struggles for power'. (Buckroyd, 1980, 170, 132, 117, 170). Elsewhere, both in her biographical study of *James Sharp Archbishop of St Andrews* and in her contribution to Macdougall's *Church, Politics and Society, Scotland 1408-1929*, Buckroyd attempts to rehabilitate the reputation of James Sharp, the apostate archbishop of St Andrews.

Inasmuch as Buckroyd has endeavoured to interpret the principles guiding those in charge of affairs in Reformation Scotland, Ian Cowan in *The Scottish Covenanters* has concentrated on the motives and objectives of the Presbyterians who challenged the authority of the crown. 'Most covenanters' states Cowan, were 'the tenant farmers and lower classes of society, many of whom had much to lose.' However, it is Cowan's view that 'the age-long debate as to whether the victims should be regarded as traitors, fanatics or martyrs' is really something of a red herring. The crucial issue, in his opinion, is that the 'wholesale fining, imprisonment and banishment was part of a systematic campaign aimed at bringing all presbyterians into conformity with the established church'. Therefore, Cowan is convinced that 'the history of the Covenanters is not entirely one of religious bigotry but rather part of a more general struggle by the church against the intolerance of the state' (Cowan, 1976, 53, 133, 149). In the end, as has already been noted, the kirk emerged victorious but it is salutary, as a final parting thought, to consider Makey's perceptive parting comment that 'the church duly achieved its independence of the state ... the castle gave way not to the cowshed but to the mansion' (Makey, 1979, 185).

What has not been discussed so far, of course, in an account which has been predominantly historiographical, are the actual reasons for the post war resurgence in Scottish history and the various revisionist arguments which have emerged. In other words, just how it has been 'manufactured'. This is no easy task but a close consideration of some of the ideas contained within Arthur Marwick's study, *The Nature of History*, would seem to be a particularly fruitful way of reaching an understanding of the more recent developments among Scottish historians. Marwick identifies three main trends which feature prominently in what he describes as 'the contemporary scene' (Marwick, 1970, Ch. 7). Thus, there has been a greater willingness among scholars to question the inevitability of events and, instead, to argue the case for discontinuity. At the same time there has been somewhat less emphasis placed on political history resulting in more attention to social and economic factors. Lastly, there has been an increasing reluctance to accept entrenched opinions and a greater willingness to challenge previous assumptions. In short, as Marwick himself notes, there has been a greater affinity with A. J. P. Taylor's precept that 'History is the great school of scepticism' (*ibid.*, 211).

Whether these are all the influences at work in the study of Scottish history since the war is possibly debatable, but Marwick's suggestions certainly appear extremely useful. Thus, Wormald in her chapters on the Reformation in *Court, King and Community* challenges the view that the overthrow of the church system was inevitable. Like Donaldson in *James V – James VII* she places greater weight than had formerly been done on the social and economic aspects of the religious upheavals. Donaldson himself in the preface to *The Scottish Reformation* specifically declares that he is not writing a political version of events but 'ecclesiastical history' based on his own research 'primarily on record evidence'. Indeed he provides an excellent example in the first chapter where he utilises evidence from the *Morton Papers*, the *Melrose Regality Records*, and his own work on the *Thirds of Benefices* to establish the fact that membership of the monastic houses was declining in the pre-Reformation era (Donaldson, 1960, 4). Then, there is Lynch's *Edinburgh and the Reformation*. Relying heavily on manuscript sources within the Edinburgh City Archives and the Scottish Record Office, such as Council and Guild Registers, Dean of Guild Accounts and Court Books, Commissary Court Records, Exchequer and Justiciary Court records as well as a wide range of Protocol books, Lynch constructs a unique account of what took place in Edinburgh at the time. The result, like other works such as Ian Cowan's *The Scottish Reformation* makes it necessary to modify or revise opinions previously held about certain aspects of the Reformation. Much the same might be said about the contributions of Buckroyd, Cowan, Ferguson, Makey, and Stevenson to the 'Century of Revolution', who, by challenging orthodox views about the Scottish Revolution, investigating the social and economic origins of the ministry, and querying the traditional version of Archbishop Sharp's career, have helped 're-manufacture' Scottish history.

In many ways, Scottish historical studies of the sixteenth and seventeenth centuries would appear to be in reasonably sound health. This however, is at university level, where Scottish history appears to be flourishing despite unfortunate financial constraints.

However there are some ominous clouds on the horizon, especially within that Vimy Ridge or Menin Road of education, the schools and further education colleges. One further education college in the west of Scotland, for instance, was the only institution to offer a higher grade course in Scottish history, and that opportunity was withdrawn by the administration in 1990. Moreover, in all branches of history in such institutions there is a constant threat from egregious carpet-baggers and lickspittles obsessed or bewitched by SCOTVEC modules. Indeed only determined trade union action in some instances has halted the slide down the slippery path to 'that grave of linguistic deformity' the modular system, with its jargon-ridden 'descriptors' and dubious assessment methods. At the same time there is little to be enthusiastic about over the new, revised Scottish Certificate of Education, Higher Grade History syllabus. Under its provisions, for example, any student interested in the Reformation will seek in vain for an opportunity to study the period for, incredibly, all that is on offer is a gallimaufry of Anglo-Scottish topics entitled 'Scotland and England in the Century of Revolution' (1603–1702)'. In other words, what is usually regarded as one of the key events in Scottish history is no longer in the Higher Syllabus and can only be studied by the comparatively small number of pupils who undertake the Certificate of Sixth Year Studies.

In the lower echelons of the educational system, Scottish history is sadly increasingly under siege, and is gradually resuming the halting gait which Bruce Lenman attributed to it forty years ago, when he described it as 'limping along'.

3

The Enlightenment

ANGUS CALDER

In 1954 that pre-eminent vent of scholarship in American colonial history, the *William and Mary Quarterly*, published a number on 'Scotland and America'. Here, two exceptionally brilliant Instructors at Harvard, with the impetuous opportunism of youth, wrote on 'England's Cultural Provinces: Scotland and America'. The future biographer of Macaulay and the future doyen of New England historiography could hardly bring their argument to an imposing conclusion, as they knew very well that eighteenth-century Scotland was an ancient kingdom, currently the vigorous auxiliary of English imperialism, a 'province' of an utterly different kind from the thirteen protesting colonies. Nevertheless, their perspective has had some influence.

Unusually, they refer to 'that remarkable efflorescence of the mid-eighteenth century, with its roll call of great names: Hume, Smith, Robertson, Kames, and Ferguson' as the 'Scottish Renaissance'. Addressing the problem of its origins, they note that, in the nineteenth century, Macaulay had attributed it to the 1696 Act of the Parliament of Scotland which had demanded a school in every parish, H. T. Buckle to the survival of energies engaged in the religious conflicts of the seventeenth century, now released in another sphere. There is 'something to be said for both these points of view', but 'neither peace nor public education' is enough to explain the Scottish sunburst, and the delayed economic benefits of the 1707 Union come 'too late to serve as a satisfactory reason for the first stages of Scotland's great creative period'. Do we attribute these to the impact of Francis Hutcheson's lectures at the University of Glasgow from 1730? This doesn't work, either, say Clive and Bailyn ... 'After Hutcheson's first year at Glasgow, at least one contemporary observer [the Presbyterian historian Wodrow] singled him out for praise because he was maintaining the cause of orthodox Christianity in a university shot through with free thought'. An 'adequate' explanation 'must take account not only of a variety of social factors at the moment of fullest flowering, but also of the conditions of growth in the preceding period.'

Here, the analogy with the American colonies comes into play. With such figures as the theologian Edwards, the *philosophe*-statesmen Franklin and Jefferson, and the painters Copley and West, these had their own 'enlightenment'. It was led by ministers of religion, by lawyers, and by some of the business men (amongst whom may be included the capitalistic, slave-owning planters of Virginia). The clubs in which it found expression were 'recruited from the professional middle and tradesman lower-middle classes'.

Enthusiastically, Clive and Bailyn point to the *Edinburgh Directory* of 1773–4, which listed citizens, apparently in order of importance, so that lawyers appeared before 'noblemen' and 'gentlemen'. Conceding that Scotland, unlike America, did have a native, hereditary aristocracy, they argue that its 'share' in 'Renaissance'/'Enlightenment' was 'contributory rather than decisive'. Its members were 'masters of the revels … [but] masters of little else'. The poverty of the 'largely' Jacobite and Episcopalian nobility was such that scions of aristocratic families were driven into trade, and Edinburgh's Old Town nurtured 'a society in which social demarcations were far from sharply drawn'. The Select Society of Edinburgh, founded in 1754, which by 1759 had come to include 'all the Edinburgh literati' among its 133 members, included at least 48 lawyers and 'along with university professors and members of the Moderate party among the clergy, it was the lawyers who played the principal role.' The close involvement of Scots and Roman law, together with liberal influences brought home from Holland by generations of Scottish students at Utrecht and Leyden were 'conducive to fresh currents of philosophical and historical thought'. Scotland is seen as almost a 'frontier' society. Clive and Bailyn point out that the one very expensive regular stagecoach between Edinburgh and London took two weeks, fully half the travelling time from New York to England. In the colonies, Royal officials were the arbiters of taste and fashion. Scotland, of course, had no petty viceregal court, but its representatives in the Houses of Commons and Lords, from 1707, 'brought back English books and English fashions. They were catalysts in the process that gave Edinburgh its own *Tatler*, as well as its coffee-houses and wits …' They felt awkward about their dialect and their accents. Thomas Sheridan, in 1761, lectured (in Irish brogue) to an Edinburgh audience of 300 noblemen, judges, divines, advocates and men of fashion on the art of 'rhetoric'. 'Scotsmen and Americans alike were constantly aware that they lived on the periphery of a greater world … A sense of inferiority pervaded the culture of the two regions, affecting the great no less than the common.' But 'compensatory local pride' also manifested itself strongly.

Conflict arose in the 'provincial' mind between the values associated with simplicity and innocence (the frontier Puritan, the 'gentle shepherd') and those of cosmopolitan sophistication. 'The complexity of the provincial's image of the world and of himself made demands upon him unlike those felt by the equivalent Englishman. It tended to shake the mind from the roots of habit and tradition' (Clive and Bailyn, 1954, 200-213).

The fact that their 'provincialism' produced among Americans the first 'democratic revolution', whereas in Scotland most 'enlightened' thinkers were politically conservative, makes the Clive–Bailyn 'explanation' merely a basis for further questions requiring explanation. The onus is in effect thrown back on general explanations of 'Enlightenment' as a phenomenon over the whole European arena. While Paris was certainly an epicentre of the phenomenon, and Diderot and Voltaire were very much its citizens, it is obvious that several major figures associated with the movement worked in 'peripheral' places. The roll call of major Scottish names is matched by the petty state of Weimar where Goethe, Herder, and Schiller operated; Kant was aroused from his dogmatic slumbers by reading David Hume in Koenigsberg, a town which without him would be almost unknown to cultural history; Vico came from Naples, Rousseau from Geneva. Even Montesquieu can be identified with Bordeaux rather than Paris: that thriving port had an Academy, energized by lawyers, clergy, doctors, and Royal officials, not altogether unlike a North American association.

Nicholas Phillipson, in a paper published in 1973, took the factor of 'provincialism' in Scottish Enlightenment aboard for a rather different, more elaborate voyage than Clive and Bailyn's. He insisted that 'there is an important sense in which the history of the Scottish Enlightenment *is* the history of Edinburgh.' The capital was, for instance, a magnet for professors from Glasgow and Aberdeen.

Like Dublin, like Boston, like Naples, and like Bordeaux, Edinburgh was the 'capital' of a province of a great monarchy. In such places, provincial élites were allowed to govern their provinces with only 'minimal interference', and preserved 'a strong sense of local pride'. They aimed simultaneously to guard local liberties and to draw their provinces, by 'improvement' from 'a state of rudeness to one of cosmopolitan refinement'.

Before 1707 Edinburgh was the seat of a provincial parliament, had its own Privy Council, Court of Session, General Assembly of

the Kirk, and University. It was the focal point of the collective life
of provincial élites interested in economic 'improvement'. In the
1690s, however, famine and the Darien disaster gobsmacked the
province's rulers, who became convinced that only free trade with
England and the colonies would make growth possible. The selfish
English parliament stood in the way. So, Phillipson argues, Scotland's leaders deliberately precipitated a crisis in relations with
England which was resolved, much as they had wished, in 1707.
The Act of Union gave them access to England's markets, while
securing the distinctive Scottish legal and ecclesiastical institutions.
(This 'optimistic' view of Union was highly debateable in 1973 and
seems unsustainable now: see Whatley, 1989). But for four decades
thereafter only the richest Scots could 'afford to play the expensive
game of aristocratic politics in London'. Until the 1750s the 'minor
nobility and more substantial gentry' were content to focus their
lives on Edinburgh, a city 'dominated by successive generations of
around 400 families of minor nobility and substantial gentry,
closely knit by kinship and by marriage'. This élite monopolized the
bench of the Court of Session and the Scottish bar. The Patronage
Act of 1712 ensured that such men could provide ministers with
livings and schoolmasters with employment. They could offer professors 'prestigious pupils' and the still more enticing prospect of
well paid tutorships which would 'rescue them from the hurly burly
of university life'. *Pace* Clive and Bailyn, the Enlightenment flourished under aristocratic hegemony.

From 1723 to 1745, Phillipson argues, the Society for Improvement in the Knowledge of Agriculture – which had its counterparts
in Dublin and Bordeaux – provided a forum for the aristocracy
which in effect replaced the lost Parliament. It concerned itself not
only with promoting the best available farming techniques, but with
linen manufacture and fisheries.

But then came economic boom. And now we come to Phillipson's
explanation of the 'extraordinary upsurge of intellectual vitality
that took place in the 1750s, which is unique to Edinburgh' (that is,
among 'provincial' capitals of the day). It was 'a function of an
ideological crisis within the governing class, precipitated by an
important change in their expectations of life which was itself the
function of rapid economic growth'.

Previously, the city's characteristic institutions of cultural life, its
clubs (ten or a dozen at any one time), had drawn on all sections of
the respectable citizenry – gentry and artisans, whigs and jacobites,
presbyterians and episcopalians, advocates, ministers, professors
and doctors. Characteristically, members were young men expect-
ing to better themselves in Scotland. 'These clubs were to the

intellectuals much as ... the Society for Improvement ... was to the aristocrats'. The belief was becoming commonplace that the economic and social fortunes of society were interconnected with its cultural momentum, and intellectuals egged on the 'natural leaders of society' while very deliberately seeking their patronage. Believing in the creative value of collective action fuelled by free will, such people had trouble with David Hume's radical suggestion, in his *Treatise on Human Nature* of 1739, that humans in fact had little knowledge of, or control over, the mechanisms governing their lives, being mere bundles of 'perceptions, made coherent by a process of association and habit'. But from 1750 onwards, Humeian determinism 'suddenly emerged as the ideological norm of polite culture'.

Aristocrats were liberated from confinement in Scotland by economic boom. Boswell typified the new hankering for London life. Edinburgh's 'society' was relinquished to the control of professional men and petty gentry. But aristocrats still wanted a home base. They had to be legitimately 'Scottish'. When Hume, Adam Smith, Allan Ramsay Jr, and eleven others set up the Select Society in 1754 to discuss their deterministic notions, it was soon bombarded by applications to join from the *jeunesse dorée*, so that its membership became 'highly aristocratic'. (The point missed by Clive and Bailyn is that lawyers in Scotland were almost invariably men of substantial family.) Most of these members were heirs to landed estates, the preponderance were on their way to high office in state, church and armed services: they were committed through the Society to a programme of social and economic improvement. While not merely 'masters of the revels', the high-born in effect deferred to literati mostly of inferior birth (Hume was unusual in having high origins among landed gentry). 'By the mid-1750s the literati were providing them with the institutional means of articulating their identity as a governing élite; they had become the guardians of the *virtu* of an aristocratic society. Men of fashion were proud of their connections and acquaintance with men of letters'. The determinism of the *literati* reassured North British lairds insecure about their provincial identity that 'the liberties and future welfare of their country lay not in their care but in that of the Invisible Hand'.

But a province within the province was to strike back. By the 1780s, Reid's 'Common Sense' philosophy, nurtured in Aberdeen, had triumphed in Scotland's universities, whence it spread to Restoration France and revolutionary and post-revolutionary America. Reid's retort to Hume made constructive free agency seem once again feasible (Phillipson, 1973, 123-147). Keith Lehrer summarizes Reid's position thus: 'Reid assumes that it is hopeless to account for our belief or the justification for our belief in the external world by appeal to sense impressions. The belief arises immediately as the result of a first principle of our faculties'. If we don't trust these 'then we should not trust reason or consciousness' (Jones, ed., 1989, 122).

At least Phillipson's extremely elegant argument gets us closer to the heart of a phenomenon worthy of very special discussion than does Clive and Bailyn's. This phenomenon takes its bearings from the arguments of the literati and assumes that the detail of these relates to a unique historical configuration which, in part, explains their especial significance for historians. But not wholly. In the end, Phillipson retreats from general explanation. If a sense of urgency informed Scottish intellectual debate in the 1750s, if it seemed to have vital social importance, then this was because of 'the genius of Adam Smith and above all, David Hume'.

Without Hume, one could argue, there is no real problem of explanation. The eighteenth century was a period when inter-continental trade and the 'commercial revolution' had widened European horizons, and secular aspirations had supplanted the fractious imperatives of religion among the growing bourgeoisie and aristocratic enthusiasts for 'improvement' alike. 'Enlightened' ideas flourished widely, in imperial courts, in metropolitan cities and in 'provincial' centres. Scotland, in contact with the England of Bacon, Newton, and Locke, with the Dutch Universities, and, through Jacobite escapades, with Paris and Italy, digested valuable foreign influences and, in an epoch of rising prosperity, the country followed England in agricultural transformation, profited vastly from intercontinental trade, and helped to launch the first 'industrial revolution'. So Scotland more or less inevitably produced manifestations of 'enlightenment'. Its rich men commissioned Adam's houses and portraits by Ramsay and Raeburn. Its bourgeoisie made Ossian, Burns, and Scott best sellers. And its universities gave ideological support to secularism and free trade, and stimulated, in their faculties of medicine, a national atmosphere in which experiment and invention produced Watt's steam engine and many other technological advances. Even Smith's *Wealth of Nations* (1776), great pioneering work though it was, can be easily and directly related to the impulse towards free trade and faith in progress consequent upon Britain's commercial and industrial prowess.

The problem of explanation posed by Hume's centrality can be stated thus: his *Treatise* antedates the most optimistic accounts of Scottish economic take-off. Antecedents in Hutcheson (who grew up in Ireland) don't account for its scope and revolutionary nature. (You would have to search hard in present-day Edinburgh to find a non-specialist owning a copy of anything by Hutcheson, let alone someone who had actually read him). Smith's economic thought has long been so alloyed by the intrusions of self-proclaimed disciples that its contemporary currency is base coin. But pure-gold Hume still stands free as the author of indispensable texts in that history of philosophy which (in present day jargon) can be called 'relatively autonomous' within general history. To extract them counter factually from 'Scottish Enlightenment' would be more drastic than to remove the *oeuvre* rather over generously attributed to 'Shakespeare' from the muddy waters of English history c1600, or to debit the mighty publicist Voltaire from the France of the *Encyclopédie*. Because of Hume we are, or profess to be, 'interested' in Hutcheson. Smith was Hume's friend and, up to a point, close ally. Reid's immensely influential contribution was inspired (like Kant's) by the need to rebut Hume. One cannot imagine Boswell without Hume, Burns without Reid, Scott without Burns and Boswell. That Hume moved in the same Edinburgh circles as major scientists probably doesn't account for Black's discoveries of carbon dioxide and latent heat, or Hutton's geology. But Duncan Macmillan plausibly suggests that his influence is present in the techniques of Allan Ramsay Jr's 'empirical portraiture', as Reid's can be sensed behind Raeburn's 'portraiture of common sense' (Macmillan, 1986, 23–25, 79–80).

Without Hume, in short, our conception of 'Scottish Enlightenment' as a very special phenomenon in its own right, rather than merely a local manifestation of a pan-European movement, would wholly unravel. Interesting theorists, clever architects, innovative poets, charming painters, even an epoch-making novelist, don't in themselves require elaborate accounting-for outside the general observation that Scotland, between 1745 and 1832 grew more populous and more prosperous, and profited from skills, *inter-alia*, in the production of books in English, buildings for English patrons, and portraits of English nobs. Indeed, the interesting question might be posed why this flourishing little country produced no composer to match Finland's Crusell, or Bohemia's Dittersdorf, let alone Hungary's Haydn. Bruce Lenman's brilliant short synthesis of the social, political and cultural history of 1746–1832 does in fact successfully digest Hume into its sub periods, noting the paradox that, in the *Treatise*, 'from 1739 or 1740 that intellectual phenomenon we call the Scottish Enlightenment had, ticking away beneath it, a time bomb capable of destroying some of its basic assumptions' (Lenman, 1982, 25). The themes of Lenman's *Integration, Enlightenment, and Industrialisation* can just about contain Hume, with the middle term bound fast between its flankers.

But Hume's major biographer makes a point that extends our problem of explanation:

The 'Science of Human Nature' expounded by Hume ... was either ignored or misunderstood by his own generation, and he did not live to know the more favourable reaction of Kant. In the nineteenth century his philosophy attracted considerable attention, but mainly for purposes of refutation. Only in the twentieth century has it met with sympathy and understanding ... [it] has now become the study of specialists in many fields, including psychology, ethics, religion, government, economics, and the social sciences (Mossner, 1980, 5). If Mossner is correct (some, Phillipson included, suggest differently) our vision of a remarkable phenomenon, 'Scottish Enlightenment' with Hume at fount, could commit us, unguarded, to attempts to explain 'historically' something which didn't 'happen' within the key period: interaction between Hume's thought and the culture of the city and nation where he lived.

By the mid nineteenth century 'Scotch feelosophy' (as Thomas Love Peacock called it) was identified with a craggy dogmatism such as would have appalled Hume himself. The followers of Smith had made political economy 'the dismal science'. The term 'Enlightenment' itself was not in good repute in the heyday of Victorian Evangelicalism: the Oxford English Dictionary gives a definition from 1865 – 'Shallow and pretentious intellectualism, unreasonable contempt for authority and tradition'. Carlyle, who had deserted Scottish 'enlightenment' in favour of German thought called the former 'Philosophism' 'sceptical, lightweight and morally dangerous'. However, John Stuart Mill, the son of an expatriate Scottish thinker, developed the 'utilitarianism' which was a legacy of the Scottish eighteenth century (Hutcheson is thought to be the first person to use the phrase 'greatest good of the greatest number') and gave countenance to the remarkable work of Henry Thomas Buckle (1841–1862) which has had enduring influence in Scottish historiography.

Buckle's History of Civilisation in England (1857–1861) is not that. Having aimed to write a history of European civilization, the ailing scholar cut his scope. Even so, only a ninth of the fragment of his grand scheme which was published deals with England, while one of the three volumes in which it entered popular reprint is devoted entirely to Scotland – four or five hundred pages in all. Buckle's enterprise was one which the Select Society would have understood: he was a 'philosophical historian', attempting, like Adam Smith or Arnold Toynbee, to find general laws at work in human societies. He pioneered in the use of social statistics. He was a rationalist, deistic in religion and vehemently anticlerical. Though he was never himself a Positivist, his thinking made sense to followers of Herbert Spencer. It appealed also to continental priest-haters, Russian nihilists, and British socialists of secular bent. For half a century, it brought Buckle posthumous international fame.

The problem which Scotland posed for Buckle was this: how was it that a land of great philosophers was also a terrain of gloomy bigotry and absurd superstition? Scotland had begun to succumb to Evangelicalism only around 1800, many decades after Anglophone North America, Wales, and England, but by Buckle's day it was, from his point of view, a disastrously pious country.

In the seventeenth century, according to Buckle, Scotland had been home of 'one of the most detestable tyrannies ever seen on the earth'. He found in Calvinist sermons 'a hardness of heart, an austerity of temper, a want of sympathy with human happiness, and a hatred of human nature, such as have rarely been exhibited in any age ...' Scotland's 'clergy, being supreme, did, Protestant though they were, imitate the ascetic, the unsocial, and the cruel doctrines which, in the Catholic Church, gave rise to convents, fastings, scourgings and all the other appliances of an uncouth and ungenial superstition'. The results for the Scottish people were disastrous. 'Whatever was natural, was wrong. ... Men in their daily actions and in their very looks, became troubled, melancholy and ascetic. ... Thus it was that the national character of the Scotch was, in the seventeenth century, dwarfed and mutilated'. (Buckle, 1970, 225, 230-1).

But at least these psychic dwarfs and cripples had directed their horrid zeal agin the government. 'The political activity which produced the rebellion against the Stuarts, saved the Scotch mind from stagnating, and prevented that deep slumber into which the progress of superstition would naturally have thrown it'. And this provides Buckle with a general explanation of 'Scottish Enlightenment' (or, in his terms, 'Scotch Intellect') which is more than faintly echoed in the influential work of our own contemporary T. C. Smout. The energies of Calvinism carried over into a new era of enforced tolerance and civil peace. 'The long and stubborn conflict with a despotic government kept alive a certain alertness and vigour of understanding which survived the struggle that gave it birth.... The boldness which, in the seventeenth century, was practical, became in the eighteenth century, speculative, and produced a literature, which attempted to unsettle former opinions, and to disturb the ancient landmarks of the human mind' (Buckle, 1970, 235).

We note again that the problem concealed in Buckle's generalizations is not really 'how do we explain Scottish intellectual life 1745–1832'? but 'how do we explain Hume?' Hutcheson was hardly an overthrower of ancient landmarks, though Buckle credits him with

launching 'the great rebellion of the Scottish intellect'. Besides
Hutcheson and Hume, Buckle surveys other major figures of
'Scottish Enlightenment' – Smith, Reid, Black, Hunter, Hutton
and so on. But it is perhaps the magnetic traction of Hume (as
Buckle misunderstood him) which pulls him into the extraordinary
generalization that the 'Scotch intellect' as displayed by such men
was always 'deductive' rather than 'inductive' – that it was anti-
Baconian, arguing from principles to particular observations
rather than the other way round. Hume, though a 'man of the
purest and most exemplary character, utterly incapable of false-
hood' nevertheless (Buckle avers) had 'a disregard of facts'. He
believed that ideas were 'more important than facts' and 'should
be developed before the facts are investigated'. In Scotland, following Hume 'deduction ... pervaded every science and governed
every phase of thought'. Thus a habit of reasoning appropriate to
religious 'superstition' persisted in Scotland despite 'rebellion'
against religious tyranny and could still be detected in the
mouthings of Scottish clerics in Buckle's own day (Buckle, 1970,
244, 283–4).

John Mackintosh, whose four volume *History of Civilisation in
Scotland* clearly marks in its title its emulation of Buckle's scope,
produced, before the end of the nineteenth century, a different
model. Mackintosh's arrangement was such that no periodized
'Enlightenment' (of '1730–1790' or '1745–1832') could emerge: the
eighteenth and nineteenth century were treated together under such
headings as 'Philosophy', 'Literature', 'Science', 'Manufacture and
Commerce', 'Ecclesiastical Movements'. The nineteenth-century
thinker Hamilton, with 33 pages, got more space than Hume (19)
and Reid (9) put together. This was Whiggish work. According to
Mackintosh Scottish philosophy was the outcome of the 'speculative movement' in Europe and England during the seventeenth
century when 'the human mind launched into the regions of speculation and scientific investigation with vigour and freedom, and in
the scientific side attained a marked degree of success'. Though the
'scrutinising spirit' had developed partly as a result of sixteenth-
century Reformation ('the great religious revolution'), Scotland was
'deeply affected' only rather late in the day. 'Hume, by his bold and
sceptical reasoning, aroused philosophers from their slumber and
greatly stimulated thought to further inquiries in various directions;
while Smith advanced an attractive moral theory and founded the
science of political economy, which has proved beneficial in suggesting legislative reform and commercial enterprise' (Mackintosh,
1895, 17, 25). So what we now call 'Scottish Enlightenment' was,
Whiggishly, a Good Thing.

And so thought other Scottish historians of that turn of the century period whose overviews remain works of reference today. Henry Grey Graham, in his pleasantly anecdotal survey of *Scottish Men of Letters in the Eighteenth Century* was full of enthusiasm for Hume's delightful private character and reassured *bien pensant* readers that 'the believing side of him was often uppermost: and in his essays the last word is usually in favour of theism' (Graham, 1901, 42). Hume Brown, whose multi volume *History of Scotland* is still so impressive and valuable, set forth an affirmative view of Scottish Enlightenment which is worth consideration, since it involved a convincing attempt at periodization, and, influentially, suggested causes.

Hume Brown notes Voltaire's remark 'that at the present time it is from Scotland we receive rules of taste in all the arts – from the epic poem to gardening'. Moving well outside Buckle's relatively narrow conception of 'Scotch intellect', he perceives 'the remarkable intellectual activity of Scotland in every important sphere of thought, and her original contribution in each of them' – not just Hume, Reid, Black, Smith and Cullen, but Robertson and also 'Ossian' Macpherson 'all mark new points of departure in their respective spheres' (Hume Brown, 1911, 295).

His overall periodization of Scottish history (1714–1745, then 1746–1789) conditions (or, perhaps, is conditioned by) his sense of the causes of this efflorescence. It has the great advantage of placing Hume plausibly in context. Like the university professors who have succeeded him in the writing of Enlightenment history, Hume Brown is highly impressed by the importance of the reform of the old Scottish Universities, which began just after the Treaty of Union. 'Regenting' was abolished in Edinburgh in 1708 and in Glasgow in 1727. Under this system, a student sat under one tutor for the full three or four years of university education: now specialist professors had chairs which carried with them the exclusive privilege of teaching their subjects. In the chair of Moral Philosophy at Glasgow in 1730 Hutcheson 'the prototype of the Scottish Enlightenment' broke from the ancient tradition of lecturing in Latin. Since, shortly thereafter, Hume 'threw out all his suggestions in economics and abstract philosophy that subsequently made the tour of the intellectual world', it is clear that 'in the sphere of thought as in the sphere of material interests' the nation, in the three decades preceding the '45 'had entered on a new stage of its development' (Hume Brown, 1911, 210–213).

Hume Brown brackets 'The Church and Literature from 1746 to 1789' together. Deism had advanced all over Europe. The Moderates – not deists, of course, but in the same swim – dominated the

General Assembly of the Church from 1752 onwards. They empha-
sized good work rather than faith, the ethical teachings of the Bible
rather than its mysteries. 'The pleasures of life were not banned, and
the member of the Church was to realise that he was also a member
of society which had its own legitimate sphere and function'. Hume
Brown is perfectly clear sighted about the social conservatism of
Moderate policy. A third of existing livings for ministers were in the
gift of the crown: most candidates for the ministry became tutors in
lairds' families. So it was not too hard for the Moderates to fill
pulpits with ministers agreeable to 'the classes whose adhesion it
was the interest of a national church to secure'. But the concomitant
of this was the growth of seceding nonconformity. In 1765 120
nonconformist meeting houses attracted more than 100 000 wor-
shippers. This development meant, long term, a crisis for the established church. In 1782 Principal William Robertson resigned the
leadership of the Moderates – in 1785 the leader of the 'popular'
party was elected Moderator (Hume Brown, 1911, 289–293).

This church history must clearly be related to the temporary
triumph of Hume, then the victory over him of Reid. Hume Brown
attributes 'Enlightenment' in Scotland 1745–89, to several causes.
Firstly, during the preceding 'play of mind', 1720–40, 'the best that
was then thought and known in Europe was familiar to the predecessors of the men who were to follow and to accomplish such
great results'. (To put it more bluntly, foreign influence was decisive.) There was, by 1740, secondly, a 'definite conception of a
cultivated society, whose aims should be at once to advance thought
and to make culture a national concern'. Thirdly, the universities of
Aberdeen, Glasgow, and Edinburgh harboured 'strenuous' teachers
whose devoted work had 'hardly a parallel in any other country and
certainly not in England'. And, finally, Scots lairds maintained the
custom of touring the continent for two or three years before settling
down: they picked up the best new thought.

Hume Brown thus suggests that external influence interacted
with a local spirit of 'improvement' and strenuousness peculiar to
Scotland. His positioning of Hume neatly relates to this: 'Hume only
systematized and gave precision to modes of thinking which widely
prevailed in Scotland during the greater part of the eighteenth
century'. And in this period 'the prevailing type of thought, most
strongly marked in Edinburgh, was a pagan naturalism for which
Christianity was a temporary aberration of the human mind'. We
might put together thus the view suggested by Hume Brown in the
tolerant era of Moderate domination in the Kirk, the Voltairean free
thought characteristic of aristocratic circles in Europe was able to
flourish, albeit undemonstratively, in Scotland's capital. Hume

Brown points out that in 1770 no Edinburgh publisher could be found to bring out the *Essay on Truth* penned by Aberdeen's James Beattie against Hume: four years before this Dr John Gregory, Professor of the Practice of Physic, had written to Beattie from Edinburgh that 'Absolute dogmatic atheism is the present tone'. However, the Aberdonian Reid's *Enquiry Into the Human Mind on the Principles of Common Sense* had appeared in 1764 and proved to be more influential in the not very long run than Beattie's popular book (Hume Brown, 295–298).

It may be that Hume Brown synthesized factors so successfully that his successors as general historians of Scotland didn't feel compelled to strive very hard for explanation. George S. Pryde (1962) produced a speciously Whiggish chapter on 'The Dawn of the Enlightenment' in which as a consequence of the 'security' resulting from 'The Revolution, the Union and the Hanoverian succession', the growth of commerce and industry fostered 'increased wealth and leisure' and 'an advance in education, literature and the arts' assisted by the 'fact that religion no longer dominated men's minds'. Amid the general 'record of progress' there was a 'steady but very slow' improvement in schools, and 'fundamental and sweeping reforms' in universities so that the 'antiquated (sic) Dutch commentators began to yield place to such "moderns" as Newton ... and Locke ...' (But if abolishing the regent system was so important, how come Reid was 'a most impressive' regent at King's College Aberdeen?) Pryde's next chapter, on 'The Athenian Age' is largely an ecstatic catalogue of intellectual and publishing triumphs (Pryde, 1962, 104–115, 162 ff.).

William Ferguson's much more impressive coverage (1968) comes in a chapter significantly entitled 'Education and Culture in the Eighteenth Century'. This is admirably detailed and subtly reasoned: one senses a distinct revival of Scottish historiography, a questioning of Whiggish platitudes. Thus, while 'a wider mental horizon' in the universities was 'stimulated by closer contact with England', 'most of the old continental influences' were still strong. There were, however, elements of continuity with Scottish tradition. 'More than a few attitudes later regarded as typical' of Scottish Enlightenment 'derive from Calvinism', and many philosophers were 'as well versed in Stair as in Hobbes, Shaftesbury, Locke, or the French "philosophes"'. Scots Law 'was philosophical in its bent: it put its faith in principles rather than in collections of dry precedents'. Hume, Ferguson and Stewart, writing on such topics as marriage and divorce did 'little more than popularise the law of their country'. If such men were 'the parents of modern sociology' this can be attributed to the Scottish insistence on the group rather than the individual. Ideas of kinship remained strong: Hobbesian atomization and 'social contract' theory cut no ice. But Ferguson never forgets the international dimension. 'Ideas ignore boundaries' – Scots sucked in ideas from everywhere (Ferguson, 1968, 198–233).

Rosalind Mitchison (1970) in a much brisker survey, links the breakthrough of Hume to the reform of the universities via reference to Hutcheson. She emphasizes the daring of Hume, who 'took further the cautious experimental method of Newton, turning it from science to philosophy, and adding something approaching the modern idea of statistical probability as the basis of scientific "law"'. She attributes the surge in which (she says) 'Scotland packed into about thirty years of crowded development between 1750 and 1780 the economic growth that in England had spread itself over two centuries' to three factors – 'the English connection', growth of population, and an intellectual life 'made possible by the structure of her educational system'. Her 'Unionist' perspective makes it hard for her to explain the educational prowess over which she enthuses – the literacy of most of the Lowland population, the availability of 'cheap and nominally obligatory' schooling in most parishes, the resulting readiness of the 'Scotch peasant' to 'argue with his "betters"'; and the vibrant life of the universities in which Smith and Reid hammered out their ideas in front of their students. Can the Act of 1707 explain all this? Never mind: education underlay Enlightenment. But its 'origin' came from 'the push to develop two particular professions, medicine and the law'.

Mitchison is refreshingly sceptical about the inane Whiggish view that the Edinburgh Medical School trained doctors who saved individual lives. Its value 'was to be shown in the public health movement of the next century'. (Western 'scientific' medicine before Pasteur, as Livingstone should have noticed in Africa, was less efficacious than the methods of witch doctors and, in Scotland, 'wise women'). Yet, as Mitchison subtly notes, medicine 'was a link between science and society and within the sciences between physics, chemistry, physiology, and geology'. While it seems likely that few of the technical advances in Scottish industry 'came directly from her own natural scientists, the society of these men provided the debate that rendered the whole country appreciative of new ideas' (Mitchison, 1982 edn. 332–3, 344–356).

Her vision of a 'special coherence' in Scottish intellectual society is like Ferguson's, and Phillipson's. But she ties in the scientists particularly well. Hume's thought is, very properly, seen as developing from Newton's and pointing forward to twentieth century science. This way of coping with Hume should have great appeal for those who, like myself, find legal theory rather tedious and the

Himalayas of philosophical speculation overtaxing of frail lungs. But, as we shall see, it's not the only way, nor, perhaps, the most necessary one.

Around the same time as Ferguson and Mitchison's contributions T. C. Smout's delightful *History of the Scottish People* (1969) devoted over thirty pages to 'The Golden Age of Scottish Culture'. We might remark in passing how much damage has been done to our understanding of Scottish history by the gilding of the eighteenth century. Before – lead or pitch. Afterwards – steel and soot. Scottish culture was not without strengths before the eighteenth century, nor has it lacked them since. But, pardoning Smout for his 'ageist' solecism, we must concede that he, too, is subtle.

He notes three striking features of eighteenth-century Scottish philosophy. Firstly:

> ... the speed of its growth from nothing. The seventeenth century was blank. ... There could so easily have been Hutcheson, then Hume as a brilliant accident, and then silence. But thanks, partly at least, to reform and development within the Scottish universities, a tradition was built up after Hutcheson which involved academics in philosophical disquisition without the possibility of interference from theologians.

Scottish philosophy, secondly, had a distinct slant towards moral problems and social affairs. 'No doubt it got this from Hutcheson, and Hutcheson got it from his Calvinism'. Thirdly, 'Scottish philosophers were avidly interested in other disciplines than their own'.

This third feature at least won't 'strike' us if we survey 'Enlightenment' as a European phenomenon. Rousseau, for instance, wrote a successful opera and a best-selling novel as well as important 'political theory'; Goethe did much more than dabble in chemistry and sought to refute Newton's optical theories; Franklin was businessman, journalist, scientist and politician; Voltaire popularized Newtonian thought in France.

However, Smout does achieve an overview in which 'philosophy' is given priority, before he goes on to display his own 'avid' interests outside his own discipline in a brilliant survey of Scottish achievements in architecture – the Edinburgh New Town is seen as an achievement 'of European significance' – and an account of literature which revels in the quiddity of verse in Scots, and brings into an overall conception of 'Golden Age' the 'greatest achievements of Gaelic poetry'.

But when the 'social and economic' Smout takes over again, he has sadly to acknowledge that Gaelic poets, unknown to their Lowland contemporaries, were outside the 'mainstream' of the Enlightenment which he now has to explain. It was a Lowland movement, and overwhelmingly the achievement was that of 'the middle class'. But great landowners were important as patrons, and the general 'lack of social and political iconoclasm' among the literati can be attributed to their identification with landed interests on whose approval they were 'emotionally dependent'. So the support of aristocrats was the first 'precondition for the golden age'. The second was the 'character of national education'. Finally 'there was the question of religion'. It is 'important to notice that the decay of the old kirk for the most part predated the cultural golden age. It was not the scepticism of Hume or the satire of Burns that blew away the clerical narrowness of the past. It was because the power of the old clerics was already waning that Hume got the chance to be sceptical and Burns to be satirical with impunity'. However – and here Buckle makes a surprising comeback;

> ... it is impossible not to suspect that the remarkable drive that so characterises eighteenth century Scotland in both intellectual and economic affairs is connected with Calvinist habits of reflection and seriousness of individual purpose. ... It is possible that the nation gained a particular stimulus from adopting in the seventeenth century an ideology with one over-riding and narrowly religious aim and then, finding this intrinsically impossible to achieve from being catapulted into an eighteenth century world where the legitimate objects of aspiration were suddenly felt to be wider and more diverse. The energy generated towards the achievement of the original objective was contained in the race for the new ones, and society for a time got the best of both worlds (Smout, 1972 edn., 451–483).

One problem, now obvious, is this: no one has done enough in the field of Scottish historiography to question Buckle's alien, under-informed and *a priori* view that seventeenth-century Scotland was a land of gloomy bigotry dominated by 'Calvinist ideology'. For this reason, and perhaps for no other, it is worth considering a typically prejudiced and bad-mannered sortie into Scottish history by Lord Dacre, as Hugh Trevor Roper, in a paper, 'The Scottish Enlightenment', published in 1967.

Trevor Roper praises the Union of 1707, absurdly, as a 'great act of statesmanship' which 'enriched Scotland materially ... enlarged its intellectual horizons ... transformed its society'. But 'The Enlightenment did not come from England only. ... The spirit which made the union possible – that liberal spirit which could see beyond the narrow glens of a tribal past – was necessarily older than the union which it made'. Could Calvinism have provided this 'spirit'? Of course not. To explain 'Scottish Enlightenment', Trevor Roper first tells us what it was like.

The Scottish literati were for the most part 'thoroughly second rate'. All, except Hume, were 'dull dogs. Their writing is flat and their conversation was dry: no *bon mot* is recorded from them'. Only half a dozen were 'real intellectual pioneers' – Hutcheson, Hume, Ferguson, Robertson, Smith, and Millar – and all *these* men were interested in, above all, was 'the social behaviour of mankind'. Hutcheson, the first of them in time 'was born an Irishman, and he drew his philosophy from English teachers: Bacon, Newton and Locke, as filtered through Shaftesbury'. So there was 'nothing very Scottish' about the stress placed on instinctive benevolent moral sense by him and his followers'. 'But', Trevor Roper now lavishly concedes, 'it was in Scotland that this English philosophy acquired its new social character', moving from philosophy to sociology, to political economy and utilitarianism until Millar, last of the six, 'annexed Hume's philosophy to Whig politics' and begat, as it were, Macaulay and J. S. Mill.

So, why was it the *Scots* who were preoccupied with social change? After 1680, the internal condition of Scotland forced men to think in a new way. Faced by horrific economic decline, 'Scots, by resuming their broken contact with Europe, discovered themselves'. The Reformation had cut Scotland off from Paris and other jolly good European places. The Dutch universities used by Scots were blinkered. Despite a 'brief flicker of Enlightenment ... reflected from the pikes and muskets of Cromwell's army' in the 1650s, the last half century before the Union was 'a dark age of introversion and social war'. But, the cavalry arrived in time, or rather the Cavaliers....

Episcopalians and Jacobites, the Dacre-to-be tells us, broke out to Europe and drank in fresh streams of thought. 'Almost all the foreign culture which reached Scotland in its dark age' came through Episcopalians. 'Jacobites' were exiled to France by the 1689 revolution, and in the 'movement' towards Enlightenment from about 1680 to 1715 'and even beyond' almost every man 'of intellectual distinction ... was at least half a Jacobite'. Quite a proportion of children could point out to Lord Dacre that Jacobites *opposed* that liberating 'act of statesmanship', (to quote his weird phrase again), the Union. He has one useful point: James II, as Duke of York, with the Earl of Perth and Perth's protegé, Sibbald, set up the College of Physicians in Edinburgh. But to say that Kames and Hume were 'Jacobites' is somewhat to stretch evidence. However, let the erstwhile Trevor Roper proceed.

Saviours did come, he concedes, from Holland, with William of Orange, including Carstares who reorganized Edinburgh University's Arts faculties on Dutch models, and set up new chairs in

fashionable subjects. Why was Holland no longer backward? Because it had ceased to be Calvinist, silly.... Arminianism was tri-
umphing there. So the strange picture is clarifying itself: Presbyterian dominance of the admittedly important universities has to be
conceded, but the 'educated laity' of the Episcopalian-Jacobite
north-east were the key factor in ensuring that new ideas from
abroad were entertained. And the ideas of Montesquieu in particular made a huge impact on Scotland because they suggested a path of
progress out of an archaic, closed, tribal society, mired in darkness,
where 'Hutcheson was lecturing on Locke and Shaftesbury in Glasgow while carts were unknown twelve miles away'. Hume and
others were provoked into 'that analysis of human progress which is
the peculiar contribution of the Scottish Enlightenment' (Trevor
Roper, 1967, 1635–1658).

The only value of Trevor Roper's farrago of prejudices is that the
few truths which lurk in it do point to contradictions in Scottish
intellectual, social, and political development. They suggest that
matters were much more complicated than Buckle, or even Smout,
Mitchison, and Ferguson suggest. The intellectual life of seventeenth
century Scotland was certainly not as richly multifarious as that of
its incurably violent but quite largely prosperous southern neighbour (where Samuel Johnson's Club later would meet in London
while less than twelve miles away his favourite beverage, tea, was
being carried by large, untameable gangs of armed smugglers into a
city as turbulent as modern New York). However, it was certainly
not characterized by monolithic and unchanging Calvinism. That,
indeed, was what the Lowland violence was about – the inability of
the Presbyterians, except for one brief period, to impose their vision
on the country.

So, far from being a land of 'savage tribesmen', Scotland had
produced, in the Renaissance period, fine minds acknowledged all
over Europe; not only Buchanan, but John Mair (or Major), born,
near Haddington, in 1467, provost of St Salvator's College, St
Andrews, when he died in 1550, having previously been principal of
Glasgow University. If Alexander Broadie (1990) fails to establish
any very direct intellectual-historical connection between Mair's
catholic philosophical circle in Scotland and Hume, he can argue
strongly that the eighteenth century was not the first in which
Scottish philosophy flowered, that by Hume's day the country 'had
acquired a rich philosophical tradition, and it is past belief that in
the absence of that tradition the philosophy of the Scottish Enlightenment could have been written' (Broadie, 1990, 3).

One route down which some of the legacy of Mair, Buchanan,
and the Scottish Renaissance might have travelled is traced in David

Stevenson's pathbreaking study: *The Origins of Freemasonry: Scotland's Century, 1590–1710* (1988). At the very least, Stevenson's work makes it possible to see how the distinctive achievements of Scottish architecture from 1660 onwards can be related to a 'masonic' enlightenment associated with secret societies where freethinking lairds mingled with craftsmen. To be brief about a fascinating matter: Scotland clearly long preceded England in developing what became a central institution of Enlightenment from the Thirteen Colonies to St Petersburg – the masonic lodge. (The English masons of course, invented a history of freemasonry which obliterated this awkward fact.)

Sir Robert Moray, from a minor Perthshire landed family, is a figure discussed by Stevenson who perhaps exemplifies one of the roots of later 'Enlightenment' in the seventeenth century. Born about 1607, son of a minor Perthshire laird, he combined practical skills in surveying, which must, Stevenson thinks, explain his acceptance in 1641 into the Lodge of Edinburgh (he was a kind of craftsman himself) with a Christian Stoic philosophy, scientific interests and acquaintance with advanced European thinkers – with Jesuit scholars and with the hermeticist polymath Athanasius Kircher. Initially a Covenanting General, he later became a hot Royalist. He ended his life at Charles II's court, experimenting in chemistry. As Stevenson concludes, 'In his interests in Hermeticism, Rosicrucianism, alchemy, and symbols he typifies the sort of late Renaissance influences which had given birth to Scottish Freemasonry [in 1598–9]. In his scientific interests, his deistic tendencies, his cult of friendship and sociability he reflects influences which look ahead to the age of Enlightenment....' (Stevenson, 1988, 166–89).

R. A. Houston (1985, 21–2, 256–7) suggests that eighteenth century levels of literacy in Lowland Scotland were not dramatically different from those in Northern England and in certain other parts of Europe. But what Scotland did possess was a remarkable 'song culture' in which higher and lower ranks of society participated. Thomas Crawford (1979) has helped us position Burns not as a unique one-off or revivalist, but as the inheritor of a continuous tradition of poetry and song. His favourite metre, 'Standard Habbie', was, apparently, the invention of a seventeenth-century laird. He also used the fourteen line stanza associated with a poem by Alexander Montgomerie – a Catholic at the court of James VI – *The Cherrie and the Slae*. This poem had remained in circulation during the period conceived by Buckle and Dacre to have been an age of savage bigotry and darkness. Its metre is as difficult to handle, perhaps, as any devised by Western man. We should never think about Scotland between 1603 and the era of Fergusson, Burns, and Scott without imagining song in the air and pithy verses to go with the fine tunes.

Hume himself was far from immune from a patriotic preference for Scottish literary and musical traditions: as Fiona Stafford has illustrated, it was the circle in which Hume drank and argued with the young leaders of the Moderate tendency in the Kirk which encouraged and promoted 'Ossian' Macpherson, and the great philosopher-historian was at first a hot supporter (Stafford, 1988, 166–8).

Yet David Daiches, in an excellent short survey (1986) writes of 'the failure of the Scottish Enlightenment to cope adequately with works of the poetic imagination'. He mentions Hume in particular, who admired not only 'Ossian', but also Home's once-famous tragedy, *Douglas*. Hume was in good company in both cases; these works remained famous, read, and, presumably, enjoyed, into the nineteenth century. (Perhaps one day persons will marvel that intelligent critics c. 1950 took such a turgid writer as D. H. Lawrence very seriously.) However, Daiches' point – making Hume the key example – illustrates that we still have an obstinate problem. Having shown how the Scottish 'enlightenment involves national continuities traceable back to the fifteenth century, how it can be seen as a splendid local expression of an international phenomenon, supported by rapidly rising prosperity and involved in complicated cross currents and contradictions, it still will not dissolve. There is an indigestible core to the phenomenon and its name is Hume'. Smout engagingly concedes 'Certainly, it would be a rash man who believed that he could discover from the study of the past the recipe to bring a new Hume into the world' (Smout, 1972 edn, 471).

Hence there is much to be said for the egregious, seemingly eccentric approach of G. E. Davie in his Historical Association pamphlet of 1981, in which he intricately positions Hume, Reid, and Smith in relation, not to the history of philosophy in general, where specialist philosophers usually put them, but to the history of thought in Scotland, about Scotland, from Fletcher of Saltoun onwards. The philosophical breakthrough begins to seem more like a 'Scottish breakaway', part of an attempt to rescue the nation from the crisis which had brought about Union. A. C. Chitnis's monographs on the Scottish Enlightenment (1976, 1986) gather together for those who want them, compendiously, the range of facts which are generally taken to comprise the phenomenon. Davie's short study, however, might valuably stimulate others in trying to find ways of explaining how Hume was Scottish and why Scotland only could have produced Hume.

4

An Uninflammable People?

CHRISTOPHER A. WHATLEY

'The Scots', observed Daniel Defoe at the end of 1706, as the Scottish parliament debated the terms upon which it would surrender to Westminster rule, were a 'hardened, refractory and terrible people'. Although he was familiar with the vociferous London mob, he was convinced that the Scots 'rabble', was 'the worst of its kind'. In 1778, in Glasgow, a small Roman Catholic congregation, which included some 'poor Highland women', gathered to worship, only to be besieged later by a dirt- and stone-throwing mob, who 'continued their outrages till night...in a grosser manner', a *Scots Magazine* correspondent reported, than he 'ever knew in Britain'.

Other sources hint at the presence in Scotland of a rumbustious people. In Aberdeen in 1731 for example, Andrew Ferguson, a piper, was banned from playing at night, as this tended to 'raise mobs & tumults in the Streets'. Kirk session and burgh court records provide vivid testimony of widespread drunkenness, sabbath profanation and observable sexual licentiousness, although the last was rarely conducted as openly as in the cases of John Dunlop and Jean Ferguson, two Glaswegians who in July 1707 were accused of 'some very immodest and unchaste carriage together in the Barony church in the time of sermon'.

Neither in the workplace was the ordinary Scot always easy to control: during a dispute involving coal miners near Lochgelly in 1745 it was remarked that, 'its these Cattles' principle & practice to Stand no longer to their bargain, than they have good profit, if they possibly can Slip the Head'. Nor, apparently, did Scotsmen confine their unruly and undeferential behaviour to Scotland. The Tyneside keelmen, amongst whom Scots migrants were in the majority, were the most 'turbulent' workers in the north-east of England, and took part in several serious disturbances during the eighteenth century (Fewster, 1957, 32–3).

Rightly or wrongly, the characteristics conveyed in these few examples are not reflected in the image of the ordinary Lowland Scot which has long been portrayed to the public by historians. The view generally conveyed is that despite the strains of major political, cultural, and economic upheaval in the eighteenth and early nineteenth centuries, the traditionally stoical and acquiescent Scot engaged in few public demonstrations of distress or disapproval. Until not much more than a decade ago, the impression was readily obtained from the writings of an enormously complacent Scottish historical establishment that, except for a handful of popular disturbances, the main visible signs of an oppositional culture in Scotland before the French Revolution were the Jacobite-inspired risings of 1715 and 1745. The Union, in this view (which has its roots in the eighteenth century itself), transformed Scottish manners, and rescued Scotland from barbarism, anarchy and unruliness and introduced in their place economic development, socio-political order and cultural enlightenment (Beveridge and Turnbull, 1989, 25–30).

Thus, 'Quiet and law-abiding', is how the hugely influential historian Henry Grey Graham portrayed the Lowland Scots in his once widely-read *Social Life of Scotland in the Eighteenth Century* (1899). Even in the rapidly growing trading and manufacturing town of Glasgow, the people were for a long time, 'well-ordered folk'. Hardly distinguishable from the kailyard tradition in Scottish literature, other writers of popular historical works reinforced Graham's views in books like W. Sanderson's *Scottish Life and Character* (1904), where chapters such as 'But and Ben', 'At the Ingleside', and 'Hamely Fare', were accompanied by H. J. Dobson's sentimental paintings of a deeply religious, contented and homely people, resigned to their fate, whether it was signing a new lease or confronting old age. It was a world of mutual interdependence and social homogeneity, of full and rewarding employment.

Such couthy and enduring images had lost little of their appeal in the 1960s, although in his *History of the Working Classes in Scotland* (1920) Thomas Johnston had made a valiant attempt to introduce conflict and class into Scottish history. Even so, G. S. Pryde, in his *Scotland From 1603* (1962), one of the 'New History of Scotland' series, was still 'struck by the relative stability of society on the farms and in the towns'. And although T. C. Smout's seminal *History of the Scottish People* (1969) heralded a new era in Scottish social history, on this issue he was not inclined to challenge conventional wisdom: the failure of the United Scotsmen (a proletarian radical movement which operated from 1797 until 1802) to attract much support was ascribed not only to the success of the government's repressive tactics but also to 'the uninflammable character of the Scottish populace as a whole'. Smout however did devote more pages of his book to riot and disorder in Scotland than most of his predecessors. He concluded though that in Scotland from the time of the French Revolution there were substantially less of the 'anxious moments' which the authorities faced in England, notably during the Luddite disturbances of 1812 and the events surrounding the Peterloo massacre of 1819 (Smout, 1969, 210–211). By contrast, rising social tension in Scotland was seen to have culminated in what has elsewhere been described as the 'pathetic' rising of 1820, the so-called 'Radical War' (Lenman, 1981, 152).

The problem for Scottish historians to consider, it was urged, not so long ago, was 'the relative lack of social discontent and either urban or peasant unrest' (Larner, 1981, 50). The aim of this chapter is to examine the ways in which this has been done, but more importantly, to ask whether the 'orthodoxy of passivity' is as watertight as it appears, and to suggest that new and modified pictures and interpretations are possible.

Rural Certainties – and Doubts

Modification rather than radical revision does seem more appropriate as far as the countryside is concerned, for compared with some other regions of early modern Europe, there was in Lowland Scotland a striking absence of overt and direct social protest against agrarian improvement and its social consequences. In attracting national attention, the sole exception was the 'Levellers Revolt' in Galloway in 1724. Comparison of Ireland and Scotland has pointed up sharply the contrast between the appearance of relative rural tranquillity in Lowland Scotland, and Ireland, where every decade between 1760 and 1840 'was punctuated by at least one major outbreak of peasant unrest' (Devine, 1988, 127). It was an earlier comparison of Scotland with England however which had first demanded explanation. In 1830 the Englishman William Cobbett had asked why it was that 'the Scots were quiet while the English burnt the ricks' (Smout, 1969, 303).

Two broad categories of factors have been used to account for the Scots' silence in the countryside. The first are social and cultural, with emphasis being placed on the delicate bonds of paternalism and dependence, and the deference-creating role of education and the Kirk (Lenman, 1981, 11). In fact, according to Smout, the church played a negative role as far as the peasants were concerned: far from providing leadership for their flocks in the face of oppression (as they had done during the Levellers revolt), ministers generally took the side of the lairds and preached a gospel of submission (Smout, 1969, 308–9). It has also been established that agricultural change brought many benefits to rural dwellers, with some being raised to the rank of tenant farmer and most experiencing real increases in their living standards in the last decades of the eighteenth century.

Although overlapping with the first, the second category of explanation focuses on material factors. The 'exceptional insecurity' of the Scottish peasant, who had no right to pass his tenancy on to his heirs has been described as 'an excellent structural recipe for docility and deference' (Larner, 1981, 50). The most important example of reasoning of this sort however has been advanced in a series of articles written over the past 15 years by T. M. Devine (Devine, 1978; 1984; 1988). Basically, Devine's case, which has become increasingly sophisticated over time, is that Scottish rural society in the Lowlands operated on lines which tended to remove the most likely causes of large scale dissent. Thus, unlike farm workers in southern and eastern England, who by the end of the Napoleonic Wars were frequently hired on a daily or weekly basis, agricultural workers in the lowlands of eastern Scotland were commonly hired for six months or a year. In large part, it is argued, this reflected the very different labour market conditions north of the border, where labour was in short supply. That Scottish agriculture tended to be mixed added to the rural workers' security of employment by providing jobs throughout the year. At the same time, the argument runs, as the hiring fairs involved individual bargaining between farmer and servant, group organization was less likely to develop. With a substantial part of the farm workers' wage being paid in kind, some shelter from the vicissitudes of the open market was obtained.

To date, the materialist explanation of rural quiescence has not been challenged, although some minor queries might be raised about aspects of it. For example, although the arrangement whereby the harvest earnings of the wives and family of ploughmen were used to pay the cottage rent benefited married men with a fit wife, daughter, or son of working age, the compulsory requirement of hinds to provide a 'bondager' for service on the farm caused deep resentment amongst those not so favoured, and ultimately, far from ineffective collective action was taken to end it. Nor did the system of long engagements work entirely in the interests of labour, and in itself it was not necessarily an order-inducing arrangement. Thus one Victorian commentator on agricultural affairs was sure that there would be no combination amongst the ploughmen of East Lothian 'because the moment they struck the men would come under the whip hand of the law', and be liable to heavy fines or even imprisonment for breach of contract, the latter being used on occasion, in the words of a Perth sheriff, 'as a sort of terror' (Houston, 1957, 321).

The part played by the law then in repressing overt displays of dissent in the countryside, should certainly not be overlooked. Indeed in a recent comparison of justice and law in eighteenth century Scotland and Ireland, one Irish historian has concluded that the Scottish courts were more likely to convict a defendant than their English or Irish counterparts (Connolly, 1988, 121). It is a topic which if extended into the nineteenth century would benefit from further investigation.

It is conceivable too that the broad brushstrokes with which the picture of rural tranquillity has been painted may have concealed from view the localized conflicts and instances of peasant resistance or agrarian discontent which are to be found in the much underused regional and district archives, as well as in court records. As the process of agrarian improvement was patchy and uneven, we should not expect to find great national or even regional risings. It was on the individual farm or corner of an estate where hurt would be felt, and in appropriate circumstances, would provoke a reaction. A couple of smaller disturbances, for example, occurred at Irvine in Ayrshire in 1749 when the local council's attempts to enclose grazing ground and later to fence off part of the town's moor to construct a linen factory produced a 'great clamour among the lower sort of inhabitants' (Strawhorn, 1985, 71, 84). They were not alone in Ayrshire, and elsewhere too accounts of small-scale skirmishes, and of landowners' agents fleeing wigless, as they were chased by angry crowds, show that change was not undertaken without shows of anger. At present however, the number of known instances of this sort is not great.

Much more substantial are the doubts which have recently been expressed about long-held assumptions concerning the extent and manner in which the church acted to create a homogenous and socially conservative rural society in Scotland. On the contrary, it has been suggested, the 'Scottish churches were the vehicles for expressing many of the antagonizms of Scottish society at large'. Class antagonizms were reflected not in opposition to the Presbyterian religion, but through the numerous secessions which racked the church in Scotland after c 1740. Within the church buildings themselves, social divisions were exposed and widened as, for example, lairds and heritors erected lofts or reserved large numbers of fixed pews for themselves and their dependents (Brown, 1990, 91–3). As far as the debate about social relations and the role of religion is concerned, perhaps the most significant finding concerns patronage disputes, that is where a new minister, appointed by a landowner under the terms of the 1712 Patronage Act, found his presentation disputed and often violently opposed by large crowds of angry and hostile parishioners. There were many of these, with perhaps half of Scotland's parishes experiencing a disputed settlement between 1713 and 1874. Further, it has been argued that more than any other form of protest, patronage disputes reveal the emerging social fracture in Scotland's rural parishes. They were the 'most persistent and geographically widespread cause of popular unrest in Scotland between 1730 and 1843', and following as they did the main phases of agricultural improvement, they were the 'Scottish equivalent to rural protest in the rest of the British Isles' (Brown, 1987, 104).

Although not without weaknesses, this is a powerful assault on the case for blanket rural quiescence. Those at the sharp end of schemes for agrarian improvement and reorganization were not unresponsive to their changing circumstances. In a society where the reformed church had dug deeply into the popular consciousness, distress and outrage appear to have been channelled differently. Yet even where the hold of the kirk was strongest, in the arena of sexual morality, recent work by two female historians has shown that there was a 'substantial minority who...defied the Church's discipline' (Mitchison and Leneman, 1989, 201).

A further doubt, or at least a qualification, arises from another direction. An extensive study of riots in England and Wales between 1790 and 1810 showed that only seven per cent of identifiable riots in that 20–year period occurred in the countryside, leading to the conclusion that 'agrarian society was nearly untouched' by rioting (Bohstedt, 1983, 166). In short, riot was largely an urban phenomenon. Perhaps Anglo-Scottish differences have been exaggerated and the significance of the relative absence of rural riot in Scotland overstressed, at least prior to the outbreak of serious post 1815 rioting in various parts of England, most notably the Swing riots in the south in 1830. It is worth observing that in both countries rural opposition to the Militia Acts of 1796 and 1797 was substantial, violent, and ugly, and involved large numbers of people.

It is striking that the general absence of overt collective action has not been interpreted as evidence of docility or an undue deference of the ruled towards their rulers south of the border. Rather, it has been suggested, in the rural situation, where for a variety of reasons collective action was less likely to surface than in the towns, when resentment and hostility did occur, they manifested themselves anonymously, with individuals being subject to intimidating threats, trees being cut down or barns and haystacks set on fire, and gates being lifted from their hinges. It was the English social historian E. P. Thompson, who first drew attention to, and defined, the 'anonymous tradition' (Thompson, 1974). It was, he said, 'exactly in a rural society, where any open, identified resistance to the ruling power may result in instant retaliation', that one finds these 'acts of darkness'.

No serious research along these lines has so far been conducted in Scotland, although with its immensely powerful landlords (at least until 1747), unforgiving courts and influential and all-pervasive Kirk sessions, it might be considered an ideal test-bed for Thompson's hypothesis. Only the odd impressionistic survey can be consulted (Whatley, 1987a). Forays into the available evidence indicate that a more systematic investigation may get behind what was conceivably a very thin veil of public deference and uncover the ugly face of hitherto unrecognized rural tensions. For example, although the anti-Militia disturbances of August and September 1797 were quickly and firmly put down by the complementary measures of judicious military action and the expeditious conviction of those accused of fomenting unrest, it was with extreme reluctance that the local yeomanry turned out to take part in the suppression of disorder. The tenant farmers and others of similar rank who comprised such forces were painfully aware of the potential dangers of rounding on rioters who were their own servants and who knew them personally. 'You quell the riot', wrote one of their number from Midlothian, 'at the hazard of your *Life, Family and Property*, because you are stationary in the place, amongst those men you compel, and who you cannot live without, which if enraged, will never hesitate to destroy you, and your effects' (NRA(S), Maitland MSS).

A more commonplace and usually less physically threatening symptom of changing rural relationships, was wood stealing. Illicit wood-cutting remained a problem on the Perthshire estates of the Dukes of Atholl throughout the eighteenth century, as tenants and others insisted on retaining their customary rights to cut timber (Leneman, 1987).

On Monymusk estate in Aberdeenshire, as agricultural improvements got under way, Sir Archibald Grant found it hard to persuade a reluctant tenantry to obey his instructions and suffered as green wood was cut, timber stolen, and dykes were pulled down. Almost half a century ago, such actions were interpreted by one of the few Scottish historians to peer beneath the surface of rural society, as 'ignorance, carelessness and a failure to appreciate the new conditions' (Hamilton, 1945). Nowadays, influenced by the perceptions of English historians such as Thompson, who has attacked the condescending attitudes of some of his predecessors towards ordinary people and their actions, the same evidence can reasonably be interpreted as the conscious acts of a tenantry which resented their loss of customary rights to kindling and firewood, and to roam at liberty and graze their animals on land which had served these purposes from time immemorial.

The growing gulf between master or tenant farmer and man or wage labourer which occurred as the process of rural proletarianization quickened after c1760 gave rise to tensions too, which in the Carse of Gowrie resulted in a petition which was sent from thirty-six 'Gentlemen, Landholders and ... Farmers' to the justices of peace of Perthshire in 1786. This complained of the increased 'Insolence' of their servants, and alleged that men were leaving at will, failing to carry out orders or executing them 'in a very Indiscreet and Grudging manner', and 'overdriving' and beating their masters' horses.

In large part this can be attributed to the exceptionally rapid rate of change which took place in this locality and also to the heavy nature of the soil, which demanded frequent ploughing (Gray, 1984, 12–13). A full time labour force of ploughmen was created, but of unmarried rather than married men, as unlike many of Scotland's other farming districts, there was little requirement for the additional assistance which the families of farm workers were expected to provide during rush seasons of the year. Housed in the squalid bothies of the type described by an appalled Hugh Miller (Rosie, 1981, 109–12), these workers had cause and were in a better position to develop a collective strength than most other rural employees, and indeed it is notable that Perthshire provides most of the early instances of agricultural trade unionism in Scotland. What the example points up is one of the most important developments in Scottish history of recent times, the clear recognition of the dangers of unqualified generalization and of the need to take account of local and regional circumstances in explaining many historical phenomena. As in England, there is a pronounced regional geography of rural crime which would repay further study (Mingay, 1989, 1–8).

A fuller investigation of the extent and nature of covert protest in Scottish rural society is for the future. At present it has to be conceded that the case for the existence of a turbulent undercurrent beneath the tranquil surface of the Scottish Lowland countryside may be strongly suspected but has not yet been proven. There are much more solid grounds for revising the older view of social calm in the towns as well as in the arena of industrial relations.

Turbulence in and around the Towns

No respectable historian has ever denied the existence of urban riot in eighteenth- and early nineteenth-century Scotland. What is at issue is the extent of this activity. So too is its meaning and significance, which are not matters of fact but interpretation. There is a belief that notable riots were few in number (no more than three or four in some accounts), lacking in political inspiration, and compared to England, 'remarkably unviolent'. Accordingly, eighteenth-century popular protest has been rather dismissively described as 'sporadic, largely spontaneous and short-lived... just a trial run for the working-class struggles in the nineteenth century' (Logue, 1980, 109). Why? In part, it has been argued, because after 1707, the state in Scotland was able to exercise its authority and suppress dissident voices (Smout, 1969, 211–2).

Such judgements however have been based on an exceedingly slim body of evidence. Furthermore, writers of general textbooks on Scottish history have almost invariably viewed their subject through the spectacles of the articulate, polite, and improving classes, and until very recently it was only exceptionally that anyone was inclined either to look further down the social scale, or more importantly, to try to comprehend the world as it was seen from below. The painstaking and systematic research work which has been carried out by historians elsewhere (eg Rudé, 1964; Tilly, 1969; Stevenson, 1979) is at an early stage in Scotland.

A start however has been made, and at least four notable developments have taken place within the past two decades or so. First, detailed studies of most of the major riots in Scotland have been published, while Kenneth Logue's *Popular Disturbances in Scotland 1780–1815* saw the light of day in 1979. Notably, it was as recently as 1981 that a reviewer of Logue's book could report the relief he felt on discovering 'that the population of Scotland...was not quite so cowed as it sometimes appears and that a popular political life went on despite the smothering 'management' of the Dundas family and the intimidation of Braxfield and his kind'. It is a lesson which has by no means been universally learned. Yet contemporaries from the upper ranks were frequently made aware that there was something of an uneasy contradiction between their own perceptions of their position and the respect which the lower orders should have shown them, and what was actually the case. Thus in 1724, John Gray, baillie of the burgh and barony of Duns, complained indignantly that his attempts to put a stop to the townspeople's annual game of football had led to an attack on his house, during which the 'mob' used 'manie execrable oaths that they would destroy the complainer and bereave him and...his family of their lives'. What apparently appalled him most was that he had believed that his 'authoritie in the burgh was sufficient to have defended him against anie insult' (Hist. MSS Commission, V, 1909).

Marxist-inspired challenges to the older view of Scottish calm and classlessness have also appeared, and given some shape to the nature of Scottish protest. J. D. Young's strongly argued but weakly-supported views in *The Rousing of the Scottish Working Class* (1979) however have found little favour in more conservative historical circles. An earlier assault from the left, again with a nationalist slant, P. Beresford Ellis and S. Mac a' Ghobhain's *Scottish Insurrection of 1820* (1970), was a landmark of sorts, but the discovery of serious flaws and clear errors of interpretation comforted those whose certainty about the stability of Scottish society in the early nineteenth century might otherwise have been shaken. Nevertheless the conceptual frameworks adopted by the Marxist writers in particular have been of undoubted interest, and have introduced radically new perspectives into Scottish social history.

Thirdly, and very recently, the papers presented at a series of scholarly seminars on 'Conflict and Stability in Scottish Society, 1700–1850', held at the University of Strathclyde in 1988–89, have been published. Significantly, the editor of the collection felt justified in concluding that 'both overt and covert protest was more common, enduring and diverse' than had formerly been recognized, while social dissent in Scotland was 'vigorous and widespread' (Devine, 1990, v). Finally, eighteenth-century industrial relations in Scotland have at last begun to receive serious attention. The cumulative effect of this has been to weaken considerably the older notion of the 'uninflammable' Scot.

Certainly there seems little support for the view that Westminster rule had a restraining influence upon Scottish society in the first half of the eighteenth century, or that urban mobs 'never made serious trouble for the government before the Malt Tax Riots and the Porteous Riots twenty or thirty years later'. Indeed there may be a case for suggesting that the opposite was true and that the first decades of Westminster rule led to an increase in disorder which was both widespread and unstoppable.

Older accounts have presented the Shawfield and Porteous riots of 1725 and 1736 respectively as isolated incidents. This tendency however, to note only major disturbances, was not, until around thirty years ago, confined to Scotland. And indeed inspired by the revisionist work of historians furth of Scotland, a preliminary survey of riot and disorder in the eighteenth century north of the border has shown that Scotland's two major riots of the first half of the eighteenth century were part of a nationwide series of popular disturbances which surrounded the activities of customs and excise officers (Whatley, 1990). Although these were not a post-1707 phenomenon – the surveyor of customs at Leith complained in June 1690 that an assailant had 'thrust him thryce in the buttock' in a struggle over some smuggled brandy – their incidence increased steeply from that date. The parliamentary union of 1707 not only raised the level of taxation in Scotland, but also introduced what was designed to be a far more efficient system of tax collection, with 'Shoalls' of excise officers being reported as coming north on the very day that the Union came into effect.

One well known result of this was an increase in smuggling. The challenge to the notion of the 'uninflammability' of the Scottish people however comes not from this, but from the popular sympathy there was towards smugglers and the bitter animosity felt towards customs and excise officers. Most historians of the period have long been aware of this, but have either simply noted it (Donaldson, 1980, 114) or been inclined, consciously or otherwise, to make light of attacks on customs and excise officers. Smuggling itself has been described as a 'national sport' (Lenman, 1977, 61). Inasmuch as during the first post-Union decades all ranks appear to have been involved in this business, and united in opposition to the new tax regime, such a term is partly adequate. What it fails to convey however is the seriousness of the situation to which widespread smuggling gave rise, notably the numerous violent assaults on officers who seized smuggled or 'run' goods.

The size of the crowds could be from a dozen to several hundred. For the unfortunate officers who were their targets, they presented a fearsome prospect. In June 1718 for example, near Dumfries, officers who had seized some smuggled tobacco found themselves 'opposed' by twenty or thirty men in disguise 'and about forte or 50 Women...who with long poles Clubs and Stafs beat and abused the said officers and their two horses and kept them prisoner till the tobacco was Carried off'. It is worth remarking that while this type of riot is being discussed here within the context of urban protest, crowds such as this one seem principally to have comprised country people. In reality there was no sharp dividing line between urban and rural society. Such was the number and ferocity of such attacks, which invariably resulted in bloody and bruising beatings, that in large areas of the country, such as Galloway, Fife, and Angus, officers simply would not go out. Even soldiers who were despatched to assist found the constant struggle to maintain order exhausting: at Dundee in 1736 the local military commander had had to beg for another company as the 'Duty of late has been so hard his Soldiers are not able to bear it'. In short, as long as this activity raged, which it did until mid-century, the coastal regions of Lowland Scotland were virtually uncontrollable, which to date appears only to have been recognized by an English political historian (Riley, 1964, 135).

What has been described as 'guerilla war' of this sort was in England largely confined to the coasts of Sussex and Kent, and to a single decade, the 1740s. In Scotland things were particularly serious during the 1720s and 1730s, when as many as sixty fatalities may conceivably have occurred as a result of soldiers firing on crowds in efforts to restore order. Significantly, the early and mid 1720s witnessed much greater civil disorder north of the border than occurred throughout the country during any of the Jacobite risings.

The decade opened with a series of food riots which spread like a 'fire or contagion' up the coasts of Fife and Angus between January and March 1720. In various parts of Galloway in 1724 and sporadically into 1725 huge crowds of 'Levellers' pulled down dykes and maimed cattle (Leopold, 1980, 4–8). Although this event has invariably been written about in isolation by historians, the authorities saw things somewhat differently, with the hard pressed customs office at Dumfries urging their superiors in Edinburgh that seized goods would only be safe in their warehouse in Kirkcudbright if the two troops of dragoons 'who were come into yt country to keep ye peace thereof agt a Mob that have gott up there of late to Demolish park dykes' remained in town. Several serious assaults on customs and excise officers took place between 1724 and 1726 in Galloway, while others happened later in the decade at Aberdeen, Ayr, and Perth. It was amidst this catalogue of violence that the well-known Shawfield Riot occurred in Glasgow in 1725. Yet protest against the malt tax was not confined to Glasgow, which is the impression frequently obtained from even the most authoritative texts; it commenced in Hamilton and erupted in towns as far afield as Ayr and Elgin. They would be worth looking at.

Events however did take their most serious turn in Glasgow, where order was only finally restored by heavily-armed forces commanded by General Wade two weeks after Captain Bushell and his men had been driven off to Dumbarton Castle by an enraged mob. It was little wonder that afterwards, the British Secretary of State, the Duke of Newcastle, reflected that the disturbances had been 'of a very extraordinary nature...the first of the kind that ever happened', for in effect this was a popular insurrection of astounding dimensions, involving a ferocious crowd. One feature of the Glasgow riot was the prominence of butchers and fleshers, the repulsive character of whose work and familiarity with blood and sharp instruments could excite awe in their fellow rioters and terror on the part of those who incurred their wrath throughout Europe.

Explanations for assaults on customs and excise officers have centred upon anti-Union and anti-English feeling, and suggestions that the smuggling which normally preceded them may have been more prominent where Jacobite sympathies were strongest (Lenman, 1980, 101). It is entirely reasonable to suppose that each of these sentiments played their part. Yet neither separately nor together do they stand up to close examination as satisfactory explanations. As has been pointed out, attacks on customs and excise officers in Scotland pre-dated the Union, so that cannot have been the primary cause. Nor did they only occur in areas where Jacobite sympathies were strong, such as Arbroath and Montrose, but also in staunchly Presbyterian regions such as the south-west. In short, the older analyses suffer both from parochialism and an unspoken assumption that the lower orders who comprised the bulk of the mobs were motivated by the same concerns of state and party as their social superiors. It is a view which governed interpretations of English crowd behaviour until recently. Mobs could certainly be raised in support of some noble cause or other, but these were by no means the only occasions on which large numbers of ordinary Scots gathered to take direct action. By borrowing analytic tools which have been used to explain similar crowd behaviour elsewhere, a much more convincing case can be made.

Pressing poverty for instance has been used to account for the degree of popular involvement in and support for smuggling in Sussex in the 1740s (Winslow, 1975, 149–50). In France too, where life was precarious, smuggling represented a source of extra income. It is quite possible that the longevity of such activity in Scotland is to be explained by the precariousness of lower class living standards in the first half of the eighteenth century. When these rose, the numbers of assaults of the sort examined here, fell.

It is reasonable too to suppose that the underlying explanation for anti-customs and excise rioting is that in Scotland, as in other parts of early modern Europe, the tax gatherer was an object of popular hatred, whose presence frequently led to some of the more violent outbursts of disorder (Bercé, 1990, 197–243). Although most Scottish mobs lacked the ferocity of their French counterparts, it would surely have been remarkable if in Scotland there had been an absence of community-based hostility to the encroachment of the increasingly powerful (after 1707, British) state and its freedom threatening, centrally generated regulations (and taxes), of which the customs and excise officers were the most public and easily identified representatives.

Earlier, reference was made to a series of food riots which swept up the eastern seaboard of Scotland in 1720. It was, as far as is known, the most serious outbreak of popular protest concerning food in Scottish history up to that time. There was at least one fatality, in Dundee, where a merchant's house was also sacked; in Dysart a crowd which may have numbered as many as 2,000 overran both the magistracy and the military; and not far short of eighty of the most prominent rioters found themselves in a court which was asked to believe that they had been involved in a combination to 'set ye Country, once more by ye Ears'. Yet the historical record is largely silent, for only recently has the case been trawled up from the vast and largely untouched sea of High Court of Justiciary minute books and papers which are held in the Scottish Record Office.

Indeed in a recent survey it was concluded that the incidence of popular protest in Scotland was less than in England. (Fraser, 1988b, 289). The contrast however may have been overdrawn: notable food rioting occurred in Scotland in 1699, 1709–10, 1720, 1727, 1740, 1756–7, 1763, 1767, 1771–4, 1778, 1783, 1794–6, 1800–1, indeed during all of the major waves of food rioting which have been identified for England in the eighteenth century. As the *Scots Magazine* seems to have been the main primary source used by generations of Scottish historians looking for riots of this sort, it seems entirely likely that systematic searches through local archives will add to the list. When the scattered references to food riots in Scotland in 1740 are aggregated for instance, the number grows substantially, with known outbreaks in Aberdeen, Ayr, Banff, Dingwall, Edinburgh and its environs (more than once), Hamilton, Leith, Montrose, Musselburgh, Prestonpans, Tain and other un-named 'Towns in the North' (Whatley, 1990, 14–15).

Nevertheless, in the absence of an exhaustive list, at present it looks as though there were proportionately fewer food riots in Scotland, certainly in the west. Why this should have been so has been explained by reference to several factors, including rare harvest failures and uniform prices; market regulation for longer than in England; bulk buying by trade incorporations for distribution amongst their members; co-operative purchase of grain by some groups of weavers; charity and paternalism (Fraser, 1988b, 273–6). Only later in the century, it has been argued, as the bonds of paternalism and deference weakened in the face of market forces, and as towns became larger and the social gulf wider, did riots become more numerous and take on a more serious, threatening tone. This however only provides a partial explanation.

It does not take sufficient account of earlier, equally violent, food riots, notably those of 1720 and 1740. The immediate cause of the 1720 riots appears to have been the fact that meal shortages were either apparent or anticipated, at a time when food should have been in ample supply, as the harvest of 1719 had been good.

Encouraged by an act of the pre-1707 Scottish parliament and an additional clause in the Act of Union which offered a bounty to exporters, grain and meal exports had soared after 1707, and indeed these reached their eighteenth-century peak between 1717 and 1722. The rioting which resulted was a classic instance of what E. P. Thompson has called the 'moral economy' of the eighteenth-century crowd, which asserted that food merchants had no right to excessive profits at their neighbours' expense. That there is little evidence of actual food shortages, but rather of the fear of them, is an indication that this series of disturbances was motivated primarily by felt injustice rather than hunger.

In this, urban artisans, servants, and others who formed the body of the crowds in Dysart, Dundee, and the other towns and villages where riots took place, shared with their counterparts throughout Britain, and indeed much of Europe, an ideology of how the world works and the way it should work.

However, that this belief apparently inspired few food riots in Glasgow and other west coast manufacturing towns is not necessarily an indication of an inherent Scottish timidity. Shortages alone rarely led to riot anywhere. Most food riots occurred in places where grain was being exported, causing fears of local scarcity in the producing regions. Glasgow was a grain importer, drawing its supplies from Ireland and the south-west. Unlike Edinburgh, its inhabitants were far removed from the farmers and grain merchants who were commonly the targets of urban mobs. They were not therefore in a position to take direct action, while they were in the fortunate position of being able to purchase grain from Ireland.

Where the circumstances were appropriate however, the Scots were prepared to resort to collective violence when their perception of justice was threatened.

It has been argued in respect of England and Wales, that riots were 'quintessentially local politics'. Not only were they tests of the rioters' and magistrates' resources of force and persuasion, but they affected local policies; they were direct contests of coercion with uncertain outcomes, and while they were commonplace, they were not approved of by the authorities (Bohstedt, 1983, 4–5). All of this applies to Scotland in 1720 (and beyond). In Dysart the authorities' powers were tested and found wanting by a crowd which included a woman armed with a bayonet. In Montrose it was only by conceding to the crowd's demands and selling meal 'cheaper than current prices', that the magistrates were able to maintain any semblance of authority.

What close study of the riots also makes clear is that the Scottish crowd could be forceful and effective. Vital to a proper understanding the dynamics of Scottish society in the eighteenth century is an appreciation of E. P. Thompson's contention for England, that class relations were not one-sided, but reciprocal, with the crowd defining, 'in the largest sense, what was politically possible' (Thompson, 1974).

Thus for example, when meal shortages threatened and the first murmurings of discontent were heard, the provosts and magistrates of Scottish towns conveyed with great urgency to their inhabitants the soothing information that they were doing their best to obtain supplies from elsewhere. Intervention in the grain market by the authorities is said to have been a major reason for the relatively few food riots which occurred in London. A similar situation may have prevailed in Scottish towns such as Edinburgh where the indications are that a fund was established to enable the magistrates to intervene in the grain and meal markets and keep prices for the poor down.

Although Scottish riots in the eighteenth century were certainly not insurrectionary (apart, possibly, from the Malt Tax and Porteous riots), contemporaries who were charged with the maintenance of order in the localities were much less sanguine about their character than most historians have been, with good reason. Although it may not usually have been visible (deliberately, as its presence was a major source of social tension), the army was frequently called in to quell disturbances. Indeed in 1783, the provost of Aberdeen urged that a campaign be fought by the burghs against disbanding the army, 'for in order to keep the necessary Peace in Towns when an uncommon Scarcity prevails, a Military strength may be wanted'.

A Scottish Safety Valve?

It seems then that riot was a more important element in the dynamics of urban life in Scotland than has formerly been allowed. Indeed there is a sense in which it was essential. This can be clearly seen in the case of the king's birthday riots, about which remarkably little has been written, other than 1792 and 1796, when at least in Edinburgh they appear to have become overtly political in tone. Normally, it has been argued, the king's birthday was an occasion for 'boisterous and inebriated celebration' (Logue, 1979, 133–43). It was much more than this. Yet the day has disappeared into a sort of historical 'black hole', noted by contemporaries and early antiquarians, but neglected by late Victorian and Edwardian historians, even those who professed an interest in holidays and festivals (Cumming, 1910). Did they simply overlook it, or judge it to have been of little significance – or perhaps did it mar the otherwise comfortable images of Scottish society they were constructing?

From the time of the Restoration of Charles II, the Scottish church and burghs, and later some employers, had orchestrated festivities on the king's birthday. The more spectacular celebrations involved flag raising, bell-ringing, firearms, and cannon fire and military displays, as well as the public drinking of loyal toasts by the towns' leading figures. By the end of the eighteenth century however the last hours of the day had become a chaotic and apparently senseless orgy of fire and fury as the 'mob' turned on the authorities and pelted them with dead cats, stones, and other missiles. Sometimes the situation could become extremely serious, as in Glasgow in 1819, when several buildings were set on fire, and some looting took place, or 1821, when a cavalry charge, which resulted in a number of fatalities, had been required to restore order on the Green.

Nevertheless, no matter how unpleasant such behaviour was for the respectable classes, in response to a demand that the activities of the 'savage' and lawless mob be curtailed, the editor of the *Dundee, Perth and Cupar Advertiser* in June 1817 warned that this would be a most unwise course of action. In fact (and again borrowing from the ideas of historians working outside Scotland), the king's birthday riots look very much like a Scottish variation of a northern European phenomenon, the regular 'carnivalesque' occasions when the world was 'turned upside down'. These were permitted because the authorities, well aware of the inequalities of wealth, status, and power within their societies, recognized that this was a vital means for their subordinates to 'purge their resentments and to compensate for their frustrations' (Burke, 1978, 178–204). Although the king's birthday riots could give the appearance of being out of control, they were in fact a means of maintaining social control. Without the deluge of temporary disorder they released, it is at least arguable that the potential flammability built into Scotland's burgeoning urban mass might have been more likely to burst into flames.

Thus far this survey has focused on crowds which were normally composed of people, male and female, especially in the younger age groups, from a variety of occupations. By contrast, almost always, collective action which was related to workplace grievances usually involved only a single occupational group.

Workplace conflict

Combinations, or early trade unions, strikes, and other forms of collective action within the workplace, have until recently been noticeable by their absence in the historiography of pre-nineteenth-century Scotland.

Yet work done within the last two decades has begun to reveal a substantially different picture. Most recently, struck by the contrast between the growing evidence of extensive collective activity amongst the artisans of England and France, and the apparent docility and disinterest in organization of Scottish workers, W. H. Fraser has dug deep into the mass of surviving but largely unexplored legal records in Scotland and demonstrated that far from being cowed and docile, 'the tradesmen in Scottish towns were organized effectively [as far back as the 1720s in some cases], boldly pushing their claims, facing prison sentences, and challenging the action of their employers' (Fraser, 1988a, 1–10). Scottish workers, it seems, made much use of the courts to pursue their interests, and therefore had less cause than their English counterparts to engage in 'collective bargaining by riot'.

Also indicative of the new ways in which the workplace in early modern Scottish society can be portrayed, is the sea change which has taken place in perceptions of the coal and salt workers. Generations of historians have evidently delighted in exposing the horrors of 'old' (ie pre-1707) Scotland by reference to the peculiarity of the collier and salter 'serfs', miserable and degraded inhabitants of the coal mines and salt pans who, in the words of Lord Cockburn, were 'a separate and avoided tribe'. It was a powerful image, from which historians have found it exceedingly difficult to break free. The older mould began to crack when empirical work published in 1970 showed that the collier serfs were far from servile (Duckham, 1970, 240–313), while in 1983 a perceptive and detailed study of the colliers at Lasswade in Midlothian c1650–1750, whose author was armed with conceptual apparatus which hitherto had rarely been applied in Scotland, revealed 'a process of negotiation over work and leisure where the workers were far from a passive, inarticulate group' (Houston, 1983, 8).

Further investigation (Whatley, 1987b) made it clear that the Lasswade experience was not atypical, while underlining the point that historians must be careful that they understand the meaning of words in their contemporary context. The numerous references to 'desertions' in coal papers, which had served to reinforce the idea of collier misery, in fact in many cases referred to collective withdrawals of labour on the colliers' part. The term 'strike' did not come into use until much later. Pejorative language such as 'cattle' and 'vagabonds', used to describe colliers (and other sections of the lower classes), could mean simply that an exasperated coal proprietor could not obtain the acquiescence of his workers. Such indeed was the collective strength of the colliers' 'fettering bonds of brotherhood', that the so-called 'Emancipation Act' of 1775, which was largely master-led, was designed to free them rather than their work-people from the burden of serfdom. Through collective action the colliers had in fact managed to obtain high wages for three, four, or five days work a week. In historiographical terms, the world of the colliers (and salters), who not so long ago were said to have 'suffered a degradation without parallel in the history of labour in Scotland', has been turned on its head.

Historians and 1820

Although there is insufficient space here to consider either the Radicalism of the 1790s or to do more than skirt round the complex question of class formation in Scotland in the early nineteenth century, it is important to say something in the concluding stages of this essay about the years surrounding 1820. This is because as far as the related issue of the 'uninflammability' of the Scottish people is concerned, there is a deep divide of historical opinion, which has its roots in the 1820s themselves, and the competing Tory and Whig interpretations of events, the last perpetuating the 'myth' that 'the working-class radicals were innocent, passive, and constitutional reformers who were caught up in an elaborate Tory plot' (Young, 1979, 62). This, by and large, is the view which has dominated historians' thinking until relatively recently. In stark contrast is J. D. Young's view that 'mounting plebeian discontent challenged the very foundations on which Scottish society rested' (Young, 1979, 60). A similar view has been taken by W. H. Fraser in the most recent assessment of this issue, where he concludes that 'the events [of 1819 and 1820] in Scotland were more serious than anything in England, not excluding Peterloo' (Fraser, 1988b, 286).

This is not to say that Radicalism in Scotland was nationalist or republican in character. The evidence for such a proposition is extremely weak (Clarke and Dickson, 1988, 302). The perpetuation of this myth simply serves to detract from the real significance and meaning of working-class activity north of the border at this time. What has been demonstrated however is that the extent to which sectional interests divided the working class has been exaggerated. Although minimally, even the colliers were involved in the Radical movement in 1820, and while support was strongest amongst the handloom weavers (not surprisingly given their numerical supremacy in the west of Scotland), it also came from cotton spinners and other occupational groups (Young, 1979, 59).

Savage sarcastic reference to the 'huge horde consisting of 35 Glasgow radicals' is a valid literary means of puncturing left-wing pretensions about the 'Radical War' and the 'battle' of Bonnymuir (Lenman, 1981, 153). The pathos of this event however, should not detract either from the fact that as many as 60,000 people apparently struck work in support of the Radical cause, or that working-class feeling on a variety of current issues was intense. Nor should the continuing fears of the upper and middle classes for their security necessarily be discounted as unwarranted paranoia. The degree of adherence to Radicalism, and its demands for universal suffrage and annual parliaments, is but one measure of popular discontent. The assumption that the alleged 'failure' of Radicalism in 1820 is in some way indicative of the acquiescence of the working classes throughout Glasgow and the west of Scotland in the new order of rampant free market capitalism, is based upon a dated and patronizing assumption that the only 'political' statements worthy of note are those which were directed towards Westminster.

That many mass meetings and riots took place in the post-Napoleonic War period has long been recognized. Less attention however has been paid to the significance of these disturbances. Some of course were clear demonstrations of support for Radicalism. Others centred round strikes or were attacks on privilege, as on the king's birthday, or protests against the level of poor relief or local taxes. These were the diverse public faces of working-class discontent and protest, horrifying for the middling and upper classes, as streets were taken over by working-class marchers, who smashed windows and extinguished street lights along the way.

Yet newspaper reports reveal that there were numerous other 'outrages' which heightened tension during 1819 and 1820, notably incendiarism, at Shotts Iron Works and in a number of cotton mills, and on at least two landed estates near Glasgow. What is also of note is that fearsome disturbances, both large and small, continued to occur after the Radical defeat at Bonnymuir. In June 1820 for example, a riot in Glasgow's Saltmarket, involving soldiers, the police and the inhabitants, was described by the *Glasgow Courier* as being the worst that had ever happened in the city. As has already been noted, the king's birthday in Glasgow in 1821 saw riots, 'as violent and as uncontrollable…as have ever been experienced here'. As late as 1823 in Glasgow, after a party of Inniskillen dragoons had dispersed a crowd of 2–3,000 people, who had destroyed dykes which had recently been erected on Westhorn estate on the bank of the river Clyde, the procurator fiscal had written to the Crown Agent in Edinburgh that, 'if any such assemblages under any pretence are to be permitted here…the people would soon get a head of the Authorities' (SRO, AD 14/23/241).

Some historians have tended not only to compartmentalize the labouring classes by occupation, but also by type of action, with urban protest, rural protest, industrial protest, and political protest being looked at separately. While organizationally convenient, this has the unfortunate effect of dispersing the full force of the historical moment. For what close scrutiny of contemporary newspapers and legal evidence reveals is that whilst there were occasions when cotton spinners or weavers or colliers were engaged in discrete battles with their employers, the same individuals (and sometimes the same leaders) might at other times join forces, not so much on the basis of occupation, although they may have had shared interest in this regard (Clarke and Dickson, 1988, 300), but the solidarity of neighbourhood. Sometimes protest was focussed on political objectives or tinged with Radicalism, sometimes not. Thus of the forty-three people arrested after the attack on the above-mentioned dykes, which were viewed within the surrounding communities as an illegitimate bar on their inhabitants' traditional right to walk along the river side, twenty-seven were weavers, but the other eleven were cotton spinners, colliers, and other tradesmen who resided in villages such as Parkhead and Tollcross, in Glasgow's mushrooming Barony parish. Radicalism in this context had little to offer. Collective and highly organized direct community action (which included the use of firearms), in the face of an unwanted intrusion did.

Conclusion

This essay has examined an issue which is still in a state of flux. By no means all of the revisionist work reported here has met with critical acclaim, and much more requires to be done, not least in the direction of tightly-structured comparisons with other societies. When the dust settles however it looks as if the old picture of the passivity of ordinary Scots will have to be repainted. New evidence, and fresh ways of looking at old representations are the main tools of those reworking this subject. The older views are certainly not without foundation though, especially in the stress on the absence of overt opposition to change in the countryside.

On the other hand, the long standing belief that the Scots were characteristically quiescent, or less likely to resent the intrusion of outsiders, or more likely to welcome the cold winds of market forces, or indeed that the working classes in Scotland were peculiarly receptive to the arrival of industrial capitalism, look less secure than they did in the past. A balance needs to be struck between the older complacency and the more extreme claims of the overheated left. Clearly there were occasions when Lowland Scots felt passionate, and mobilized the collective strength to which the lower orders turned in similar circumstances throughout Europe, although until the early 1800s they did so without the same degree of violence. The many small fires which were lit across Lowland Scotland between c1707 and the 1820s did not become a conflagration.

5

The Whig Interpretation of Scottish History

MICHAEL FRY

When I first began to read and think about modern Scottish political history twenty years ago, I discovered a strange thing: that next to no books on the subject existed. There was naturally any number of British political histories, a few with passing reference to Scotland. There was an ever growing number of excellent Irish political histories. There was even a Welsh political history. Scotland herself had general histories, social histories, economic histories, cultural histories – but really no works on political history to speak of, not at least for any event beyond the first two or three decades of the nineteenth century.

To be sure, just at the time when I started feeling my way round this void, Nationalism was stirring. I soon discovered that it already had a literature behind it stretching back quite a long way, recently summed up (Hanham, 1969) in a good if quickly outdated book. But all the evidence of my own eyes and ears told me that Nationalism, while no doubt significant and interesting, was not by itself the sum of Scottish politics. I could otherwise perceive a range of the British state's and of the British parties' appendages, though all vying with one another to proclaim their Scottishness. Might it really be true that they had no present or past life of their own, that the diligent inquirer could not usefully reflect on them except as mere shades of a greater Britishness? And if that was not true, why had no diligent inquirer actually ever done so? I eventually got on and wrote up the political history of modern Scotland myself (Fry, 1989), since there seemed to be no answer to these questions. But here I shall turn back to them.

'This is the historical age and this the historical nation' declared David Hume. Indeed, so consuming was the interest in history of Scots during the eighteenth century, so fruitful their investigations of it, that they were able to generate in consequence most of today's social sciences. Nor were they shy of showing off this achievement in England, where notions of history remained largely mythological. The Scots therefore did the English a good turn by rewriting their history for them. As with other instances of such fellow-feeling after 1707, the effort was not much appreciated south of the border. In the end the English were to exact an insidious revenge.

That prevailing mythology of theirs was grounded in the idea of the ancient constitution, which the Glorious Revolution was held to have restored. The more imaginative myth-makers, such as Sir Edward Coke early in the seventeenth century, had discerned quasi-parliamentary institutions even among the ancient Britons. More often, original authorship of the constitution was attributed to the Germanic tribes which had rid Britannia of Roman despots: Anglo-Saxon breasts already nurtured ideals of liberty tempered by reverence for tradition, first clauses in the contract eventually sealed between rulers and ruled. Though the Norman conquest of England set things back for a while, before long the same imperishable qualities in the national character induced Edward I to invent Parliament. Freedom under the law was thence progressively established as the unique English way of life. So it would have gone on, had not the alien, Scottish house of Stewart disrupted this development by importing its nasty, foreign notions of absolutism. But it had got its come uppance in 1688. Now, with the ancient constitution not only restored but even perfected, England would continue to be a light among the nations.

It was Hume himself who exploded this complacency. He refused to believe that freedom could be guaranteed by constitutions. There were in his day, of course, no written ones (except in Poland, seldom thought to be an admirable model), nothing more than working arrangements more or less cloaked in more or less misleading mythology. In this, England was not superior to France, Holland, or the Holy Roman Empire. According to Hume, her superiority lay in her faster social and economic progress. That was what generated liberty – and he impudently asserted that in other circumstances an enlightened despotism might just as well have delivered the goods, and elsewhere might deliver them still. He had great fun deriding the notion that Anglo-Saxons differed from free and virtuous modern Englishmen only in having lived a long time ago. What came afterwards, he said, was mere feudal anarchy. He reserved special venom for the revered Edward I. He wrote with feeling how, especially in the matter of Scotland the 'iniquity of that claim [to the throne] was apparent, and was aggravated by the most egregious breach of trust'; fortunately, 'the barbarous policy of Edward failed of the purpose to which it was directed'. Furthermore, under the

Tudors the English had been no freer than the subjects of the Grand Turk: what liberty was there then for the Stewarts to subvert? (Hume, 1763, chs. 13, 55). Scots were notorious for ganging up – Adam Smith and Adam Ferguson followed Hume in insisting that the Glorious Revolution neither restored nor confirmed the ancient constitution, that liberty was not ancient, but modern.

All this apparently so shocked the sensibilities of the English that they were quite unable to formulate a response, which had to be left to an Irishman. Edmund Burke was to point out that, even if they could not claim to have preserved an ancient constitution, they had at least enjoyed unbroken continuity in their organic political evolution. That was still unique, and justified English national pride. The Scots yet refused to climb down. No doubt their knowledge of Scotland's own national experience informed their outlook, but they were not merely setting one nationalism against another. On the contrary, their view was altogether cooler and more cosmopolitan. It observed in the progress of civil society a general European phenomenon, with English constitutional liberties as an assuredly welcome, yet also local and atypical, version of it. With the same generosity of spirit, they also took Burke seriously, and sought to integrate with their own thinking what he had so obviously and so strikingly got right in his warnings against a meretricious modernism in civil affairs. Something might be conjectured to vindicate English worship of the ancestors even on Scottish assumptions about the value of social progress.

This meant, then, a compromise between Hume and Burke. For example, in his *Historical View of the English Government*, John Millar of Glasgow still rejected the idea that there was anything precociously constitutional about the Anglo-Saxons, as an explanation of differences between the English and other nations. Instead he looked to the work of nature, to the insular situation that kept England out of wars and fostered her trade and commerce – a recognizably Scottish form of historical interpretation. By personal conviction, however, Millar was not a Humean Tory but a Whig. He believed Hume had to be wrong in his views of the constitution under the Tudors and Stewarts, and would not for a moment allow that the royal prerogative, rather than any contractual principle, might have the weight of historical legitimacy behind it (Millar, 1803, i, 373–4; ii, 470–2). A Scots Whig historian of the next generation, George Brodie, reversed the whole argument to accuse Hume (and, by implication, the Scottish political regime in his own day) of excessive constitutionality. Tories, he said, erred in defending the royal prerogative 'as if they deemed it as a sufficient reason for consigning the people to slavery, that they can plead the precedence of former times' (Brodie, 1823, i, 4). The Scots had twisted, but also turned, and ended up conceding that there was after all some essential continuity, not absolutely linear yet clearly there, in English liberties and representative government. England was yet a light among the nations.

All these threads were drawn together and woven into a seamless finished garment of Whig history by Lord Macaulay. A Scot by blood, he made his name in the *Edinburgh Review*, and later sat for the capital in Parliament. In his account of the constitution he explicitly and eagerly adopted the Scots' sociological context to a greater extent than any English historian. His materialism was of positively vulgar dimensions. This in no way sapped his awe of the constitution, which moved him to lyricism even after admitting that liberty was not ancient, but modern: 'neither Greek nor Roman, but essentially English. It has a character of its own – a character which has taken a tinge from the sentiments of chivalrous ages, and which accords with the peculiarities of our manner and of our insular situation. It has a language, too, of its own, and a language so singularly idiomatic, full of meaning to ourselves, scarcely intelligible to strangers' (Macaulay, 1828, 136).

Despite his breadth of vision, there is at the same time little so arresting in Macaulay as the strength of his Whig pieties, except perhaps the strength of the animosities arising out of them. By any standards, and certainly by modern ones, Macaulay's judgements in his *History of England* were violently dogmatic. The fire of his rhetoric often warped the truth or scorched away the inconvenient details that might damp it. Once he had found a man guilty of Toryism, nothing could be pleaded in mitigation, for even Tory virtue was suspect. But a Whig counted *ipso facto* as a better human being, whatever his vices. Thus James VII and II was wholly bad, William of Orange wholly good; the Duke of Marlborough's victorious generalship could never compensate for his deficiencies, while the Master of Stair's involvement in the massacre of Glencoe was subtly underplayed. These blatant double standards were the great blemishes on Macaulay's work. Why did he thus detract from the value of it? One answer doubtless lay in the naturally combative and partisan character of 'cocksure Tom': he was, after all, a practising Whig politician. He did really seem unable to concede that the opponents he imagined himself facing if he had lived in the past had any more to commend them than those he actually faced in his own day.

This was the attitude identified as the essence of the Whig interpretation of history in Sir Herbert Butterfield's classic examination of the subject: 'It is part and parcel of the Whig interpretation of history that it studies the past with reference to the present ... The Whig historian stands on the summit of the twentieth century, and organises his scheme of history from the point of view of his own day.' A vast network of ramifications followed. The Whig method was bound to over-dramatise, to send on a historical cast of heroes and villains whom the reader was supposed to boo or cheer rather than understand. It was bound, by seeking analogies to the present, to read into historical struggles motivations which they had not contained. It was bound to attribute consistently honourable purposes to progressives and consistently base ones to conservatives, obscuring the fact that most historical processes issued in a compromise between the two. Above all, perhaps, it was bound to call forth moral judgements, and encourage the historian in a belief that he ought to provide them. Yet, Butterfield asserted, 'the value of history lies in the richness of its recovery of the concrete life of the past' (Butterfield, 1932, especially 11, 13, 34, 41, 68, 107).

England was the pabulum of Whig history, and other countries were brought in, if at all, only by way of disparaging contrast. Yet Scotland, as the single next-door neighbour, could not be altogether ignored. Nor was there any disposition to ignore her at the outset. The man who may count as the very first Whig historian, Gilbert Burnet, native of Edinburgh and witness in London of the events of 1688, treated Scottish politics on a par with English politics. Indeed he was criticised by the abridger of his unwieldy *History of his Own Time*, one Thomas Stackbridge, for making Scotland 'the prime place of his action' (Burnet, 1979, vi).

Hume showed much the same disposition, even while harbouring no doubt that Scotland had been, till relatively recent times, a barbarous nation. He was on the one hand so fastidious about this that he insisted on translating all the best lines from Scottish history into English. Thus Robert the Bruce's fellow-thug, going back into the church at Dumfries to finish off the Red Comyn, is made not to growl 'I'll mak siccar', but to lisp, ludicrously, 'I shall secure him'; and the dying James V turns to the wall not with a mournful 'It cam wi' a lass and it'll gang wi' a lass' but with an insipid 'The crown came with a woman and it will go with one'.

On the other hand, Hume by no means underrated Scotland's part in his *History of England*. He still took a dim view of that part, for he saw Scottish history as little more than an interplay of feudal anarchy and religious bigotry. He did not hesitate, for example, to depict Mary, Queen of Scots as the lesser of the evils facing her country in the era of the Reformation: 'But all the insolence of the people was inconsiderable in comparison of that which was exercised by the clergy and the preachers, who took a pride in vilifying, even to her face, this amiable princess ... The ringleader in all these insults on majesty was John Knox: who possessed an uncontrollable authority in the church, and even in the civil affairs of the nation, and who triumphed in the contumelious usage of his sovereign ... He once treated her with such severity, that she lost command of her temper, and dissolved in tears before him; yet, so far from being moved with youth, and beauty, and royal dignity reduced to that condition, he persisted in his insolent reproofs'. After such a history, the advent of the Union had been a blessing, by which Scots 'have happily attained the experience of a government perfectly regular, and exempt from all violence and injustice' (Hume, op. cit., i, 13, 25–9, 31, 38, 44).

Meanwhile, William Robertson, a future leader of the enlightened Moderate party in the Kirk and principal of the University of Edinburgh, had been writing the first work which deserves the name of a modern history of Scotland. It quickly became a best-seller at home and beyond. It applied the standard analysis of conjectural history, depicting social development as progress through several stages. But while admitting that Scotland had lagged behind, he was no more than Hume prepared to swallow English views of Scotland. He too wrote of 'the malicious policy of Edward I of England'. And there was surely more than a sly dig at the southron in this: 'The nature of their country was one cause of the power and independence of the Scottish nobility. Level and open countries are formed for servitude ... Mountains, and fens, and rivers set bounds to despotic power, and amidst these, is the natural seat of freedom and independence'.

A minister of the Kirk might be expected, however, to differ from Hume over the Reformation. Of the Queen, Robertson wrote: 'The re-establishment of the Romish doctrine seems to have been her favourite passion: and though the design was concealed with care, she pursued it with a persevering zeal'. By contrast Knox 'possessed a natural intrepidity of mind, which set him above fear ... Instead of amusing himself with lopping the branches, he struck directly at the root of popery, and attacked both the doctrine and discipline of the established church with a vehemence peculiar to himself, but admirably suited to the temper and wishes of the age'. All his qualities 'which now render his character less amiable, fitted him to be the instrument of Providence for advancing the Reformation among a fierce people'.

He yet agreed that the national story had reached a happy ending. The period after 1603 was awful for Scots, because of 'their political situation, not any defect of genius, for no sooner was the one removed in any degree, than the other began to display itself ... At length the Union having incorporated the two nations, and rendered them one people, the distinctions which had subsisted for many ages gradually wear away; peculiarities disappear; the same manners prevail in both parts of the island; the same authors are read and admired; the same entertainments are frequented by the elegant and polite; and the same standard of taste, and of purity in language, is established. And the Scots, after being placed, during a whole century, in a situation no less fatal to the liberty than to the taste and genius of the nation, were at once put in possession of privileges more valuable than those which their ancestors had enjoyed' (Robertson, 1759, bks. i, ii, viii).

This envoi, sanguine to the point of blandness, formed an interesting contrast with the defence against common English prejudices that Millar later felt called on to mount. Though Scots had long been backward, even before the Union 'they had already made some advances in knowledge, and they were surrounded by other civilized nations, from whom they could hardly fail to catch a degree of science and literature'. He also rejected Hume's entirely negative view of the Presbyterian inheritance: 'The peculiar spirit with which the Scots had overturned the Roman Catholic superstition gave a particular modification to their intellectual pursuits ... Even the common mass of the people took an interest in the various points of theological controversy; became conversant in many abstract disquisitions connected with them; and were led to acquire a sort of literary curiosity'. This helped explain why nowadays the English had to put up with so many Scotsmen on the make: 'the shrewdness, cunning and selfishness, imputed to the people of Scotland, are merely the unfavourable aspect of that intelligence and sagacity by which they are distinguished above the mere mechanical drudges in the southern part of the island, and by which they are more able to discover their own interest, and to extricate themselves from difficulties, and to act, upon every occasion, with decision and prudence' (Millar, op. cit., iii, 32–3, 86, 94).

Individual historical judgements naturally varied, but the general impression we can take from these enlightened scholars is that, while all firm unionists, they were far from anglicizing toadies The same spirit seems to have been transmitted to Macaulay. Even in his *History of England*, he did not doubt the importance of Scotland, or of Ireland, nor the virtues of their peoples. Introducing the subject, he wrote: 'Scotland had, with heroic energy, vindicated her independence, had, from the time of Robert Bruce, been a separate kingdom, and was now joined to the southern part of the island in a manner which rather gratified than wounded her national pride'. He agreed all the same that after 1603 'she was, during more than a century, really treated, in many respects, as a subject province'. Union was the only answer: 'The sacrifice could not but be painfully felt by a brave and haughty people who, had, during twelve generations, regarded the southern domination with deadly aversion, and whose hearts still swelled at thought of the deeds of Wallace and of the triumphs of Bruce. There were doubtless many punctilious patriots who would have strenuously opposed a union even if they could have foreseen that the effect of a union would be to make Glasgow a greater city than Amsterdam, and to cover the dreary Lothians with harvests and woods, neat farmhouses and stately mansions'. The net benefits were overwhelming but had only been maximized, Macaulay stressed, because the English respected what the Scots themselves respected, notably their religious and educational systems. The whole story was an object lesson in the burying of hatreds between Celt and Saxon: 'In Scotland all the great actions of both races are thrown into the common stock, and are considered as making up the glory which belongs to the whole country' (Macaulay, 1849, i, 64, 66; ii, 256–7; iv, 781).

But in English historiography Macaulay has been the exception. Till very recently indeed, scarcely another scholar has assumed the affairs of Scotland, or of Ireland, to be anything better than trivial, or stopped for a moment to question his own assumption. Perhaps it was indeed the Scot in Macaulay, realizing how the Union had formed him personally, that gave him his deeper insight, and a resolve to do historical justice to the special problems in the Union's smaller members. His sympathetic and rounded account of them forms one of his major achievements.

Such respect for Scotland was only due, given the place she had occupied in the British polity till Macaulay's time. The system set up in 1707, and lasting till the Reform Act of 1832 and the Disruption of 1843, has since come to be known as semi-independence. During that period, the institutional structure guaranteed by the Treaty of Union remained to all intents and purposes intact. Insofar as the British state touched the life of the ordinary Scot, it did so through native surrogates. Macaulay alone of the Whig historians set any great store by all this. Perhaps the others took them for granted, or perhaps they preferred to stress what united Britons rather than what still divided them.

A more likely reason, however, is that Macaulay's deeper insight gave him some sense of the permanent value of the settlement of 1707, at a time when the more shallow and glib among progressives were losing it. This sense may be no more than implicit: for example, it was altogether odd that, in writing his *History*, he should have gone out of his way to praise a Kirk just shattered by the Disruption after ten years of conflict with the state, and to praise an educational system thrown as a result into confusion. The contrast becomes clearer when we turn to what other Whigs were now saying about the constitution given to Scotland by the Union. While they naturally lauded its basically English nature, they saw its local Scottish elements as deformities, excrescences of Scotland's black, feudal past. This was what Brodie had in mind when he condemned the excessive constitutionality of the Tories, who in Scotland defended the Union settlement on quasi-nationalist grounds. Such sentiment had no place in a reformer's scheme. Whigs, as scholars, could scarcely approve of a system which, as politicians, they were trying to dismantle.

In fact their partisanship on this point knew no bounds. Since 1707 it had on the whole been taken as a good thing that Scotland should be run by Scotsmen, an arrangement which Macaulay praised too as an enduring principle of the Union, and one in fact restored in our own century. But the Scots Whigs of his day had a different view. Henry Cockburn, for example, heartily welcomed the break in 1827 of the traditional system of Scottish political management, when the incoming Prime Minister, George Canning, instructed his English Home Secretary to oversee the affairs of Scotland directly. Cockburn was delighted at the end of 'the horrid system of being ruled by a native jobbing Scot' (Cockburn, 1874). Though he is remembered today for his delightful *Memorials* (1856), for his antiquarianism and nostalgia, at every point where in real life he could exert a direct personal influence, he actually wanted to make Scotland as much like England as possible.

Let a couple of examples suffice from the legions that might be quoted. The preservation of Scots law is often instanced as a vital element in national identity. But Whigs had come to regard the law, which also provided the personnel of the local ruling class, as the fountainhead of Scottish authoritarianism. The answer, then, would be to assimilate it to English law which, as an article of Whig faith, offered the supreme example to follow. Thus Cockburn wrote in 1819 to a friend on Parliament urging him to enlist English support against expected resistance to a particular legal proposal: 'The improvement is recommended by the practice of England. So that, though our Lord Advocate and Court will object, I think you must succeed in a Parliament of Englishmen'. Again, two years later, when the pair of them were discussing a wider franchise, Cockburn remarked: 'There is no chance, especially with an English Parliament, which will look on the whole system but won't pry into details or explanation, but in one broad and universal measure, and that the nearer we can propose to make ourselves to England the better'. With a political programme like that from the Government-in-waiting, it is easier to understand the remark by Walter Scott, often thought maudlinly eccentric, when he shed tears over changes in the Court of Session and said: 'Little by little, whatever your wishes may be, you will destroy and undermine, until nothing of what makes Scotland Scotland shall remain'. Cockburn's own response, by the way, was chilling: 'Properly applied, this was a comment with which I cordially sympathised. But it was misapplied by Scott, who was thinking of feudal poetry, not of modern business' (Cockburn, 1874, 4, 33; Lockhart, 1839, ii, 328).

What was this business that Cockburn had in mind, so pressing that it could justify any degree of casual disregard for the terms of the Union? He himself thus depicted the struggle for parliamentary reform which reached its triumphant conclusion in 1832: 'The sole object was to bring Scotland within the action of the constitution' (Cockburn, 1852, i, 82). Therefore, presumably, in these modern Scots Whigs' view the events of 1688 and 1707 had not as a matter of fact brought Scotland within the action of the constitution: Hume, Robertson, and Millar had deluded themselves to think so, and Macaulay too, when he came to write some years later, would still be deluding himself. The great work of emancipating Scotland remained to be done, and only these modern Scots Whigs were able to do it. Could there in truth be better proof of their inherent tendentiousness, their blindness to the past as anything other than ammunition for the partisan struggles of the present?

A contemporary Tory, Archibald Alison, wrote of their 'withering self-sufficiency'. And their typical refusal to concede any merit to their opponents, or to consider, even for a moment, counter-arguments to their own, was over the following years of Liberal hegemony to exact a heavy price. Right at the outset, it meant that the Scottish Reform Act was botched, for its draftsmen professed a silly contempt for Scots law and perpetuated many of the abuses they claimed to be curing. Nothing, however, could deflate Whig arrogance after their victory. Even in the relatively objective Macaulay, it is evident that all fears about the nature of the state were stilled forever by the extension of the franchise, the publicity of parliamentary proceedings and the growth of informed public opinion. Francis Jeffrey, to whom as Lord Advocate of Scotland it fell to pilot the Reform Act through, could write to John Ramsay MacCulloch in 1842 that he 'should be satisfied to have a clear vision of this country about the year 1900, before which, I feel persuaded, the problems we are puzzled about will all be substantially resolved'. The stupendous smugness of this new Scottish establishment has led even a sympathetic critic to see in Cockburn during his last years 'a flowing bowl of hypocrisy, duplicity and complacent self-deception' (Alison, 1883, i, 82; Cockburn, 1852, ii, 373; Miller, 272).

There was not only a political but a cultural effect. It may seem odd that the Scottish Enlightenment should have expired so promptly after emerging from the dark depths of the Dundas despotism on to the sunlit uplands of the Whig millennium. But that was indeed what happened. Among the casualties we have to count the Scottish historiography that had so far flourished in quite a satisfactory fashion, even if sometimes disguised as English historiography. Cockburn himself is in fact the only major, published, contemporary authority for the politics of the period. In him we are dealing with Whig history at its most naked, offering the interpretation that all Scottish political problems had now been, or would soon be, solved. Nothing further in such problems could therefore demand serious professional attention from historians (or, come to that, from politicians).

It was not that Scots lost interest in history. The nineteenth century was the classic age of Scottish antiquarianism, inspired by Scott and appealing to a wide educated public. But he did not thus succeed, as he had hoped, in creating a historical consensus with which all his compatriots could identify. At the same time, England developed free from further Scottish influences – through her Stubbs, her Freeman, her Froude and so on – a highly distinguished historiography, inspired by the majesty of the state and the importance of its constitution and politics, which continues with undiminished vigour to the present day. It was fed by such riches as the medieval charters, in which England was lucky enough to have a classical historical corpus meriting scholarly attention at the highest level. There existed no parallel in Scotland. Her own muniments were meagre and in any case, every Whig knew that she had no constitution to speak of. A fresh independent impetus could probably only have come from the Scottish universities. But they now found themselves drawn down into the very vortex of the cultural crisis. They were to prove themselves quite incapable of consensus on how they might adapt to modern needs. One solution often canvassed was simply to anglicize them, and an easy measure of anglicization was to obliterate Scottish history from any part of the curriculum. It was done not altogether without regret, but in a conviction that it was inevitable and on balance to the good. Cockburn had rationalized the underlying sentiment like this: 'The feelings and habits which had prevailed at the Union, and which had left so many picturesque peculiarities on the Scottish character, could not survive the enlarged intercourse with England and the world'. It actually felt liberating to close the door on Scotland's dark and cobwebbed past: 'The Reformation was freedom, the Union was freedom, the Disruption was freedom, the death of Scottish history was freedom' (Ash, 1980, 148–50). As her sons fell in with the onward march of history, Scotland moved out of it. She was locked for safekeeping in the kailyard.

Cockburn had in fact set a tone for the rest of his century: those 'picturesque peculiarities' were the sole Scottish theme worth attention, and then only by way of light relief. Dean Ramsay, author of the hugely popular *Reminiscences of Scottish Life and Character*, once wanted to lecture on changes in the manners and habits of Scotland during the last 50 years (this in the 1870s, at the height of the transformations wrought by the second stage of the industrial revolution). He chose the following points to dwell on: the growing frequency of family prayers; the banishment of drunkenness from genteel society; the lessening intimacy and familiarity between families and their domestics; the switch in the speech of the upper class from Scots to English; and alterations in the national wit and humour. This was his summarizing comment: 'Much of this change had of course taken place before any of the present generation can remember. Much has been done in my own recollection, and now there remains only comparatively the slighter shades of difference to be assimilated, and soon there will be little to notice' (Ramsay, 1873, 2). There is no reason to suppose that this witty and popular, yet patriotic and perceptive Victorian Scot held views by any means atypical: he genuinely believed everything distinctively Scottish to be vanishing before his eyes, leaving nothing behind but mocking, ghostly echoes of couthy anecdote.

Henry Grey Graham's *Social Life of Scotland in the Eighteenth Century*, published in 1899 and reprinted as late as 1937, perpetuated the outlook and tried (with no great success, according to today's experts in his field) to bring the couthy anecdotes together in a somewhat more robust scholarly structure. But this was a time, before the Second World War, when attempts at social history still had to be justified according to the scholarly criteria set by the dominant British (that is, English) political historiography. Graham said he ignored Scottish politics because it consisted chiefly in 'obscure intrigues and factions, Whig and Tory, Presbyterian and Jacobite, measures managed by leaders of Scottish business, who were servile followers of English ministries, manoeuvres of Scots nobles and placemen who travel southwards on horseback or in coach to win favour with great statesmen at Westminster or courtiers at St James – figures not very real to us today as they flit across the stage, 'transient and embarrassed phantoms'. To the end of the century ... political life in North Britain was virtually non-existent' (Graham, 1937, vi). This was actually, leaving aside some differences in terminology, a perfect description of English politics in the eighteenth century as revealed to us by Sir Lewis Namier – which nobody otherwise suggests to be unworthy of notice. The purple passage may, however, have been a cloak for Graham's true thesis, that 'after all, it is in the inner life of a country that its real history is to be found' (*ibid.*, vii). And the inner life of Scotland, notoriously, was played out in the kailyard.

This was one consequence of the Whig interpretation of Scottish history. But there existed also a higher Whiggery, still producing Scottish history of a kind but continuing to stress that at bottom it consisted in dangerous and reactionary nonsense. The purpose thus lay in proving that Scottish history was in all essentials over.

An exponent of that view was H. T. Buckle, in his *History of Civilisation in England* – a peculiar title considering that by far the greater part of it concerned Scotland. He had much to say on what he called 'the real difficulty of Scottish history', which he identified like this: 'that knowledge should not have produced the effects which have elsewhere followed it; that a bold and inquisitive litera-ture should be found in a grossly superstitious country, without diminishing its superstition; that the people should constantly with-stand their kings, and as constantly succumb to their clergy; that while they are liberal in politics, they should be illiberal in religion'. He repeated the now standard Whig view that the Union had only imperfectly corrected the national failings, notably a curious taste for theological polemics. But at least with the Enlightenment there had come 'a tendency to turn aside from subjects which are inacces-sible to our understanding, and the discussion of which has no effect except to exasperate those who dispute, and to make them more intolerant than ever of theological opinions different from their own' (Buckle, 1861, ii, 160, 316).

Even those unwilling to accept Buckle's strictures did not assert, as Millar had, that disputation might be useful as mental training. They merely claimed that he had been uncharitable in doubting the Whigs' official view that they had solved, or could solve, all Scot-land's problems. Here is the riposte of J. Mackintosh in his *History of Civilization in Scotland*, a title which suggests a deliberate at-tempt to counter Buckle: 'The population, wealth, industries and commerce of Scotland have greatly increased during the last two centuries .... I see no necessity for taking a gloomy view of the future. The resources of the human mind are not exhausted. The incidental suffering associated with the existing industrial system may be gradually remedied, as the moral and intellectual state of the people becomes more perfect. Let us all endeavour to eradicate injustice, and embrace every opportunity of ameliorating the conditions of life and human happiness' (Mackintosh, 1896, iv, 495).

The *summa* of this higher Whiggery came with Peter Hume Brown's *History of Scotland to the Present Time*. It rested on three propositions. The first was that the Union had been in every important respect inevitable and beneficient: 'It was thus the pressure of events beyond [Scotland's] control that drove her into that closer Union which was, in truth, a necessary consummation for the existence of both.' Any base motives among those Scots who had pushed it through against clear popular opposition could be entirely discounted: 'The men who carried the Union threw themselves into their labours with an ardour which no bribery could purchase; and, if from sentiment rather than reasoned conclusion a majority of their contemporaries denounced them as traitors to their country, the consenting testimony of a later time has approved the far-sighted wisdom of their policy' (Hume Brown, 1911, 58, 101–2).

This was the classic Whig judgment of the past by the present, but Hume Brown assimilated, secondly, the more modern Whig view that all the distinctive political arrangements to survive 1707 were rotten to the core. One would have thought that it somewhat contradicted the first proposition, and several of his young colleagues had to work hard to substantiate such an obviously dubious point. H. W. Meikle, in *Scotland and the French Revolution*, took as the central fact of modern Scottish history the emergence of radicalism in the 1790s, naturally casting as villains the rulers who had suppressed it. W. L. Mathieson embarked on an elaborate project of linking up, in several volumes, the political and ecclesiastical history of the previous three centuries. It was a demanding task which sometimes got too much for him: he would then relieve himself through pages of invective against the corrupt and reactionary Tories. In either case, since no virtue might be allowed to the Union's distinct constitutional arrangements within Scotland, one could assume that total political assimilation had been the only right and proper course in the long run.

Hume Brown held, thirdly, that the Scottish religious inheritance was deplorable. In his crude materialism, he rivalled Macaulay. Union had come 'in an age when material interests were overriding every other'. Enlightenment spread once 'commerce and the modern spirit had vanquished the Stewarts and the political principles they represented; and they had concurrently overridden the theocratic ideals which had been the bequest of the Reformation of 1560'. It followed that 'the Disruption was a disaster to the national Church, but it can hardly be regarded as a disaster to the national religion', since tiresome clerical squabbles ceased. What remained, in this best of all possible worlds, was that progressive secularism which again had the answer to everything: 'We may conclude that the political instincts of the nation have undergone no change, and that, as from the hour of her enfranchizement, radicalism is compact with the national temperament and habits of thought' (Hume Brown, op. cit., iii, 59, 265, 345, 369). It was Mathieson who then deduced that with the Liberal hegemony Scottish history had, thankfully, come to a stop. On finishing his account of the Disruption, he wrote: 'The ecclesiastical history of Scotland, in so far as it concerns the national historian, may thus be said to end in 1843, as the political history had ended with the abolition of the Scottish representative system in 1832' (Mathieson, 1916, 373).

Even anti-radicals, their particularist scruples of a century before safely forgotten, could at last be invited to this self-congratulatory love-feast. A. V. Dicey and Sir Richard Rait numbered among their *Thoughts on the Union between England and Scotland* this one: 'Edinburgh has not lost its charm or its intelligence, yet it is all but incredible that Edinburgh, or any other town in Great Britain, including London itself, should ever have again the pre-eminence which made Scotsmen a century ago describe Edinburgh as the modern Athens …. This dying away of separate local centres of intellectual power is, like all changes, not without its loss. But one should never forget the warning of Burke, that the man who quarrels with the nature of things goes very near to fighting against the decrees of Providence. One may venture to say that some of the cries for so-called Home Rule are nothing better than lamentations over the way in which the growth of civilisation, by the very benefits it extends, limits the personal and relative eminence both of individuals and individual countries' (Dicey & Rait, 1920, 344–5).

Here, in the consensus reached by all Scottish historians and political scientists of note by about the time of the First World War, was the answer to the question I had posed myself 20 years ago. There were no books of Scottish political history because Scottish political history did not exist. What was more, it ought not to exist, at least so long as Scotland expected to continue enjoying the benefits bestowed on her when the Whigs had set out, a century previously, to arrange her final and irrevocable assimilation to England. By this means, among others, civilization was advancing and I, or anybody else with a mind to diligent inquiry, should content myself with that and kindly keep my doubts to myself.

The highest praise ever bestowed by Cockburn on an opponent was that he 'became as good a Whig as a Tory can be'. Even this Tory historian is to some extent infected by Whiggery, and in a way happy to be so: for too rigorous an effort to dissociate the past from the present also has its dangers, encouraging antiquarian or monographic history at the expense of the dramatic narrative that Macaulay wrote in the belief that great ideas are in truth the motive force of history. Yet it ought to be possible, without heavy handed moralizing, to derive from a society's view of its history, from its uses of and attitudes to its past, some revelation about what it believes and assumes to be its own destiny. For example, it seems to me from what I have recounted above that Scotland for a long time neither was nor wanted to be a full fledged political community. She was content with couthiness, and with the undemanding, unambitious, self-satisfied provinciality which that implied.

So what now when self-satisfied provinciality is no longer enough, and Scotland again aspires in some sense to the attainment of political community? The first thing to be said is that the deformations bequeathed to us are difficult to overcome. Much of the newer Scottish historiography just parrots a simple-minded leftist line that the story of modern Scotland consists largely of capitalist oppression, where it does not parrot a simple-minded nationalist line that the story consists largely of English oppression. In essence both views remain pure Whig, still judging the past by the standards of the present, still distorting the past by interpreting it in terms of the present, still searching the past for the origins and evolution of ideas and institutions to be recommended for the present. Whig history proper started by seeing a gradual, natural, inevitable progression towards political and religious rights and freedoms. It is a difference only of form rather than of substance to see a similar progression towards democracy, equality, collectivism and socialism, or a nationhood embracing these things.

A Tory historian must protest that we violate the past by fitting it to this Procrustes' bed of progress. Butterfield warned us against such anachronism, and its reduction to deterministic ideas of all the complexity, the discontinuity, and the potential unfulfilled in the event that gave the past what was unique to it, all that made it a different country, though one where the inhabitants can make themselves understood to the attentive visitor from the present. And Scotland is a fine example, for by any standards she, during a great part of the nineteenth century, was regressing as a political community, if in pursuit of the supposedly higher purposes she had set herself.

And thus a final thought for this essay is how in Scotland we need better political history. Much of our latest historiography is social and economic, and – I freely admit to bias – not very interesting because it treats Scottish themes as variants of English ones, the subject of recent complaint by a distinguished practitioner of the older generation (Campbell, 1990, 19). I dare say also that this has a good deal to do with the need for academic historians to compete in a British market for articles and theses. According to the fashion in that market the essential realities to be studied in history are the relations of social classes and the lives of the anonymous masses. And they are to be studied through mechanical application of the standard techniques of social science. Hence we in Scotland too must compete in dredging the lower depths of history from below, and in hauling up out of oblivion all the submerged groups: women, ethnic minorities, sexual deviants, criminals, and lunatics.

Yet the best and most influential of recent historiography has come from people, like George Davie and Tom Nairn, who have no wish or incentive to join in such competition and who are therefore free to concentrate not on what makes Scotland a mere variant, but on what makes Scotland unique. In accepting the Whig interpretation of their history, the Scots of the nineteenth century diverged sharply from contemporary historians in other countries, who took for granted the continuity of the past because they took for granted the political nature of that continuity, which is to say, the essentially political nature of history. It may be a good or a bad thing that nowadays political history has everywhere been extensively displaced by social and economic history. What it does allow us to see is how crucial that political dimension was to the history and culture of the nineteenth century, and thus to its belief in the continuity between history and culture, between the past and the present. By the same token, we can see how much Scotland lost.

That traditional attitude is often condemned on the ideological grounds that the sort of political history it generated, history from above, was imposed by capitalist rulers intent on denying their subjects a history of their own as part of a general mode of oppression. But let us consider for one moment the uniqueness of Scotland. For here, if it was indeed by such a process that history was generated, the rulers imposed history from below, imposed at most a history of the 'inner life' and denied that the nation had a political history of its own. If we really wish to recapture total history, therefore, this political history has to be a prime object of our attention. And in pursuing such an apparently singular and eccentric task, Scottish historians might not be endangering their career prospects as much as they fear. For Scotland is not quite unique. We do have a similar example in Ireland, which also long laboured under a denial that she had any political history usefully separable from the general history of the Empire. Who can doubt that the historiography she has developed in recent decades, considerably richer and deeper than Scotland's, is due above all to her rediscovery of her political past? The Irish have thus made their own way into a great stream of historiography, which started with Herodotus and Thucydides, and stretches down through the towering figures of the nineteenth century even to some historians of our own day: and which assumes that a polity, not always a vast empire or even a powerful nation-state, but something of the kind, was the true bearer of that 'entailed inheritance', as Burke put it, which ensured the continuity of the past and the present, and of the present and the future. Can we in Scotland do less?

6

'The Enterprising Scot'

IAN DONNACHIE

'An easy and luxurious existence does not train men to effort or encounter with difficulty; nor does it awaken that consciousness of power which is so necessary for energetic and effective action. Indeed, so far from poverty being a misfortune, it may, by vigorous self-help, be converted even into a blessing, rousing a man to that struggle with the world in which the right-minded and true-hearted find, strength, confidence and triumph.'

Samuel Smiles, *Self Help*, 1859.

While the manufacturers of Scottish history were predominantly concerned until recently with high politics and great events, a few, at least, addressed themselves to economic issues. But even the pioneers of economic and social history, some of whom are referred to in the editors' introduction, did little to modify the popularly held view that the secret of Scotland's greatness in the era of industrialization was the enterprising Scot. He (rarely a she) was largely manufactured by the Victorians who saw in him the personification of progress. Scottishness and enterprise were synonymous. The duality expressed in our title here was considered until recently as self-evident by the majority of those engaged in the manufacture of Scottish history. The 'self-made man' of the Smiles tradition is still regarded as the conventional hero of the Industrial Revolution and is not altogether a myth, yet the evidence of modern historical research suggests that he was in the minority. Men of enterprise were an amazingly diverse group and this chapter explores some of the mysteries surrounding the origins of the thrusting, entrepreneurial and apparently successful Scot (see Calder, 1986 for a very readable overview). It shows too how historians have set about reassessing a fascinating figure who certainly played a major role in modern Scottish history.

Scholars of earlier generations writing business biographies tended to indulge in hagiography hence the overt concentration on the hugely successful figures who started with nothing and made it to the top. But it has been argued elsewhere – primarily in the Australasian context – that we only know about the success stories, and many more Scots were probably failures, both as entrepreneurs and more generally as migrants. Quite likely the same was true of those who stayed at home and tried to make good. While quantification is difficult, I would like to explore this question both at home and overseas with special reference to the Industrial Revolution and Victorian eras (see the Checklands, 1984 and Slaven, 1975 for the background to this period). We will also examine the idea, developed by economic historians, that 'entrepreneurial failure' or loss of industrial leadership occurred in Scotland at the end of the nineteenth century (discussed, among others, by Campbell, Church and Payne, all 1980). This, incidentally, is a good illustration of how a major historical debate – generated mainly by English and American historians – has impinged on the manufacture of Scottish history.

So this chapter looks in turn at how historians have treated the following issues. First, how has the problem of 'Scottishness' been addressed – how much enterprise was really native, did Scots follow the English lead, and did they take substantial initiatives themselves? Second, what was the role of 'clannishness', family connexions, overlapping partnerships and the like? Third, was poverty the real driving force behind enterprise or were successful Scots already men of capital? Was 'push' more important than 'pull' relative to social mobility within Scotland and emigration overseas? Fourth, what were the origins of Scottish business enterprise and entrepreneurship, with specific reference to such facets as religion, education, social class, capital? Fifth, in which spheres at home and overseas were Scots most active? Sixth, was there, as some historians have maintained, a loss of industrial leadership by end of the nineteenth century, and if so why? Did Scottish capitalists react rationally in the circumstances? Lastly, were the Scots all that enterprising and successful relative to other ethnic-religious groups? In probing these questions we will see something of what historians have written and how the idea of the enterprising Scot developed.

Scottishness, Clannishness, Poverty

First, the problem of 'Scottishness' is especially fascinating during the period of industrialization and the dominance of the British economy internationally before the 1880s. Then, as Donaldson (1966) showed, the Scots certainly had a strong ethnic and cultural identity furth of their native land. How far can the Scottish contribution be identified and how much did others contribute to the success of Scottish economic growth? The Scottish Industrial Revolution came later and faster than south of the Border, so it is no surprise that, at least in the early stages of Scottish industrialization, much was owed to English expertise. Henry Hamilton (1932) was among the first to point out that southern entrepreneurs were attracted by cheap resources, cheap labour, and lack of legal restrictions on company formation. For example, both the iron and textile industries – vital sectors in the process – used imported technology, though generally the Scots showed themselves ready and willing to harness up the new ideas.

Carron ironworks, the first in Scotland to use the Quaker, Abraham Derby's coke smelting process, was established in 1759 by an Anglo-Scottish partnership including Samuel Garbett, a Birmingham merchant, and close associate of the university educated chemist, Dr John Roebuck, of vitriol fame. Much of the initial labour and skill were imported, but later ironmasters, like the native Wilsons of Wilsontown, were quick to cash in on the new technology when they set up their own ironworks near Carnwath in 1779. Interestingly, the capital came from successful trading enterprise in England and Sweden and was one of the first to use Boulton and Watt steam engines. But the works was so advanced in terms of its technology that it eventually over-reached itself and left the Wilsons bankrupt. Another Englishman, Richard Arkwright, inventor of the water-frame, one of several devices that made mass production cotton spinning feasible, used his patent rights to good effect by licensing his device in return for secured partnerships in new cotton mills. He was amazingly active in Scotland, as his well known (if short lived) association with David Dale, George Dempster, and other Scottish entrepreneurs demonstrates. Other Scots – like their European and American counterparts – were quick to pirate the English inventions and when Arkwright's patents lapsed there was a veritable 'Cotton Mania' throughout the Scottish Lowlands.

While the English influence was important in certain sectors, Scottish invention or adaptation in others also stands out significantly during the Industrial Revolution. The practical bent of Scottish science can, to some extent, be seen as a product of the Enlightenment in the ancient universities (discussed elsewhere in this volume). Instances of early Scottish invention abound, from the familiar improvements made by James Watt to the steam engine, which made possible its use as a prime mover in the factory system to the less familiar invention of Andrew Meikle's threshing mill, which held the key to greater productivity on the farm, but used less labour and hence forced more people off the land, and into the industrial workforce, or to overseas migration. Later Scottish innovations greatly increased the pulse of development in the iron, chemical, and engineering industries during the nineteenth century. So there can be little doubt that, at least in terms of creative invention, the Scots played a prominent role in the march of enterprise. To answer our question directly for the period to 1914, about half was due to native wit and half was imported. Some ideas sprung from Scottish minds. Others took other people's ideas and adapted them to local conditions and resources.

Second, like other ethnic minorities separated not by language (except in the case of the Gaels) but certainly by background, culture, and religion, the Scots everywhere formed cohesive groups, invariably but not exclusively dividing only on class lines. Self help and enterprise certainly could bring social mobility and it was greatly assisted by the very fact of Scottishness and 'clannishness'. Clannishness and family connexions invariably assisted migration to the industrial cities and towns, as well as overseas. The Australian historian, Geoffrey Bolton, has described how the Scots 'stuck together like bricks', saying that the cohesiveness of the Scottish community derived as much from its aspirations to make good in the colonies as from its distinctive culture. Family links and continuity through the generations were both significant. As late as 1914 a large proportion of enterprises at home and abroad remained in family hands and there were also numerous instances of overlapping partnerships and interests in most of the major businesses. One might speculate that cultural cohesiveness and links of kin, while initially beneficial, later imposed constraints on further enterprise or innovation. As we will see, what were strengths turned into weaknesses.

Third, practically all observers and most modern historians agree that for much of the eighteenth century Scotland was a relatively poor and under-developed country. Was poverty perhaps the driving force behind Scottish enterprise as men of all classes sought to better themselves during times of great change? Eighteenth century Scotland undeniably started late and from a relatively low base line compared to her southern neighbour. Yet some of the more astute individuals of the period realized the human and natural resource potential, although surprisingly little is known about what they actually thought about enterprise and the scope for economic improvement. This small group included certain members of the wealthy élite and some from further down the social scale. Political misdeeds or the legacy of entailed or sequestered estates had left some of the gentry in hard times. Moreover it was always the lot of their younger sons – the least likely to inherit – to seek their fortunes, taking the highroad to Edinburgh, London or overseas. In the eighteenth century the power of patronage was considerable and positions and preferment could be obtained for promises of political support. Not only this, kinship still counted for much and many lesser gentry and their offspring thus secured military or colonial careers offering opportunities of upward social mobility and financial reward. The best example was probably the East India Company which was virtually dominated by Scots. The same was true of settlement and enterprise in the North American Colonies (surveyed by Brock, 1982), and the West Indies, where Scots were vigorous planters and merchants. We know less about their role than we ought, especially their participation by default or design in slavery and the slave trade.

Further down the social ladder were small traders, craftsmen, shepherds, and other rural labourers who could sell their skills in the colonies, not only in North America but also later in Australia, New Zealand, and other spheres of recent settlement (investigated, among others, by Cage, 1985, Jackson, 1968, Macmillan, 1967, and Prentis, 1983). That opportunities were seen, or thought to be greater than at home, also explains the apparently magnetic attraction to the rural poor of the towns and cities of the Lowlands once enterprise was seen to be promoting economic opportunities. So the 'pull' factor (often involving chain migration) could well have been as critical to social mobility and enterprise as the 'push' which characterized the depopulation of the Highlands (considered in greater detail elsewhere in this volume) and the rural Lowlands. These migrations have been subject to close scrutiny and we can conclude that in many instances the 'pull' of urban employment prospects or new lands (as well as the preservation of culture or religion) was often as critical as the 'push' of grasping landowners anxious to develop sheep-runs or cattle grazing in place of crofts (Donaldson, 1966 and Gray, 1990 provide a useful summary of migration). For many what has been described by one Canadian historian as the 'people's clearance' was just that, as the landless voted with their feet for town work or a pioneering life in the colonies. While the impending demographic crisis might not have been obvious save to a few contemporaries, the poverty in which many found themselves must have been all too apparent. The short and medium-term impact of this influx into industrial towns was devastating, with severe overcrowding, heavy pressure on essential services, successive housing crises, and epidemics of killer diseases. We might just add that not enough attention has been paid by Scottish historians to the impact of overseas settlement on native peoples, for while poor but potentially enterprising Scots were undoubtedly pulled by the attraction of new lands, other races fell victim to the push of such vigorous and often voracious settlers (see, for example, Richards, 1985, 269–70).

Origins and Capital

Fourth, what have historians had to say about the origins of the enterprising Scot? Looking first at the kirk and the theological basis of early capitalism, the role of religion in the development of Scottish enterprise remains controversial. There is virtually no agreement on what Calvinism in Scotland is supposed to have fostered, but did not (Marshall, 1980, 31). Weber's classic view of religion and the rise of capitalism saw the accumulation of wealth as an end in itself, and European Calvinism, in its direct teaching on wealth not only made wealth and election compatible, but even sanctioned the improvement of prosperity as a duty. Scottish Calvinism argued not so much against possessing as abusing riches, and the neo-Calvinism of seventeenth- and eighteenth-century Scotland stressed both diligence and conformity – as well as saying that the *form* of enterprise (for example, a trading partnership) was also important (Marshall, 1980, 107, 278). For all this, and despite modest efforts before the Union, Scottish economic development and enterprise lagged far behind the march of capitalism elsewhere. Could it be that they were not that closely related, especially when one bears in mind that much of the early spirit and tools of enterprise were actually imported from south of the Border or from Continental Europe, circumstances seen in many pre-1707 Scottish industrial or mercantile adventures? Even in the eighteenth century industrial development was inhibited by traditional protectionist and mercantilist doctrines (partly borrowed from England), when the laissez faire approach advocated by Adam Smith might have been more relevant. Witness the establishment of breweries and distilleries well beyond burghal boundaries outside cities like Edinburgh and Perth (Donnachie, 1979; Moss and Hume, 1981), or, partly for reasons of resources or water power, it has to be admitted, the remotely located textile mills, iron works, or lead mines.

As regards education, one of the major figures manufactured by Scottish historians of earlier generations (and by the kailyard novelists and others of the same genre) was the 'lad o' pairts', a son of the soil or some rude mechanical, made good by raising his station in life. Through diligence, perseverance in the face of long odds, and perhaps with the encouragement of the local dominie and relatives, the lad (rarely if ever the lass much before the close of the Victorian era) managed to achieve a college or university education. The majority, however, appeared to reject enterprise, settling instead for the kirk or the law, traditional vocations of the university graduate before the mid-nineteenth century. Indeed, much debate has focussed on the role of education in generating not only a higher level of literacy in Scottish society as compared to that in England or the Continent, but also its role in sparking off the spirit of enquiry within a relatively conservative system. Houston's study of Scottish literacy and identity before the eighteenth century seems to indicate that there was little difference between Scotland and England, and other scholars have shown that despite the precepts of Knox and his successors the parish school system was actually very patchy (Houston, 1985; Anderson, 1983). Even in the burghs, with their grammar schools and academies the quality of provision varied widely and the curriculum was geared to very basic education. Nor, according to Anderson, was Scottish education all that democratic. Social segregation was soon well-established and only occasionally did the son of the laird or even the manse rub shoulders with the 'lad o' pairts' (Anderson, 1983). Such, however, are the myths in which the history of Scottish education has long been enshrouded! Indeed education was both a powerful instrument of social control – limiting the curriculum to essentials posed few challenges to the established order (as Robert Owen, for one must have realised) – and a means of monitoring the extent and degree of social mobility open to underlings (Smout, 1969).

With this said, by the eighteenth century both schools and universities seem to have been more committed to 'useful' or applied arts and sciences than their English counterparts and this certainly encouraged both scientific enquiry and the rise of the new social sciences (especially political economy), both of which had some relevance to enterprise. Scottish scientists of the eighteenth and nineteenth centuries were probably more interested in seeing their ideas and innovations put to practical use than their English or Continental counterparts, and this remained so until the industrialization of countries like France, Germany, and the United States got seriously underway. Practical application of ideas remained a prominent feature of some nineteenth-century Scottish educational institutions, from the humble Mechanics' Institute to the Schools of Arts and Sciences and Technical Colleges established in the major cities. Some of the most enterprising Scots of their generation, like James 'Paraffin' Young and William Thomson, Lord Kelvin, came from these stables. Both Young and Kelvin helped pioneer new technologies, but a curriculum geared to traditional subjects could not contribute much to innovation. Later some schools adopted commercial education and modern languages and Scottish universities continued to produce a high number of science graduates. Excepting those from Glasgow, the majority before 1914 seem to have eschewed business careers. Quite possibly this was a factor in the apparent loss of leadership which occurred in Scottish industry in late Victorian times.

While no one could deny that the pioneer industrialists of Scotland, who 'by laying the foundations of a new Scottish economic order ... affected the lives of all who have lived since', there is considerable controversy about their social origins and real achievements (Smout, 1969, 369). In Scotland they had a number of precursors as early as the sixteenth century, but on the whole they can be seen to have been a new breed which emerged in the eighteenth century, the 'new men' who made the Scottish Industrial Revolution, and sometimes their fortunes (Crouzet, 1985). They were markedly different from the leaders of such traditional industry as existed – soon to be overtaken by the Factory System (an old-fashioned term, but appropriate nevertheless) and the new technology. What kind of families did they come from? What were their occupations before they set up as industrialists? Where did they get the ideas and capital? Were they successful?

From the humblest level of society, the peasant or working class, with perhaps a little schooling but without many savings, was represented by self-made men and some rose from rags to riches by deploying practical skills. For example, James Carmichael started out as a journeyman machine-maker, then managed several factories before himself becoming a successful Dundee flax spinner. Again, the great civil engineering genius, Thomas Telford, was one of several Scots in that field, who had lowly rural origins – certainly something of a contrast to the prosperous and well-connected circumstances in which John Loudon MacAdam spent his upbringing.

At the other end of the social scale probably a larger proportion than in England came from the landed classes and professions; lawyers being prominent; and though often distancing themselves from both plant and management, nevertheless made a significant investment in enterprise. Although the Earl of Selkirk, proprietor of much of the neighbourhood around Kirkcudbright, refused permission for the development of a cotton mill 'for fear his mansion might be disgraced by the vicinity of an establishment of manufacturing industry', he was somewhat unusual, since, as T. C. Smout has shown, most Scottish landowners favoured economic development, including agricultural 'improvement' and other activities. Often they had fingers (and capital) in many pies. A wide range of industrial enterprise attracted their attention, coal, salt, textiles, brewing and distilling, as well as transport in the form of the turnpike roads, canals, and railways which often skirted their estates but passed through the planned villages they had created. Like the lawyers (see Shaw, 1983), the gentry were often in an ideal position to exploit local opportunities by joining in partnerships with men of enterprise intent on industrial development. Their surplus capital might be savings but invariably came from the higher rents generated by agricultural 'improvement' or less frequently successful investment in trade. The Campbells of Jura who invested in David Dale's cotton spinning enterprises at New Lanark and elsewhere, were typical of the former, while many of the 'Tobacco Lords', the Glasgow merchant elite with whom Dale associated, were already investing in both land and industry well before the bottom all but dropped out of the tobacco trade following the American Revolution (Devine, 1975).

However, as in England, the middle class was the main recruiting ground for entrepreneurship, though a strong contingent sprang from its lower strata. Many Scottish industrialists had 'humble', though not necessarily proletarian backgrounds and beginnings and must be considered self-made men – an expression which is often unjustifiably restricted to those who emerged from the ranks of the manual workers. There are numerous case-histories, but two must suffice. The Bairds, who established a huge enterprise embracing coal and iron, virtually creating the 'Iron town' of Coatbridge in the process, came of farming stock, and Charles Tennant, the successful chemical entrepreneur, was also the son of a farmer (Crouzet, 130–3).

With this said, we cannot ignore the powerful argument presented by Joe Melling who claims that entrepreneurs from different social backgrounds active in different sectors of the economy had little in common, and that these divisions actually widened as the scale of enterprise grew (Melling in Dickson (ed.), 1982, 67). The landowners, he claims, remained dominant until challenged in the latter half of the nineteenth century by financial and mercantile capitalists. This represents something of a revision of earlier views and shows how historians can use the same evidence to come to different conclusions.

The social origins of entrepreneurship are vital to this discussion, but we move now to look in further detail at what historians have written about the role of capital. Who financed the Scottish Industrial Revolution and maintained the momentum through succeeding generations? Much of the evidence so far assembled by historians would indicate that the gentry and merchant class again played an early and prominent role, and that, as might be expected, the bulk of any available surplus accrued from either the land or commerce. The time-scale has recently been revised backwards. According to current thinking enterprising landowners actually appeared much earlier than previously supposed and the origins of the Agricultural Revolution which swept Scotland in the eighteenth century are clearly to be found long before. So despite the disruptions of civil and religious disorder the accumulation of surplus capital was probably a longer-term business than might be imagined. When the opportunity to invest in new enterprises arose, some landowners as we have seen, were not slow in coming forward. In fact, they exercised considerable initiative, which emulated in enthusiasm if not scale that of the merchants and middlemen. Even in such a primitive economy it was quite natural that they should become involved in industrial as well as commercial enterprise. There was always considerable overlap: linen and cotton merchants invested in textile spinning, bleaching, and printing partnerships; while iron importers established their own blast furnaces and collieries. Some landowners, like the Buccleuchs, the Elgins, and the Hamiltons, accrued fabulous wealth on the back of coal and other minerals but none established industrial dynasties of the kind associated with the later iron, steel, engineering, and shipbuilding industries which made Scotland the 'Workshop of the Empire'. We might just note that a few men of modest capital were able to deploy both their cash and technical skill to advantage especially in the consumer sector where entry was cheaper than to heavy industry. The family brewing concerns of John and Robert Tennant in Glasgow and William Younger in Edinburgh were established respectively by innkeepers and excisemen, their knowledge of the drink trade coming from different but related ends of the business.

In the mobilization of capital, as S. G. Checkland has shown, the well developed banking system was vital, though by no means always fool-proof (Checkland, 1975). Substantial risks were to be run investing in new enterprise and there were probably more failures than successes in the period of dramatic economic expansion accompanying Scottish industrialization. How much capital was needed? In some cases entry into small scale enterprise could be bought for modest capital: a small salt-works, tannery, brewery, or flour mill might be established for a few hundred pounds and with luck the venture would flourish. What clearly was characteristic of early industrialization was craft skill, with no great emphasis on either capital or technology, but this changed as the process gathered momentum. Setting up a large cotton mill or ironworks, and sinking deeper collieries required substantial investment, and even more as time progressed.

There are no hard and fast figures for the total that went into new enterprises – say between 1770 and 1820 – but we have some idea of what individual businesses were worth at particular times and on that basis can make some guesses for a few of the key sectors. The cotton industry was new and dynamic and according to Sir John Sinclair was worth £1.4 million in 1812. New Lanark, larger than most mills, but by no means atypical, was sold in 1814 for £114 000, an enormous sum for the time, equivalent to a multi-million pound enterprise at present day values (Butt, 1971).

Iron was another highly capitalized sector. More than £150 000 had been invested in Carron by 1770 and a decade later apart from larger investments later the Wilson brothers (small Clydesdale lairds turned merchants) spent almost half that sum developing their new plant at Wilsontown. But these and other early enterprises had problems of under-capitalization which were largely solved by the time of the great expansion after 1830. It has been estimated that the industry was already worth £6.5 million by the 1840s – a situation reached in both ironworks and their associated collieries at enormous social cost. For the men of enterprise in this apparently booming industry the risks were high and the returns considerable. David Bremner, first industrial correspondent of *The Scotsman* and a pioneer of business history, reckoned the Bairds, employing 9 000 men, made 25 per cent of Scottish output and earned £750 000 a year in 1869. Typically, they deployed a modest proportion of this in morally uplifting endowments.

The Pillars of Enterprise

Fifth, Scottish enterprise found outlets across an enormous range of economic activities at home and abroad, but generally speaking the most favoured were agriculture and processing, commerce, shipping, textiles, coal, iron, and engineering – the great mainstays of British economic growth before 1914. Historians have produced some important studies of these and other sectors, but there are still major gaps to be filled.

Looking first at the domestic scene, enterprise in Scottish agriculture, after a relatively late start by English standards, caught up fast. By the early nineteenth century, at least in most of the Lowlands, it could be regarded as a leading and highly productive sector benefiting landed gentry and tenantry alike. It remained very labour intensive (and working conditions were pretty appalling), but being cheap was not yet an impediment to profit. Taken overall, Scottish farming was diverse in terms of its land use and production, and hence weathered the problems of later nineteenth-century depression better than the more specialized industry in southern England. There were many landowners and owner-occupiers with no minerals, relying entirely on their estates or farms, who prospered greatly in the Victorian era.

Sustained population growth, urbanization and rising incomes generated a huge demand for food, drink, and clothing, so it comes as no surprise that Scots led enterprise in this sector. As we have seen, entry to processing industries could be bought cheaply, a small meal mill, tannery or brewery being established in the early 1800s for a few hundred pounds. Some pioneers in the drink trade (described in Donnachie, 1979; Moss & Hume, 1981; and Slaven & Checkland, 1986), like Haig, Tennant and Younger (both Edinburgh and Alloa), Melrose and Barr, established large and profitable businesses, with dynasties, surviving in some cases, to the present day. Familiar foodstuffs producing sustained enterprise included, among others, those prime essentials of the Scottish high tea – bread, biscuits and jam! In this sector good examples of successful diversification by modest family enterprises are Baxter of Fochabers and Scott of Carluke, whose products are recognized internationally thanks partly to their Scottish origins. The retail baron, Thomas Lipton, was another who began in a small way and made his fortune (for biographies see Slaven & Checkland, 1990).

Another sector long attractive to enterprising Scots was trade and shipping. We tend to forget that before the railways coastal shipping provided a vital link for many communities and that from modest beginnings ventures could be made further afield (even by small vessels) to Europe and North America. Such initiatives made Glasgow and the Clyde a major trading centre by the end of the eighteenth century. Glasgow maintained its lead (despite the efforts of Leith, Dundee, and other ports to muscle in on some of the action) and, through the initiative and enterprise of native Scots, created a dynamic shipbuilding industry. At first its products were wooden sailing ships but these were ultimately displaced by iron steamships. Hence the close links that always existed between enterprise in shipping, shipbuilding, engineering, and iron and steel originated in the early nineteenth century (Slaven, 1979; Campbell, 1980). Some of Scotland's most successful entrepreneurs, like the Burrells and the Mathesons, were identified in different ways with merchant shipping (Slaven & Checkland, 1990, 268–70; 301–2).

Small beginnings, as we saw, could also be made in textiles and are evidenced in the careers of men of enterprise throughout the industry. For example, in 1826 James Coats began producing sewing cotton and silk thread in a small mill at Ferguslie on the fringes of Paisley. By 1860 the town was a major world centre of thread making and the firm of Coats, under James's three sons, James, Peter, and Thomas, was one of the two largest internationally. It then employed 1 100 and sales that year grossed £200 000, mostly exports. By 1883 when Thomas Coats, the effective authority, died, the firm had 3 000 employees and with its North American subsidiaries was reckoned to be worth close on £2 million. Coats himself was the first of several millionaires in the family – some of his accrued wealth being disbursed in benefactions to his native Paisley. A powerful dynasty thus established continued to respond to market forces, making it the most profitable single British firm by 1910 with assets worth £70 million (Slaven & Checkland, 1986, 329–34).

It was, of course, in the heavy industries that the Scots really excelled, and at least for a while made Clydeside the Workshop of the Empire. Coal, iron, and heavy engineering became more closely related after 1830, partly reflecting a natural affinity, and partly the overlapping interests of powerful masters like generations of Dixons, Bairds, Colvilles, Beardmores, and Lithgows, described – among others by Slaven (1975, 111–34; 163–83), A. B. Campbell (1979, 93–116), Hume & Moss (1979), and Payne (1979, 14–41). Both David Colville Sr and John Craig, iron and steel masters of different generations had relatively humble origins, the latter a son of a puddler at the former's Dalzell Ironworks (Slaven & Checkland, 1986, 97–103). In these sectors innovation was far from lacking (in marine engineering for example), yet the experience of the later Victorian era suggests that the earlier dynamism had gone somewhat by the board.

Overseas the pattern repeated itself in North America, Australia, New Zealand, and elsewhere. Historians have begun to look at the impact of the Scots in areas of recent settlement and archive linkage between such places and Scotland has already produced some interesting results. Naturally the first emphasis everywhere was on subsistence farming and simple trade, but as pioneering gave way to higher levels of economic activity, the Scots rapidly found their way into large scale capitalist agriculture (ranging from sugar planting in the West Indies to sheep farming in New South Wales) and land or real estate dealing, notably in the United States, where Scottish syndicates were especially active. Mining was another much favoured pursuit, where fortunes could be quickly made – and as quickly lost. Such activities required the support of urban industry, and as the case of Melbourne ('virtually a Scots colony' by the 1840s) so clearly shows, the Scots played a major role in development as diverse as brewing and railway engineering. Skills learned at home, and exported capital, could thus be deployed to build a new life (and for the lucky few, a fortune) in the colonies.

A Failure of Nerve?

Sixth, if Scots were so successful during Britain's rise to industrial and imperial supremacy, how do historians account for the apparent loss of leadership which occurred in late Victorian times? As far as Scottish enterprise is concerned this has to be seen in the context of Britain's changing position relative to international competitors and to some extent to industrial inertia which sprang from early leadership (Church; Payne, both 1980). Neither was failure to innovate and respond to new challenges anything like universal, nor, in retrospect did entrepreneurs act irrationally. So, as Campbell has shown, the causes are complex, and, further, the detailed analysis presented by Scott and Hughes proves beyond doubt that Scottish industry was, in any case, always the junior partner in the British economy and imperial expansion (Campbell, 1980, 1; Scott & Hughes, 1980, 258–65). Scottish prosperity as Workship of the Empire was based on export-orientated manufacturing companies and overseas-orientated investment companies. In the mid-nineteenth century the bulk of Scottish capital was concentrated in heavy industries, railways, textiles, investment, and mortgage companies – with some lesser involvement in drink, chemicals and overseas merchanting. By 1904–5 little had changed for the bulk of Scottish capital was to be found in basic industries, railways, textiles, and investment. More than ever the main areas of Scottish enterprise were linked together 'in common ownership, inter-locking directorships and bonds of kinship' to the extent that 85 per cent of the top hundred companies were so connected (Scott & Hughes, 1980, 18–21).

The mixed fortunes of the iron and steel industry illustrate the problems that confronted capitalists and leave historians puzzled about their motives. According to one scholar the ironmasters, having weighed up the relative merits and potential profitability of moving into steel or sticking with iron and coal, chose the latter (on coal, see Church, 1986). In retrospect they may have been wrong to do so, but steel making presented technical difficulties and required large-scale investment in new plant. Some of the more astute may have realized that Scottish iron smelting was in irretrievable decline and that steel might be even more risky. Not all ignored steel. By 1900 five of the largest iron-making enterprises were producing steel, but 'the effort was somewhat half-hearted'. So the Scottish iron masters concentrated on what they knew – iron for shipbuilding and railways – and, says Payne, 'who can blame them?' (Payne, 1979, 46–55).

Was there a failure of nerve as well as entrepreneurship? Payne showed that the majority of Victorian businessmen clung steadfastly to the belief that things would get better and that it often took a relatively long period of unprofitability before they reckoned that their companies had little prospect of future prosperity. This unwillingness to gamble with new ideas or investment may have had something to do with predominant family ownership, for in many enterprises far more than individual wealth or status was at stake in the event of collapse. Interestingly, by the 1870s or 80s many of the pioneers had died or retired, perhaps leaving their firms in the hands of less able or less courageous men. Inertia, in one sense, helped to preserve the known, rather than venture into the unknown. Certainly, in some instances, enterprise continued to be funded by founding families, though increasingly institutions had a growing stake which forced modernization and more professional management. But in many cases it came too late – as in the heavy industries, whose reliance on the old ways was simply compounded by the onset of the arms race and the Great War in 1914 (for a good account see Harvie, 1981).

So we return to our final and most difficult question. Enterprising Scots of the Industrial and Imperial eras were a mixed bunch, much influenced by their environment. This was dominated by the Calvinist tradition, ideas of Enlightenment and enquiry, and a certain degree of commercial drive which had its roots in relative backwardness and poverty. Given the nature and timing of early industrialization Scots were in a good position to adapt English ideas to local conditions and to innovate of their own accord. In doing so probably a high proportion, upwards of three-quarters, were either never much of a success or outright failures – if the evidence of those sectors investigated in any detail by historians can be taken as typical of enterprise as a whole. Some traditional characteristics of the Scot on the make – ability, ruthlessness, determination, pride, and clannishness were to be found in other ethnic groups, the Welsh and Cornish being readily distinguishable instances. And this may be a significant aspect of the myth-making process. For Scots – at least furth of their native land – stood out from the crowd by virtue of their numerical minority and socio-cultural cohesiveness. Did the English or Irish, numerically stronger, even jealous of success, invent the hard-headed Scot, or did he invent himself? The Scot, supposedly asked by an Irishman what the Scots had achieved in Australia replied, 'Well, we own it!'

If Scottish history can be de-mythologized and we come to understand more about the way myths and legends have been both manufactured and perpetuated for cultural, moral, or political ends, so the role of the enterprising Scot might be further re-evaluated. Undoubtedly, as history tells us, the Scots were enterprising (in diverse activities other than business, which we have not had space to consider here), but, while there were some successes, there were also many failures. As I have said elsewhere, we know most about the success stories, and it seemed logical for historians of previous generations to make the most of them. Dictionaries of business biography at home and of national biography in North America and Australasia still bulge with entries on successful Scots. For every one success there were certainly hundreds of failures who replaced the poverty of existence in their native place with the grind and misery of urban work or the harsh conditions of pioneering on the Canadian prairie or the Australian bush. The mute testimony to failure at home are the thousands of sequestration books found in the Court of Session records in Edinburgh. In any case, if the revisionist view is accepted the enterprising Scot had rarely come up from nothing and the majority were of the middling rather than the labouring class. Enterprise seems to have held little attraction for the 'lad o' pairts' and as time progressed entry became more difficult except for really talented individuals, 'self-made' or otherwise. Finally it has to be said that successful men of capital and enterprise, as well as raising their own status, helped create modern Scotland, irrecoverably changing the economic and social fabric. Were they responsible for the ills that beset Scotland after the Great War? If they had acted differently would the outcome have been any different? I'm afraid this takes us into the realm of speculation and certainly well beyond the myths surrounding the enterprising Scot and how historians have seen him!

7

Red Clyde, Red Scotland

JOHN FOSTER

Most readers of Willie Gallacher's *Revolt on the Clyde* remember the sharp, photographic quality of its imagery. It opens with Gallacher describing the drab back streets of working-class Glasgow at the outbreak of war – 'what a terrible attraction a war can have! The wild excitement, the illusion of wonderful adventure and the actual break in the deadly monotony of working-class life'. Working people celebrated the declaration of war. Fifteen months later we are shown the Glasgow Sheriff Court in Ingram Street. Thousands of women rent strikers are joined by columns of workers marching in from the great armaments works and shipyards to the north, south, and west. Anti-war socialists, John Maclean, Gallacher, Maxton, address the crowd from improvized platforms, poster boards taken from shopfronts, and balanced precariously on the shoulders of riveters and platelayers. January 1919 provides another image: George Square on a grey winter's morning, crammed with tens of thousands of strikers. Rain had fallen during the night and the square was wet and muddy. Many sections of the demonstration are jammed in the surrounding side streets and cannot get access to the square. Gallacher addresses the demonstration from the plinth of the Gladstone monument while a deputation goes into the City Chambers to see the Lord Provost. Suddenly, without warning, a signal is given. The massed lines of foot and horse police in front of the city chambers charge the rear of the demonstration. Initially the demonstrators retreat. 'Men were sprawling all around, and just beneath where I was standing a woman was lying on her side and on her face were the marks of a muddy boot'. From the period after the war Gallacher gives us a final image. May Day in 1924, Gallacher leads a march. It is very small: one hundred at most (Gallacher, 1936, 18, 227 and 243).

Gallacher's account sums up both the paradox and symbolism of the Red Clyde. For the first half of this century the evidence shows quite plainly that working people in Scotland were less unionized and less likely to vote Labour than their counterparts in England. In general the leadership of the Scottish trade union movement and of the Labour Party was also far more committed to right-wing perspectives. Gallacher does not hide this reality. The chauvinism, the religious bigotry, and the desolation of the post-war depression are all there in his account. But against this are balanced his moments of near revolutionary mobilization. There can be no doubt that Gallacher, like many other participants, did believe – perhaps with hindsight – that something special had occurred on the Clyde during and immediately after the first world war. In the mid-1930s, when he wrote *Revolt on the Clyde*, he considered that a moment of near revolutionary potential had been reached, and missed, on 31 January 1919. The 60 000 strong gathering in George Square came three weeks after the massive demobilization mutinies in the south, when the Glasgow police were on the verge of strike action and when on Clydeside demobilized soldiers had joined shipyard workers and miners to demand shorter hours and full employment. Had the George Square demonstrators marched to the Maryhill barracks instead, and fraternized with the disaffected soldiers there, the outcome, Gallacher believed, could have been very different.

From different perspectives many other participants also believed that the two million people of the Clyde Valley, concentrated around the biggest of Europe's heavy industry and munitions centres, represented the most serious potential threat to the existing order in Britain. This was certainly the position of at least some of those responsible for defending that order. And on Clydeside it became part of an abiding popular conviction. John Maclean, the Glasgow school teacher and Marxist lecturer, twice imprisoned for his opposition to the war, was its human symbol for well over a generation after his death in 1924. Indeed, to some extent this conviction underlies a belief among many Scots today that as a nation they are somehow more proletarian and more militant than the English. Red Clydeside, Red Scotland.

Our immediate concern is with how far this conception of the Red Clyde is a historical creation: the promotion of a 'heroic episode' to compensate for a far more humdrum reality. A number of new histories researched and written over the past two decades have asserted just that. They argue that Red Clydeside was a legend invented years after the event by left-wing propagandists such as Gallacher, Tom Bell, and McShane. The gist of these new interpretations is that the major transformation on Clydeside during the first world war had very little to do with the revolutionary left. The industrial battles led by the Marxist shop stewards during the war were in fact conservative rearguard actions to defend the privileges of the skilled craft elite – and defeated. The real changes occurred at the level of the community not industry. It was moderate, reformist politicians such as Wheatley and Dolan who, during these years, and especially in the three years after the war, created a mass Labour vote and did so by their patient work on housing, rents, and municipal services. This dramatic transformation was not achieved through industrial struggle but by the creation of new constituencies of support among those hitherto excluded: women, the unskilled and unemployed, and particularly the Catholic, Irish minority. This, so the new line goes, provides a far better match with what followed than the overdramatized tales of Willie Gallacher.

Our task here is not to develop any new interpretation but to review the process by which these various histories have been constructed. Obviously some assessments of what did actually happen will be inevitable and necessary: to pretend there is no ultimate reality is a dangerous game for any historian. But we do not have the space to attempt a full documentary reconstruction. Nor can we compare in any evenhanded way what people said or thought at the time, with what they said about it later. We need to remember the inherent bias of the situation. Almost anything done by Red Clydesiders was technically illegal. A chance remark about the war to a neighbour on a tram could and did lead to arrest and imprisonment (Caledun, *Call*, 17 October 1918). No newspaper was allowed to report activities which could be construed as harmful to the war effort, and even relatively moderate newspapers like *Forward* suffered temporary suppression for this reason. The offices of more radical organizations such as the Socialist Labour Party (SLP) and the British Socialist Party (BSP) were repeatedly raided for evidence which might permit the prosecution of their members. We cannot therefore assess subsequent accounts against any real evidence of what the principal protagonists might have thought at the time because the evidence just will not be there.

Our objective is a far more modest one. It is to compare the different ways the history of the Red Clyde has been written: starting with the participants – reformists, revolutionaries, and government figures – and working our way through the conventional histories, to the revisionists of the 1970s and the further revisions of the last decade. As we will see, the vigour with which this episode has been contested and redefined, the sheer refusal of its ghost to disappear, bears witness to its continuing importance for the way Scots define themselves today.

Participants

Gallacher's account we have already noted. We will take one other viewpoint from the revolutionary left, that of Tom Bell, a member of the syndicalist SLP in contrast to Gallacher's more orthodox BSP. As might be expected, Bell focuses on the origins of the shop stewards movement, the individuals within it, and the Marxist education work of John Maclean. The events of 1915 and early 1916 are given somewhat perfunctory treatment, partly perhaps because Bell was working mainly away from Glasgow for the first two years of the war. More attention is given to the growth of militancy in 1917 and 1918. Bell, an iron moulder and an executive member of the Associated Ironmoulders of Scotland, credits his union with a significant part in this. He sees its three-week strike in September–October 1917 as a major factor in securing one of the turning-points in wartime industrial relations: the concession of the 12½ percent bonus. The Russian Revolution comes as the 'culmination of a tremendous movement of mass discontent with the war'. He talks of 'serious repercussions on the troops' and a 'stimulus to the widespread discontent and war weariness' among the working masses. The visit by Sir Auckland Geddes to Glasgow in January 1918 provided the catalyst for opposition to the war and to further conscription. In the City Hall meeting Bell describes the climax as being reached when, an ex-soldier, secretary of Discharged Soldiers and Sailors Committee, came on to the platform to challenge Geddes. A whole chapter is given to the Forty-Hour strike of January 1919. Bell describes it thus: 'starting primarily as a Scottish movement, it spread rapidly to all parts of the country, and at one time assumed all the possibilities of a general political strike'. Bell instances the actions and threats of solidarity action from electricity, underground and rail workers in London, shipbuilders in London, Barrow, and Birkenhead, electricians in South Wales and the parallel general strike in Belfast. Bell stresses the unusual characteristics of the strike – as being jointly called by unofficial and official union structures, as addressing its demands to the government and as demanding shorter hours with the intention of 'absorbing the unemployed', specifically discharged soldiers and those laid off from the munitions industries. The episode in George Square on 31 January was, Bell claims, deliberately set up by the authorities with the intention of intimidating the strikers (Bell, 148–158, 160–173).

Another central figure in the 1919 strike was Emanuel Shinwell who progressed from youthful radicalism to the centre-right of the Labour Party. He published his main work of autobiography in 1973 and did so from the vantage point of the House of Lords after a long ministerial career.

Shinwell's account of the period moves through the growth of the shop-stewards movement, a product of the wartime 'failure' of the official Labour and Trade Union Leadership, to the 1915 meeting with Lloyd George and the suppression of *Forward*. As a member of the Independent Labour Party (ILP), he highlights the work of the Glasgow branch of the Union of Democratic Control in campaigning against the war and secret war aims. He claims that Glasgow's reputation as a 'trouble centre' emerged soon after the war broke out and focussed particularly on the issue of housing. Interest in the Russian Revolution was not, he says, 'ideological', but 'as a possible way to end the war'. Shinwell notes that 'many' of those who took part in the demobilization mutinies in November and December 1918 were 'natives of Glasgow'. Shinwell does not minimize the scale of the 1919 general strike. Then chairman of Glasgow trades council, he presents it as a gesture of 'self-sacrifice by shop stewards and trade unionists, to help the workless'. The government's response, on the other hand, was caught up in 'a neurosis about red revolution'. The government, and Churchill in particular, was determined to pursue a 'propaganda ploy of dividing the nation as between 'the public' and the 'workers', and hence refused to consider any of the demands put forward. Shinwell quotes his own speech made as chairman of the 11 January conference which called the strike. The demand for forty hours was 'not revolutionary in character. It is attributable solely and entirely to the fear of possible unemployment'. He sees the confrontation with police in George Square as part of a plan by which the government sought to get public opinion on its side (he cites Churchill's advice to the cabinet about 'going gently at first') before bringing in troops (Shinwell, 1973, 37–45).

Shinwell blames the same type of right-wing propaganda for the mistaken attribution of revolutionary intent to the Clydeside MPs. 'In the euphoria of the hour, Neil McLean, who had won Govan in 1918, told the cheering audience that the old parliamentary order was finished'. 'Massive propaganda from London succeeded in persuading the middle and upper classes in England that the new Scottish MPs were rebels, under the influence of Moscow if not actually in its pay'. Shinwell adds that what McLean really meant was that he wanted 'to change the composition of parliament, not to abolish it' (Shinwell, 1973, 20).

Tom Johnston, another reformed rebel who became Secretary of State for Scotland, gives much the same explanation in his autobiography published in 1960. The Clydeside MPs were, he claimed, victims of scare stories in the London press. Johnston had been editor of *Forward*, the Glasgow weekly paper most closely associated with the ILP throughout the war. *Forward* was the only paper with relatively mass circulation open to the working-class movement in Scotland and it drew material from all its political trends. It was a highly professional and successful publication which played a crucial role in informing working-class opinion. Johnston, however, gives us very little on this. Only eight pages are devoted to his long years as editor. Only three cover the war years and these are almost entirely taken up with the government's suppression of the paper in January 1916. Johnston describes it as a hilarious bureaucratic bungle by the military censors. He recounts his interview with Lloyd George in London six weeks later when the latter described the episode as a complete misunderstanding. With that Johnston wipes clean his slate. He makes no mention of the 1919 General Strike, in which *Forward* played an important role, nor of the industrial battles which preceded it (Johnston, 1952, 37–38, 46, 47).

Our last Clydesider is David Kirkwood, elected MP in 1922, he had previously been a key rank and file leader, convener of shop stewards at Beardmores and very close to John Wheatley, the Catholic ILPer. By the time he wrote his autobiography, *My Life of Revolt* in 1935, he had broken with the ILP and took a centrist position in the Labour Party. Both Lansbury and Churchill contribute Forewords to his book. His autobiography focuses on his role as a mass leader during the war when, in March 1916, he was one of those deported along with Gallacher by the military authorities. However, of the eighty pages devoted to the period all but a dozen address the period prior to his deportation and the months of deportation itself. The other two years of the war, during which Kirkwood still held an important position in the movement, are passed over in virtual silence. The 1919 General Strike, in which Kirkwood played a leading role, warrants only two pages – and these are used mainly to highlight his acquittal when tried alongside Shinwell, Gallacher, and others for sedition (Kirkwood, 1935, 80–162, 171–174).

 Comparing these accounts one preliminary impression emerges. While all of them describe roughly the same landscape, the perspective from which it is viewed tends to be quite sharply different. For Kirkwood and Johnston the heroic period, the 'revolt' on the Clyde, is identified with the early years of the war when organised labour is seen to confront government and secure a recognition of its legitimate demands. For Shinwell the 1919 general strike is discussed at some length. But it is principally to enable him to press home his contention that the labour movement's demands were essentially limited. For Gallacher and Bell, on the other hand, the early years are seen as preparatory. They form part of an escalating series of actions, the humiliation of Lloyd George, the strikes of 1917–18, the routing of Geddes, the agitation around Maclean's imprisonment and the May Day strike of 1918. The culmination is the 1919 strike. It is this which is seen to mark the high point of revolt and political consciousness.

But, whatever the differences, it is clear we are dealing with the same, generally familiar landscape. When we turn to accounts by figures from the other side of the class divide this is by no means always the case.

The most authoritative and often used account is the Official History of the Ministry of Munitions. This twelve-volume compilation was printed but never published and reviews the ministry's work up to its closure at the end of the war. Created in 1915 to oversee the production of war materials, the ministry's precise responsibilities were subject to considerable bureaucratic conflict (from the Admiralty, the War Office and the Ministry of Labour among others) and these conflicts tended to become sharper and more rancorous as the war went on. For the first year of its existence the ministry was headed by Lloyd George and for its last eighteen months by Churchill. Both politicians still held leading government positions at the time when the history was compiled.

Reading the Official History it is quite easy to gain the impression that labour unrest on the Clyde peaked in 1915, was administratively diffused and channelled early in 1916 and thereafter remained at a relatively low level. A total of 480 pages [volume IV, Part I to Part IV] are devoted to labour relations on the Clyde between June 1915 and March 1916. The picture we are presented with is one which has become familiar through frequent repetition: of the new ministry having to tackle a chaotic situation created by autocratic managers, greedy landlords and inept intervention by other government departments (particularly the Admiralty) which was being exploited by a few anti-war extremists. The Ministry of Munitions is credited with recognizing the real grievances of workers, tackling old autocratic management styles and winning enough confidence among the patriotic majority of trade unionists to ease in a significant element of labour dilution. The ministry's final bureaucratic triumph was its ability to isolate the anti-war element within the Clyde Workers Committee and remove them from the Clyde in March 1916.

This level of detail is in stark contrast to the sixteen pages [volume II, pp 91–92; volume V, pp 177–192] devoted to the War Bonus debacle of 1917–18. In a bid to increase productivity and halt the loss of skilled labour (and no doubt also to gain some credentials with organised labour), one of Churchill's first acts in the summer of

1917 was to grant a 12¹/₂ per cent War Bonus to skilled time workers in engineering. The result was a reverberating series of strikes as workers in all other war industries and all other grades took action to secure the same rise. The wave of unrest continued till February 1918. Far more days were lost through strike action over the war bonus than over dilution in 1915–16. The interruption to production came at a critical moment in the submarine war, when munitions were short on the Western Front and when the success of strike action gave strength to a shop stewards movement increasingly radicalized by events in Russia. The Ministry of Munitions many enemies in other ministries were quick to attribute the sharp deterioration in industrial relations to Churchill's blundering intervention (Gallipoli in 1915; now this on the home front in 1917) and, in an ultimate humiliation, secured the establishment of an interdepartmental committee headed by the Ministry of Labour to sort out the mess.

Churchill's own account bears fulsome testimony to his embarrassment (Churchill, 1932). What labour unrest? The bonus crisis is not mentioned. The book's appendices reproduce in great detail the departmental memoranda that flowed from Munitions to the War Office and elsewhere on production levels and the development of Churchill's pet weapon, the tank. But there is nothing on those that came back about the disruption of supplies or on the ministry's harassed attempts to deflect the blame on to steel suppliers and the Admiralty (Churchill, 1932, 1070–1125).

Lloyd George's *War Memoirs* tend to confirm this foreshortened view that labour troubles on the Clyde were largely at an end by 1916. Lloyd George attributes this outcome largely to the impact of his bold decision to visit the Clyde over Christmas in 1916. 'The visit, for a time at least, had a quieting effect and a quickening influence on production. Some weeks later we had further trouble and strong action had to be taken in the way of deportation of some of the leaders and the prosecution of others (Lloyd George, 1938, 188). Lloyd George presents the matter as essentially that of meeting legitimate grievances and dividing moderates from extremists. He describes his reception at Beardmores at Christmas eve. 'A man who seemed to be their leader stepped forward and started haranguing me on the servitude of labour in private establishments. He was a strong man, with a fine open face. This was my first acquaintance with Mr David Kirkwood … he was a fundamentally reasonable man to deal with. […] There was another spokesman who seemed to me to be a natural savage. He came right up to me with a threatening mien and locked fists, talking in an ill-tempered and angry vein … Later on I met Mr Gallacher, a Communist' (187).

Once he had relinquished direct control at the Ministry of Munitions, Lloyd George does, however, note the scale of labour unrest. This was particularly so during the Russian revolutions of 1917. 'The coming of the Russian Revolution lit up the skies with a lurid flash of hope for all who were dissatisfied with the existing order of things. It certainly encouraged all traditional malcontents. In Russia, they pointed out, the workmen formed a separate authority coordinate with the Government ... Why not in Britain? This was the question asked in every workshop and at every street corner' (1146). As previously, the Clyde 'was always a danger spot for labour trouble' but Lloyd George decided not to visit in person on this occasion. Instead he sent the king. 'In September [1917] the King spent some four or five days there, and visited more than two dozen shipyards and steelworks. So far as I can recall', and the note of caution is interesting, 'neither these nor any of the innumerable visits ... were marred by any kind of unpleasantness' (1163).

One final witness from the establishment side might be William Beveridge, assistant general secretary at the Ministry of Munitions. Always a frustrated advocate of state compulsion schemes for labour, he was described by Ernest Bevin in 1916 as one of the 'sinister crowd of Civil Servants' who stood behind Lloyd George. Beveridge's account also focuses on the early period, when he acted as principal architect of much of the legislation. However, while spending some time on the success of his parliamentary drafting, Beveridge has little to say about the details of the labour unrest it was meant to defeat. Similarly, he describes Lloyd George's dexterity in justifying the suppression of *Forward* without telling us why it was done. Beveridge focuses on the way Lloyd George avoided parliamentary censure by linking its suppression to that of the more radical, *Scottish Vanguard:* 'defending the suppression of one paper in the main by attacking a different paper. It was a Parliamentary triumph exceeding in dexterity the trick cycling which I had just seen at Drury Lane' (Beveridge, 1959, 133).

This mixture of evasion and discretion typifies most public recollections of those responsible for containing labour unrest during the war, and poses for us the question we need to tackle next. Given the almost total censorship during the war and the limited circulation of the left-wing press afterwards, how and in what form did Red Clydeside pass into history during the two interwar decades?

Passage into History

Two main sources might be suggested – both largely propagandist. One derived from the struggle within the British Labour Movement about its political direction after the war. The other was the no less propagandist output of those defending the existing social system.

For the Communist Left wartime Clydeside provided the clearest possible evidence for the viability of a new type of working-class movement. The exchanges between Gallacher and Lenin, widely disseminated in Lenin's *Left Wing Communism*, were based on the assumption that the character of the British Labour Movement had decisively changed during the war. A new, active non-reformist trend had emerged in the form of the shop stewards movement. Gallacher claimed that the new forms of unofficial workers committee were similar, in their representative and non-sectional character, to the Russian workers' councils or Soviets (Lenin, 1920/1966, 79). This interpretation figures regularly in most contemporary Communist accounts. The historical section of *Communist Party Training* (CPGB, 1927, 46–65) refers to the 'revolt against the bartering of the trade unions to the imperialists' which took place on the Clyde. It gives particular prominence to the government's creation of the joint employer-worker Whitley Councils as marking a recognition by the state of the scale of the revolt and also of the potential 'value of the workers' organisations when led by labour imperialists'. In Scotland a not dissimilar interpretation was given by John Maclean and those organised around his Scottish Vanguard. The movement against the war had revealed the potential for fundamental anti-imperialist struggle among Scottish workers which was not present in England. 'We on the Clyde have a mighty mission to fulfil', wrote Maclean in November 1920, 'We can make Glasgow a Petrograd, a revolutionary storm-centre second to none' (N. Milton, 1978, pp. 220–232). A somewhat different, though parallel, line was taken by that trend in the ILP represented by the Plebs League. This linked events on the Clyde to the perspectives of guild socialism. The National Council of Labour College's main history textbook was Mark Starr's *A Worker Looks at History* (1927). Here the emergence of the shop stewards movement 'notably on the Clyde', is seen to demonstrate the failure of the old craft unions in the face of demands for workshop control. 'So insistent became the cry for workers' control that in 1917 the Whitley Committee issued its report ... The Russian Revolution (1917) and its Soviet administration greatly stimulated the move towards workshop organisation.'

These trends of analysis, the Communist, Maclean's and the Plebs League, represented the main centres of active interpretation within the organised working class movement. While an appreciation of the finer doctrinal points of difference may have been restricted to a fairly narrow band of activists, these general assessments were nonetheless much more widely influential in disseminating a knowledge of 'what had happened on the Clyde'. They formed part of the assumed geography of political reference at a time when the character of the Labour Party remained politically undecided and when, between 1919 and 1926, millions of workers were being drawn into active political and industrial action for the first time.

It was precisely this very fluid political situation that informed government attempts to mould public opinion. From 1917 onwards there was growing concern that, as in Russia, attitudes at home could turn against the government. Starting early that year much greater emphasis was placed on domestic propaganda. Two main organizations were responsible: the Ministry of Information and its home-front sister, the National War Aims Committee. Unfortunately, the papers of both departments are missing from the Public Record Office. From comments in other files it appears that they were removed and probably destroyed in the inter-war period. It was only in 1940-41, when a new Ministry of Information was being created, that a few scrappy historical files were reassembled and it is on these that we largely depend for any assessment of the scale and character of these activities.

The main responsibility for domestic propaganda rested with the War Aims Committee. Its objectives, as stated in a confidential memorandum of 1917 were 'to strengthen national morale … to counteract … pacifist publications … to dwell on the democratic developments and improvements in the lot of the working classes which state control and other war changes had already secured … to explain the meaning of a German peace … to inspire war workers at home … to encourage unity and stifle party and class dissensions. …' ('Home Publicity during the Great War', INF 4/4A, Public Record Office). This propaganda campaign was principally waged through the production of pamphlets, the insertion of centrally produced stories in the press and the organization of local meetings. One surviving statistic is the number of public meetings held across Britain during the fourteen days 25 September to 10 October 1917. The total amounted to 899. The department produced regularly updated speakers notes and organised the speakers. Its budget for the six months ending 31 March 1918 reveals that particular attention was being paid to Scotland – with £5 000, about 5% of the total, being allocated to additional 'special expenses'. The Ministry of Information was, theoretically, only responsible for propaganda in neutral countries, but under Beaverbrook from February 1918 it also intervened inside Britain. An undated memorandum by Sir Robert Donald notes that in addition to the production of films there was domestic activity in other areas: 'the Advertisement Manager of the *Daily Mail* works under the Ministry of Information in connection with labour on the Clyde' ('The Ministry of Information', INF4/8). This is confirmed by John Buchan's biographer who speaks of Beaverbrook's drive to 'repopularise the war' on Clydeside and in South Wales (Janet Adam Smith, *John Buchan*, 1965).

The novels of John Buchan, written and published in this period, give a close approximation of the government's preferred assessment of events on the Clyde. Buchan was Director of the Department of Information when it was within the War Office and from February 1918 Director of Intelligence in the Ministry of Information under Beaverbrook, and it was from Buchan's mass circulation thrillers set in Scotland – with their fast cars, aeroplane chases, and networks of German spies – that most non-activist readers outside Scotland probably got their first inside information on what the 'trouble' on the Clyde was really about. Buchan, a social imperialist, did not attribute blame to the trade unions themselves. On the contrary, he provided a largely sympathetic portrayal of the aims of organised labour – as long as it remained patriotic.

In his novel *Mr Standfast*, published in 1919, the honest trade unionist is personified by Andra Amos. Amos, a skilled craft worker in shipbuilding, was one of the older generation of trade unionists. He was not too proud to take a small retainer from the government (Buchan seems to think this was quite normal behaviour) to assist in combating anti-war agitators, who Buchan presents as mainly alien elements, Irish and Jewish, manipulated by German spies. Amos is made to reassure readers about the basically patriotic sentiments of the native born worker: 'I don't say there's not plenty of riff raff – the pint and dram gentry and the softheads that are aye reading bits of newspapers and muddlin their heads with foreign whigmaleeries. But the average man on the Clyde, like the average man in either places, hates just three things, and that's the Germans, the profiteers, as they call them, and the Irish' (Buchan, 1919, 85). At the same time, in order to maintain the dramatic tension, Buchan has to make it clear that working for the government could be a dangerous business. Amos himself had to be careful: 'I've to keep my views to mysel, for these young lads are drunken daft with their wee books about Cawpital and Collectivism ...'

This assessment, like Lloyd George's contrast between the 'open faced' Kirkwood and the ugly, violent Gallacher, reflects the emerging wartime consensus about the new boundaries which could be set for 'democratic developments', for the role of the state in improving conditions and, within this, the new status allotted to a constitutional Labour Party. Increasingly for the purposes of this interpretation the acceptable face of Red Clydeside was refocussed on to its elected MPs. These men, portrayed as passionate fighters for their constituents, were, while socialists, ultimately dependable and sensible individuals. Churchill himself said so in his Foreward to Kirkwood's autobiography.

The question remains, however, as with all propaganda, as to how far this version of events did inform opinion. There is always a delicate balance in propaganda work between focussing hostility and directing undue attention. In the immediate post-war years, when covert government propaganda continued at a high level, the judgement of those responsible may not always have been very reliable (Jones, 1969, I, 139; Skelley, 1976, 36). There was also the degree to which those with a direct knowledge of events continued to inform opinion within elite circles in British society. Britain had a relatively small and tightly knit community of big businessmen and financiers, and a significant number of those had interests on the Clyde. At this level a strong opinion appears to have persisted that quite unusual dangers existed. In the *Economic Survey of South West Scotland*, produced for the Board of Trade in 1932 by a team of Glasgow University economists, it was noted with concern that altogether no new external investments had come to the Clyde during the previous decade. The authors directly related this to an impression that 'the district is one seething with unrest which is of a subversive character' (Scott, 1932, 140). The authors are at some pains to point out that this is far from the truth. While 'there is a small amount of Communism', it had little mass influence over the 'mass of working people': 'no more steady and dependable body is to be found in any similar area'.

The passage of Red Clydeside into history was, therefore, a process that was, perhaps predictably, dislocated and incoherent. Within the political and economic establishment there was a public position that seems in many cases to have been quite different from views which, though privately held, nonetheless determined decision making. Within the Labour Movement there were also strongly diverging views – and probably also different positions held in public and private. As we have seen, the ILP and Guild Socialist tradition stressed the issue of workshop control, and from the late 1920s this was articulated in the successive editions of G. D. H. Cole's *Short History of the British Working Class Movement* (Cole, 1927, III, pp. 127–130). The Communist tradition stressed the direct challenge to state power culminating in 1919. By the late 1930s this was embodied in A. L. Morton's *People's History of England* and Allen Hutt's *Post War History* and the literary output of Grassic Gibbon and James Barke. Finally, there were the autobiographies identified with the parliamentarian trend of Labour politics. These started to appear in the 1930s and tended to swim with the tide of establishment public opinion. They typically identified a heroic phase in 1915–16 when Labour challenged for its legitimate rights – suffering imprisonment and deportation – and then jump quickly to the period after the war when the battle for decent conditions, for housing and welfare, took the Clydesider MPs down to Westminster. In many ways this continued as the official Labour version of events into the early 1960s when Henry Pelling's *History of British Trade Unionism* [1963] could discuss Clydeside industrial relations during the war without mentioning the 1919 General Strike.

New Interpretations

It took the release of previously unavailable private papers and public records to break the logjam of these received positions and begin a new cycle of re-interpretation. The first work of this kind was Keith Middlemass's *The Clydesiders* published in 1963. Middlemass had access to the papers of Viscount Davidson, Chairman of the Conservative Party, confidant of both Bonar Law and Baldwin and, for periods in the 1920s, politically responsible for the security services. This material convinced Middlemass that the government had taken very seriously, and far more than had previously been acknowledged, the threat of revolutionary turmoil during the final phases of the war and immediately afterwards. He was later to use this contention as part of the basis for his argument, in *The Politics of Industrial Society* (1979), that it was fear of the potential influence of the revolutionary Left which precipitated a decisive turning-point in British politics. Middlemass argued that the 1920s saw the origins of a long-lasting partnership between business, the state and the organised trade union movement which sought to contain otherwise ungovernable social conflicts. His account was written from a centrist standpoint which was not particularly friendly to the socialist Left. He talks of Clydeside's 'evil reputation' and saves most of his praise for those on the reformist wing of the Labour Party who achieved practical benefits for their supporters. Gallacher is portrayed as something of a clown – creating opportunities for action he was unable to utilize. Wheatley, on the other hand, is credited with immense organizational talents. It was his careful work behind the scenes that made it possible to create an authoritative, purposeful and effective Labour Party out of the ruins of wartime militancy. Where Middlemass's reconstruction of events broke new ground, however, was to reveal for the first time the scale of governmental intervention throughout the war and the degree to which the strike of January 1919 was of unprecedented size and character.

James Hinton was able to draw on a still broader range of previously closed archives. Wartime government records finally became available in the 1960s, and his *The First Shop Stewards Movement* used those of the Ministry of Munitions and Cabinet office. Writing in the early 1970s when the shop stewards movement was once more challenging the legal government, Hinton argued that he had found evidence for an authentically British revolutionary tradition. 'Whatever distortions were later to be imposed on the British revolutionary movement by its subordination to the heirs of a degenerated Russian Revolution, the post-war victory of the theory of soviet power over both syndicalism and parliamentarianism rested on the authentic, if ambiguous, experience of a section of the British working class movement during the war years' (Hinton, 1973, p. 17). As far as Clydeside was concerned, Hinton's focus was on the years 1915–16. It was then that the first 'Worker's Committee' had been established and when, in terms of Ministry of Munitions records, government intervention was most detailed and skillful. Later Hinton switches his attention to Lancashire and Sheffield and the industrial action which flared in these regions against further dilution, and then in 1917–18, against conscription. Very little space at all is given to the postwar 1919 forty hours strike.

Hinton's principal contribution was to integrate a narrative of the conflict between the stewards and the government into a wider social analysis of the origins of the shop stewards movement. He was able to detail the changing balance within the key trade unions, especially the engineers, as the number of workers in munitions work rose dramatically during the war years, and then relate this to a detailed reconstruction of the dynamics of the Clyde Workers committee. Taken together with Middlemass's *Clydesiders* and Terry Brotherstone's 1969 article on the suppression of *Forward* (Brotherstone, 1969), this research appeared to give scholarly credentials to at least some of the claims of the revolutionary element among the Red Clydesiders. Neither Hinton or Brotherstone did so uncritically, and their own interpretations tended to shift the emphasis of traditional accounts back towards the positions of the guild socialists and GDH Cole. Those shop steward leaders who subsequently entered the Communist Party, Gallacher, Bell, McManus, are shown as more prone to temporize with the more backward looking sections of the skilled workforce, and, by contrast, Maclean and MacDougall are presented as more effectively upholding a principled opposition to the war. But, whatever the emphasis, research appeared to show that there had indeed been a Red Clyde and that its emergence was closely associated with the wartime organization of workers, especially new and non-craft workers, in large scale industry. On the basis of this, Cronin could argue, somewhat like Middlemass, that there existed a perceived revolutionary threat and it was this which induced governments to modify policy in favour of welfarism and an expanded role for the state (J. Cronin, 1979). By the late 1970s, therefore, Clydeside's revolutionary potential had become sufficiently recognized to be integrated into a larger rewriting of British history.

It was this new orthodoxy that McLean and Reid set out to challenge in the 1980s. McLean's *Legend of Red Clydeside* was, as its title suggests, a comprehensive assault. Although Labour did rise to political power on Clydeside after the first world war, this, he claims, had nothing to do with wartime industrial militancy or the emergence of socialist class consciousness. It was the product of careful, cautious Labour reformism working outside the yards and factories, focussing on the humdrum issues of rents, municipal amenities and transport. McLean presents two major pieces of evidence. One is an elaborate statistical analysis of voting patterns in Glasgow. This demonstrates that the crucial jump in Labour's support occurred after the 1918 General Election and most sharply in those wards worst affected by poor housing conditions and unemployment and, by and large, where there were less skilled workers. McLean's other area of evidence derives from a reworking of the Ministry of Munitions materials used by Hinton. Although he points up a few inaccuracies in the accounts of Hinton and Brotherstone, his main drive is to challenge the logic of their inter-pretation. Granted the record shows a high level of militancy in 1915–16, is it not more significant that it was successfully handled by the government and did not recur? McLean makes a great deal of the fact that the socialist shop steward leaders only retained mass support to the degree that they championed basically backward-looking, sectional demands of skilled workers. Having established this point, McLean then takes it forward. It was, he argues, precisely the success of dilution and the defeat of sectional craft influence (attributed to joint skills of Wheatley and generally welfarist civil servants) that opened the way for a broader, more generous Labour Movement rooted in the communities, among women and the unskilled. Hence, he concludes, far from assisting the development of mass Labour support on Clydeside, the manipulative and extrem-ist politics of Gallacher and McManus stood in its way. Their irrelevance was finally proved by the failure of those supporting a soviet-style revolution to gain any electoral support after the war.

The work of Alastair Reid takes us still deeper into the territory of Andra Amos and the commonsense working man (Reid, 1985).

Reid uses Admiralty records to look at industrial relations in the shipyards. Focussing on the period up to the end of 1917 he finds absolutely no indication of a shopfloor revolt. On the contrary, two findings emerge which again seem to refute conventional left-wing wisdom. First, full-time trade union officials retained the trust of their members; negotiation throughout these years took place through the official structures. Second, a genuine partnership is seen to emerge between these trade union officials and those in the Admiralty Labour Department, and elsewhere in government departments, who were trying to introduce rational and effective methods of production into the shipyards. According to Reid it was this experience, in which Fabianism, trade unionism, and progressivism found common purpose against old style capitalist management, that determined much of the success of the Labour Party's 'class alliance' politics after the war. It was, for Reid, precisely the wartime penetration of state administration into the yards which created a new mutual trust which thereby made possible the marginalization of the left. With this, therefore, we are brought full circle to the remit of the War Aims Committee 'to dwell on the democratic developments and improvements in the lot of the working classes which state control ... had already secured'.

The last decade has seen a number of responses. One has been to shift the search for Clydeside's revolutionary politics outside the workplace and into the surrounding communities. Sean Damer, accepting much of McLean's criticism of the Clyde Workers' Committee, argues that the real force for change was among the women who became mobilized on the issues of rent and housing (Damer, 1980, 1985). Seeing this as an example of an autonomous (non-class) 'social movement', he presents the housing struggle as rooted in the wartime emancipation of women. Forced by the war to take on new roles, Clydeside's women are seen by Damer as bringing a radical rejection of the patriarchal institutionalism of old style Labourism. It was this, he argues, which, fused with the radical socialism of Maclean, created a mass community base for Labour politics on Clydeside.

Other responses have more directly challenged the assumptions and scholarship of Reid and McLean. A statistical reconstruction of strike activity for the period has revealed that, far from peaking in late 1915 and early 1916, Clydeside's strike activity rose to considerably higher levels in the final phases of the war and reached its climax in 1919 [Foster, 1990]. This finding is linked to a challenge to McLean's electoral analysis. If industrial activity peaked after the 1918 election, then it is somewhat less easy to claim that the rise in the Labour vote after 1918 had nothing to do with it. It is even less so when the full range of electoral results is taken into account. McLean restricted his analysis to the city of Glasgow – and thereby excluded many of those areas of Clydeside where large-scale industry was most heavily concentrated and strike activity had been most marked. When these areas are included, very significant votes can be found for Left-ILP and Communist candidates, and, no less significant, electoral support for these candidates increased at just the same rate between 1918 and 1922 as it did for those taking a more right-wing Labour position.

This linking of strike activity and voting has been complemented by research on the special character of the Scottish ILP and its links to skilled workers in industry (Melling, 1990; 1991). Joseph Melling challenges both Reid and McLean's claims about the political orientation of Clydeside's skilled workers in engineering and the shipyards. He demonstrates conclusively the degree to which rank and file militancy did emerge in the later stages of the war and the degree to which previous historians have been misled by the self-serving history by the Ministry of Munitions. He also demonstrates how this unfolding industrial militancy was matched by a transformation within the Scottish ILP. This party had always been more to the Left than its counterpart in England. During the war its members had worked closely with the activists of the BSP and SLP, and by its end the Scottish ILP was, by a large majority, in support of affiliation to the Third International – a vote repeated in that organization's Scottish conference in 1919 and 1920. Alan McKinlay's research has now identified those branches which most firmly backed this position and finds that they were those based in industrial and shipyard constituencies (McKinlay, 1991). Accordingly, McLean's attempt to pose a sensible, reformist ILP against the revolutionary politics of Gallacher and Maclean begins to look like a somewhat unhistorical attempt to read back a division which only became real some years later.

However, perhaps the most important piece of evidence which had recently come to light brings us back to what people were actually saying at the time – although from a quite different viewpoint from those with whom we started. It is the minute book of the Clyde Shipbuilders Association, lodged, since the nationalization of shipbuilding, in the Strathclyde Regional Archives (Strathclyde Record Office TD 241/1/18, ff 144–159). This reports the discussions which took place among Clydeside's employers, sometimes virtually hour by hour, during the General Strike of 1919, and places these events much more centrally within the waves of mass strikers which spread across Europe at the end of the war. It makes clear that local employers thought the strike to be political. Its leadership was dominated by the explicitly socialist Clyde Workers Committee and its objectives were to force the government to sustain full employment by a drastic limitation of hours. It also makes clear why they thought the strike was so dangerous. It had created an active alliance between the tens of thousands of recently discharged soldiers (demobilized only weeks before in circumstances of real and threatened mutiny) and the most radical sections of the industrial workforce. It was the ex-soldiers, organised in the Discharged Soldiers and Sailor's Federation, who were providing much of the backbone for the mass pickets. These pickets had already stopped virtually every industrial workplace and were now threatening the one remaining source of electricity supply. By 30 January the employers were gravely concerned at what they saw as a slide to collaboration and compromise by the local civic authorities. Early on the morning of Friday 31 January a deputation met the Lord Provost. He was reprimanded for talking to the strike leaders earlier in the week, and then asked how he intended to deal with the 'unruly mob' assembling in George Square. Over a hundred West of Scotland employers met through the day to consider further action. They agreed to the formation of a Civic Guard. 'It was felt that quite a number of loyal workmen and Employers would join the Guard with a view to opposing the Strikers and protecting workmen against "massed pickets" or intimidation'. At the same time they realized that a Civic Guard would be of little use until they could drive a wedge between the demobilized soldiers and the strikers. The problem was how to respond to the soldiers' demands for employment without giving legitimacy to the strike. Eventually they decided to remit a motion that the 'Employers should issue a Manifesto to the effect that two months from this date should there be a number of demobilised soldiers still out of employment, the Employers would either by reduced hours or other means give them employment'. Finally, the meeting turned its attention to the manufacturing of history. It was agreed to 'interview the Press Representatives with the object of a judicious cutting down of statements in the Press concerning the unofficial strike and eliminating from Reports the names of the Strike Leaders.'

8

Snug in the Asylum of Taciturnity: Women's History in Scotland

JOY HENDRY

Writing this essay ten years ago would have given me a malicious sort of pleasure. The task would also have been much easier, given the then much clearer and simpler story: for an age women had been almost totally ignored by historians in Scotland, writing as if human beings came into the world as Pallas Athene did (sprung fully formed from their father's head) though the noteworthy chips off the old block did not share her gender.

Things, now, are more complex. A welcome change has been coming about. It needs charting, and some indication needs to be given of future directions, in both practical and ideal terms. Yet that age of neglect is also more than worthy of investigation. It is very much part of history overall. If Scottish history could die (cf. Marinell Ash's *The Strange Death of Scottish History*) it is presumably also susceptible to various dietary deficiencies, marked by odd behaviour; saying unaccountable things or persisting in curious silences. The diagnosis of such problems, and their treatment, might be thought a matter for specialists, if there are any in the field.

I am not a professional historian and cannot pretend to write as one. I am, however, as a writer and editor, profoundly interested in the state of historical scholarship in Scotland and in the widespread dissemination of it in books, and in our educational institutions where, until comparatively recently, there has been woeful neglect based on the ridiculous premise that Scottish children need British (i.e. English) history and not their own. Some residue of those attitudes remain, but in almost all areas of intellectual and cultural life in Scotland, people seem to have wakened up to the fact that neglect of our own character actually diminishes us as participants in an international dialogue. I am also a woman and have spent the last twenty years of my life untangling a mess of masculinist and anti-Scottish prejudices inculcated in me by Scottish education. It would be reasonable to assume that many other women have laboured under similar misconceptions, and some consideration of how this has affected their lives is relevant here.

The subject of this book is the manufacture of Scottish history, and the pun 'man-made' is irresistible as more than appropriate. I also can't resist making the other obvious point that I am the only woman contributor to this volume. Almost a century ago, Henry Grey Graham produced his wonderful book *Scottish Men of Letters in the Eighteenth Century*, (1901). It's an informative and beautifully written study of the men of the Scottish enlightenment: David Hume, John Home, Principal Robertson, Adams Ferguson, and Smith etc. In keeping with his times one could have expected him to be happy to include no women at all – indeed his title would provide all the excuses he needed to make such his policy without a qualm. Yet he interrupts the parade of distinguished men with a chapter devoted to 'Women of Letters': Lady Wardlaw, Lady Grisell Baillie, Mrs Cockburn, Jean Elliot, Lady Anne Barnard, and Lady Nairne, who account for 35 pages out of 430. Less than 10 per cent, you may complain, but daring for the time, and revealing too in that plainly Grey Graham would have liked to write more about women.

He is almost free of prudery when writing about them, witness this lovely aside in his treatment of Lady Anne Barnard, not about the lady herself, but about someone who had come to her estate of Balcarres for a little visit and stayed for 13 years. This was one Sophia Johnston, 'daughter of the coarse, drunken laird of Hilton'. Graham relates with some relish that:

> She had grown up, according to Hilton's hideous whim, without training, or education, or religion, only furtively learning to read and write from the butler. She was able to wrestle with the stable-boys, to shoe a horse like a smith, to make woodwork like a joiner, and to swear like a trouper. There she was, the strange creature, working at her forge in her room at Balcarres, playing the fiddle, singing songs with a voice like a man's, dressed in a jockey coat, walking with masculine stride, speaking broad Scots in deepest bass, which would roll out a good round oath.

There is some clue in Graham as to the nub of the problem, and it gives what is one of my main themes in this essay. Graham felt it necessary to devote about a quarter of his introduction to apologizing to the 'shades' of these women for including them at all. Referring to his chapter title 'Women of Letters', he explains:

> strictly speaking it describes women who were not literary persons, like their learned sisters in England. Their whole output consisted of one or two songs; yet those have survived

the laborious contributions of women of letters south of the Border. An apology is certainly due to the shades of those high-born dames for bringing them into the company of men who wrote for vulgar fame or money; seeing that their life-long anxiety was to conceal from the public the fact that they had ever written a line or composed a verse. Each of these ladies desired, as the erudite Miss Aikin said of Joanna Baillie, 'to lie snug in the asylum of her taciturnity'.

The rest of this essay could profitably be spent unravelling and analysing the attitudes implicit in the above. One or two key things emerge, however. First of all, and this is confirmed in Graham's most famous work, *Social Life in the Eighteenth Century*, Graham has at least an unarticulated notion that literary and historical importance is not just an academic matter; and that the fact that the songs of these women were ubiquitously sung was deeply signifi-cant. He tacitly applies the Scottish refusal to distinguish between literature on the one hand and song on the other. How different from twentieth-century literary historians who dismiss them as 'one-song poetesses' (Lindsay, 1977). Graham is also refreshingly free of snobbery, saying with approbation that

'High-born ladies of those days did not keep aloof from the common affairs of the common people; they spoke the broad Scots tongue themselves, and the work of the byre and barn, the wooings of servants and ploughmen, were of lively interest to them in the parlour and drawing-room, and did not seem themes unworthy of their verse.'

One writer who might be expected to be alive to the distaff side of things is Agnes Mure MacKenzie, and her trilogy *Scottish Pageant, 1513–1802* (1949) doesn't ignore women totally, although the emphasis is still much on masculine reality. Her idiosyncratic selec-tion, if it might lack something in historical respectability, is at least a source of documentary material not readily available elsewhere; and worth plundering on this and other matters. Here, from the third volume, is a fragment on women in action aboard the ship 'Goliah' during the Napoleonic Wars, under MacKenzie's heading 'Great Grandmother Wrens': 'The women behaved as well as the men, and got a present for their bravery from the Grand Signior ... One woman bore a son in the heat of the action. She belonged to Edinburgh.'

MacKenzie's attention to women and to domestic and social detail might be dismissed as undue interest in tittle tattle, a common complaint underlying the low repute of her work. No enormous claim need be made for it overall, while insisting that as a woman she saw that not everything outwith the accepted understanding is irrelevant and insignificant. Things have too long been seen from a man's, rather than a human, point of view, according to the Scottish philosopher John Macmurray, a writer only too happy to acknowledge a great debt owed to his artist wife. If Agnes Mure MacKenzie does not qualify as a Historian, Macmurray equally tells us that history is not exclusively the business of Historians.

The important point here is that of the relationship between the public and the private domain, and the relative importance of these two things. The way history is written, which is to say seen, does to an extent determine how people see themselves, and shape their assumptions about what matters in life. Just how much this is so is impossible to measure, because it is more subtle, various, and pervasive than many academic minds find convenient. Certainly reading history as in a sense past and done with and therefore given, unarguable, and inevitable, a fact, something unchangeable, has a powerful effect on women's perceptions of what is open to them in the present and the future, and of how they see themselves within their own sphere of influence. Yet is the 'history' people read not something else? Is it not rather a lot of statements about what happened, rather than 'what happened', to people living difficult but ordinary lives, whose contribution to history few have cared to record.

One of the key problems here is that both men and women, from the eighteenth century onwards have perceived the public sphere as the playground of the men, and the private sphere as that of the women. How men and women perceived each other and their roles prior to the Reformation is more difficult to document given the paucity of evidence. It's likely that it was much the same as after, for despite the Reformation the presiding crude theology of those kirk sessions was fundamentally mediaeval. And while the mediaeval Catholic church in Europe had at one time such great figures as the abbess Hildegarde of Bingen (1098–1179), philosopher, mystic, and musician, it had long before the Reformation fallen under a ban against the extraordinary female monastic culture she represented. Thirled to the terror-doctrines of 'Federal Calvinism', which in fact misread even Calvin, the Kirk from the seventeenth century came to exercise control over social behaviour, discouraging wildness and deviations from the accepted norm. Supposedly free of the evils of prelacy, and with the bible open before it, the Kirk lapsed into the counting of sins, fear of hell and temptation, without such warrant. Where did the prejudices come from?

Women may indeed have been more ready to speak out in the public sphere prior to the seventeenth century, though from points of view which were not perhaps pleasing to the male. Their place in commerce may be suggested from the fact that, in Edinburgh, for example, women actually lost ground when, with the establishment in 1596 of the Edinburgh Society of Brewers, brewing was made a members-only activity. This discriminated not specifically against women but generally against the 'economically and politically weak, rather than women as gender' (Houston 1988). That is part of the story. A Stirling woman, Marion Alexander, was actually prosecuted in 1621 for brewing and selling ale. One effect of the Reformation and its immediate aftermath was to push women more effectively into the private domain. Women were also constrained to accept this as desirable morally and socially – hence Grey Graham's '*apology*' for dragging his women out of the snug asylum of taciturnity. To this day some women are still distressed at the prospect of any of their activities becoming public.

The next consideration is the unquestioned value judgment that the public is of paramount importance and the private safely ignorable as insignificant. Until perhaps as recently as ten years ago, we had, by and large, the history of the public sphere, with such commendable exceptions as Grey Graham leaning a little on the barriers, but most historians confidently writing about the public domain and mentioning women only insofar as they were accepted to have impinged on that. Given the impact of Marxist theory, or feeling, some historians have recognized the importance of giving consideration to working class or peasant life, but have got hardly much nearer to the secret, private world of Scottish women.

This is not original or new as a train of thought, but worth stating in this context. It would be both easy and tedious to spend this essay scanning the pillars of Scottish historical writing for neglect of women, but a little of this is in order. Take J. D. Mackie's *A History of Scotland* (1964) for instance – a work on the shelves of every tourist office large enough to sell books. There you find almost no women mentioned apart from royalty and the nobility. Some women have inignorably affected the welfare of the state, and omission is impossible. Others are ignorable as a matter of course.

Still more worrying are cases where women are not ignored, but where in the telling the full extent of their effect is, as often, diminished. Margaret (Saint), Queen of Scots, is referred to twice in Professor Mackie's book of almost 400 pages, but the enormous influence she exercised over the Scottish court and social and religious life is reduced to her finding 'irregularities in the Scottish practice' of religion (a parallel one must say, with the Abbess Hildegarde in Europe). Other matters of lingering importance even today, such as the decline in Gaelic for which she was personally responsible, are given no mention. She is simply the wife of Malcolm

Canmore. Eric Linklater in *The Survival of Scotland* (1968), gives more credence to her influence: 'Nothing in Malcolm Canmore's life was of more abiding significance than his marriage to this remarkable woman' – and gives a better account of her life but still without putting his finger on the crucial part of her inheritance to modern Scotland. Not written by a historian, Linklater's book is more alive to the real influence of noble or royal women, and his account of the career of Mary, Queen of Scots is nothing short of inspired, making full use of his imaginative skills as a novelist (though I cannot vouch for its historical accuracy in every aspect), but he falls into the same trap of viewing history as an account of the public domain, which by definition largely excludes women.

Even though under obvious pressure of space, the general *An Economic History of Modern Scotland 1660–1976* by Bruce Lenman (1977) might be expected to give some analysis of the contribution of women to the commonweal. No. 'Women' don't figure in the index at all; the woman most mentioned is Queen Anne (referred to, not just in passing, five times) who is not listed in the index. Anne, Duchess of Hamilton, who is listed, is commended as 'remarkable' for having stumped up £3,000 for the Darien venture. Her other 'remarkable' accomplishments are not mentioned, but include great efforts to relieve local poverty, (and posthumously she was honoured above other women in having a male descendant, Lord Anne [sic], named after her!). The only general reference to women in this book is under the heading of 'human fertility', the increase in childbirth due to the fact that Scotswomen were marrying earlier, with a disturbingly blunt reference to famine as an effective mass contraceptive. Other than that, across the length and breadth of Scotland, all we learn of what women did concerns the north east, where some wove cloth into gloves and stockings.

I make no attempt to judge this book in other regards, but it is particularly bad in this one, lacking any analysis of women's role in agricultural life, or account of women's work in the factories. In particular, there is no reference at all to the interesting phenomenon of Dundee, where for a very long time there was female employment and vast male unemployment and the women held the city together. It seems that in Dundee 'the jute industry could use extremely cheap labour' – 'female' not specified. Lenman says a good deal more about whaling, – a male-dominated activity. Similarly there is no reference to Paisley, for instance, or the extent to which women were involved in home-weaving.

That historians should do this is unremarkable, and I don't propose to indulge in a warlock-hunt. There is a simple mechanism in operation – if you don't expect women to do anything much, then you are likely to miss the import of what they do accomplish. Women are as capable of doing this to other women as men are, and the operative assumptions and psychological habits are what I am trying to uncover in order to redress the balance and suggest practice for the future. There is no point in blaming a writer for reflecting biases of the time in which he wrote, but there is considerable point in strongly indicating shortcomings of his or her analyses and his or her wrong assumptions.

A classic instance of this is John Stevenson's *Popular Disturbances in England, 1788–1878* (1979), which mentions virtually no women at all, except the Queen Caroline affair when George IV wished to divorce her and her cause became a focus for radical dissent. One Mrs Armistead, otherwise unknown to the pages of history, is listed in the index: the reason – that at the time of the mobbing of William Pitt the Younger at Grocer's Hall, London in 1784, supposedly instigated by Charles James Fox, she was providing Fox with the perfect alibi by being in bed with him.

The truism illustrated here is simple: women are awarded a place in history only if they are the wives of Kings, nobility, poets (very occasionally), mistresses, or mothers of important men. Otherwise their existence goes unremarked (I think this is the key word, a remark being a solitary and isolated linguistic utterance). But the non-remarking of individuals is a mere peccadillo in comparison to the non-remarking of the woman's world. Not only is the being of woman marginalized, her contribution to her family and her community goes quite unnoticed, a much more serious crime. Public is public, private is private, and never the twain shall meet.

It has to be a ringing condemnation that, at least until very recently, the liveliest and most detailed account of the texture of life for a clever, ennobled Scotswoman comes from Henry Grey Graham, a century ago. He even manages to work in lively accounts of the antics of women of the 'lower orders'. But if the distinction between public and private domain is accepted both by men and women there will also perhaps be the added discouragement that men would not wish to pry into a world universally recognized as private? This is not an excuse which twentieth century writers can reasonably plead.

A famous, central, and still recent work of Scottish historiography is T. C. Smout's standard and in many ways admirable *History of the Scottish People, 1560–1830*. Like most related works short on the mere mention of women, it at least lets them figure in the index, and under the heading of 'female labour' has quite a few entries, and a reasonably full discussion of women's roles in, for instance, agriculture, mining, and the cloth industry. Smout is full of sympathy for the plight of young girls employed in the mines, of whom he comments: 'The labour they were capable of doing almost defies belief'. Citing among others Margaret Leveston, who at 6 years old carried half a hundredweight of coal, and Jane Johnson, who at 15 carried 2 hundredweights, Smout quotes a large chunk from Robert Bald's *General View of the Coal Trade of Scotland* (1812), emphasizing the suffering caused by this ruthless graft:

> '... they go for eight or ten hours almost without resting. It is no uncommon thing to see them when ascending the pit weeping most bitterly from the excessive severity of the labour.'

This is certainly not male chauvinism. What we see is the beginnings of an outline of the work done by women in society, urban and rural. There is, however, no discussion of the overall role and status of women in different classes and during different periods. References to women are scant and so slight sometimes as to be hardly recognizable as such. Sex and its vast social ramifications is dealt with in a formal way under headings like 'population' but hardly discussed in terms of how women's lives were variously controlled and shaped by it. Smout's account of Scotland's developing educational system is highly regarded and thorough, but one question he ducks almost altogether is the important one of the education of women. Almost throughout he talks as if male and female are allowed equal opportunity, but makes an occasional aside to the effect that some schools were girls only, or had an especially large proportion of girls. Attitudes to the education of girls as opposed to boys go quite unexamined. Only with reference to the founding of the Andersonian Institute is there any elaboration of this question. Smout tells us 'About half the number [between 500 and 1000], rather surprisingly, were women', and quotes Thomas Garnett that it was 'the first regular institution in which the fair sex have been admitted to the temple of knowledge on the same footing as men'. Revealingly, Smout goes on:

> It is impossible not to exclude a suspicion that many of these students were not serious: two out of the three physics and chemistry courses offered were described as 'popular' and consisted of 'pleasing and interesting experiments' ...

The term 'the fair sex' and the association of women with dilettante learning is not encouraging. Quite apart from that, there is little discussion of what might be called 'the distaff side' of life. While some attempt is made to describe women at work, there is little attempt to analyse and summarize their overall contribution, socially, culturally, and economically, to their own times. This is not so much the failure of Smout's diligence as a historian, but a reflection on the perception of the times which devoted no particular study to it. The private world remains private, the public world is the domain of men.

Smout's follow-up volume, *A Century of the Scottish People, 1830–1950* is a little different. Women are still a rarity as far as individual mentions go: Queen Mary (the ship) gets more mentions than any other 'she' with the exception of Queen Victoria. However, at least there is a better treatment of the private domain: things concerning the daily fabric of life are much more adequately dealt with: domestic life and conditions, diet and food, drink, poverty, land and housing, living standards and recreation are more prominent; a chapter is devoted to 'Sex, Love and Getting Married' and there are more references to women under a wider spread of headings – even a sympathetic reference to housework and its arduous nature. Smout quotes Kellog Durland's *Among the Fife Miners* (1904), recollecting:

> I have seen a son of one-or-two-and-twenty order his mother across the room to get his pipe which was on a shelf directly above his head a few inches out of his reach from the chair where he was sitting.

On what Durland sees as women's 'slavery to men', a minor who had read the volume commented: 'Instead of "slavery" you should call it "devotion".' Of the complexities of these perceptions Smout offers no analysis. He does, however, write something about the independent, wage-earning women of Dundee and the role of the 'dry nursing' men. The analysis of the provision of education for women is however at least as poor as in the previous volume. Nothing specific is said about primary or secondary education for women, and there is only a parenthesis about women's struggle to be admitted to the universities, but a brief account is given of women's basic literacy taken from the 1871 census. There is a single mention of suffragettes which, despite its presence in the index, I was unable to find; there is a little about the Glasgow rent strike. Some of these mentions are so fleeting as to be confined to the use of the word 'woman', which leads me to suspect that the indexer to this volume had a sharper awareness that women had to be seen to be present. Although the private world figures more largely here, the neglect of women is still evident.

I do not wish to single out Professor Smout for special approbrium, but his widely-read books cannot be ignored. Less public, so to speak, is his analysis (with Ian Levitt) of the parish statistics gathered for the Scottish poor law commission which reported to Parliament in 1844, in *The State of the Scottish Working Class in 1843*, (1979) which is determined not so much by the preoccupations of the editors, but by the questions put to the informants. However, this volume does reveal a good deal about the fabric of daily life, for women and children as well as men, providing in some instances separate statistics, for example about women's industrial employment. The editors, indeed, are to be commended for perceiving the historical potential of these statistics. Such detailed scholarly work makes advances in what is available to scholars. It remains private in its own way unless it can be brought into the more widely read historical literature. The public/private dichotomy I have so far attacked fits well with what Edwin Muir said sixty years ago about other widespread misapprehensions of Scottish history. It resembles nothing so much as a bad poem.

I can claim the precedent of 'Metaphysical Scotland' for citing a passage from Aristotle's *Poetics*. What is the nature of history, when all is said and done. Aristotle says:

> Poetry is more philosophical and more weighty than history, for poetry speaks rather of the universal, history of the particular. By the universal I mean that such or such a kind of man will say or do such or such things from probability or necessity; that is the aim of poetry, adding proper names to the characters. By the particular I mean what Alcibiades did and what he suffered.

Many have seen this as a rejection of history, but it is really a contrast between the accepted procedures of some poets as analysed by Aristotle, and the demands the historian must always be aware of, and aware of much of the time almost inevitably falling short of.

Both history and poetry (including in the definition narrative fiction, stories, plays or novels) are founded on and utterly dependent on the particular. Why otherwise praise characterization, or remember characters rather than through ideas? The imagination registers universality by finding almost mysteriously revealing particulars, not manipulating generalities. The point to be made however is that particulars do not come ready made. We begin with, and are always coming back to, if not bad poems then usually generalities. What Aristotle is talking about as the more philosophic and weighty character of poetry – and he means *very* good poetry – is the range of meanings it can express. It is in a sense condensed history, and Hugh MacDiarmid was neither the first nor the last to dismiss Scott's historical novels as a bastard genre, attempting to combine what the poet knows, with the complexity of historical detail, what unknown Elektras did and suffered. Great poetry may carry extraordinary insight into human society and the soul, but if it handles any amount of historical detail it is likely, at best, to give a limited view of the historical setting. At worst it may be a distorted interpretation of history.

In the eighteenth century, to say nothing of William Robertson, among other of Grey Graham's *Scottish Men of Letters*, David Hume produced his *History of England*, often described as a pioneering work in the gradual movement toward modern historiography. His factual resources were limited, and he does argue from inadequate evidence. The book belongs on the whole to the history of history. The exceptions are parts of it concerned with the history of the English constitution, and judged as modern 'history' they seem to suffer from too much interpretation on too little evidence. They are certainly not poetry, but they are philosophical. Hume's *History* is in part political theory, and that in a kind of combination with his own partisan political views. The other part of his big work is a kind of historical journalism, based on limited material resources. Modern historians have rightly sought to improve standards of evidence. This has led them also to a hypersensitivity with regards to what can be argued on the basis of historical evidence. They are very careful about what is said, and inclined to reject, sometimes out of hand, more daring analyses. They are also inclined to oppose statements other than their own, so that sometimes they are not considering the soundness of such arguments as George Davie ventures for instance, in *The Democratic Intellect*. They merely say that this work was not written according to the canons of modern historiography, and, by amassing a great deal of less obviously interpretative statements, propose undoubtedly sound enough conclusions, whose scope and validity may be quite remote from the larger concerns about which we need to be informed. They do not write poetry, they may even tell us how a latterday Alcibiades felt, with some certainty of detailed evidence. What do they not even try, or know, to be able to try to tell us?

What's all this to do with the manufacture of women in Scottish history? It brings us back to basics, the real problems which confront us in the manufracturing [sic] of history to date as far as women are concerned, or also the dis-manufacturing of history. History is there for Scottish women: they have done many things, and they have suffered, in the broader sense of the word. Without the valid particular we have nothing: no history, and no poetry either. You have to ask the right question, and too many historians have seemed to vindicate another great philosopher's statement that that is the most difficult thing of all.

I recently had contact with some 'British Canadian' Indians of the Nisga tribe. Their pride in their Indian heritage has been revived over the recent generation, and when women of the tribe wanted to learn the art of button-blanket making, they turned to literature and anthropology, and found nothing. Where could they learn this art?

Just in time they went to the 'elders', the old women, and absorbed as much as they could. The anthropologists had been there, with their notebooks, but the anthropologists had been men, sympathetic enough, but they had talked to the men about their forbidden totems and written all about them. They hadn't thought the women had anything to say, sitting in the corners, sewing away at their buttons.

There were two consequences of this, one unlucky, for the young Indian woman seeking to recover her lost heritage: with nothing recorded in print, or printed pictures. She had to, and fortunately could, go back to the source. The other was fortunate indeed: before the sympathetic anthropologists came, there were other, hostile visitations from forces of evangelism and the law who sought to forbid the making of totems, as a heathen activity, worshipping false gods. But these visitors didn't realise that the women, sewing away in the corner, were doing precisely the same thing on their button-blankets as the men had done on the forbidden totems. So the women sewed on long enough, until the younger generation realized the politics of what was happening and came flocking to re-learn an old craft.

There are lessons in this to do with the manufacture of Scottish history. It demonstrates in an emotive way what must be obvious. In Scotland, the anthropologist/historian has come in with his note-book, right enough, but being a male person, he will unthinkingly record what is important according to masculine values: the affairs of state, 'intellectual' discourse, great inventions – the things obviously of the public domain. He will ignore the women singing a waulking song in the kitchen. He will dismiss their conversation as prattle, and put his pencil in his pocket. Yet as Sorley MacLean tells us in an outstanding essay, in 'The Old Songs' composed without writing, by not least forgotten women, we have the most clear testimony as to a great deal of historical highland life (MacLean, 1970). This is not all history but a part of it, a part without which it marches with military precision. The female expression of a national character is vital, indeed indispensable: O gentle dames, Scotland hath need of thee.

Not until recently have Scottish historians thought women's daily lives to be of the slightest importance. Women only merit the recorder's ink when sex, and preferably witchcraft, is involved, like breaking their arm by using it as a bolt, in support of a regime subsequently very male. Otherwise the most interesting thing a woman can do is to be one of those four-times offending fornicators, who notch up five stars in the kirk session records. That is true of most general historical accounts, and of Gordon Donaldson's *The Shaping of a Nation* (1974), which makes almost no reference to women at all. Even the chapter on 'Society' is dumb about the female sex, talking about the bondman, but not his female equivalent, and the 'working man', and so on. Among the less regarded academically, the popularly addressed Plantagenet and Fiona Somerset Fry's *The History of Scotland* (1982), falls into the typical pattern of mentioning royals only with Jenny Geddes, whose stool-throwing fame is now discredited, and Flora Macdonald as slices of lemon. Even the academic professional Rosalind Mitchison's *A History of Scotland* (1970) slips into the general pattern.

The problem of dealing adequately with women's realities has, I am pleased to say, begun at last. A new perspective is visible in books like *Sexuality and Social Control* (Mitchison and Leneman, 1988), which bring out interesting facts. For instance while in the National Covenant of 1637, by 1654, the renewal of the covenants, the men were pledging everything, including their women, to God, as if they had automatic rights. Once you change the perspective all manner of things begin to emerge. Mitchison and Leneman point out with clarity that although in principle the Reformation regarded woman and men as of equal concern to God, they were still second or third class citizens in the eyes of both Church and State. If, for example, a man committed fornication, he would indeed be chastized, as was a woman, but if he subsequently became guilty of a relapse, a trilapse, or, God help us, a quadrilapse, he was not further pursued, whereas women were chastened with all the weapons, emotional and actual, at the Kirk Sessions's disposal. As late as 1977, the Kirk was pointing the finger at promiscuous women for being at the heart of Scotland's moral problems. Mitchison and Leneman effectively isolate male historians who discuss extramarital fertility purely in terms of women. They also reject the legendary notion of the exercise of the *droit de seigneur*, of the laird having the first bite at the cherry as his unalienable right and property. If there was no such literal institution, one need not be Aristotle to see the 'philosophical and weighty' character of the legend.

Leah Leneman's volume in honour of Rosalind Mitchison ('the doyen of Scottish social historians') pinpoints salient factors largely ignored by the general historians. Geoffrey Parker's essay, for example, on the 'Taming of Scotland' by kirk sessions, point to the cultural and social importance of the Book of Discipline, which has failed to earn historical notice partly because of its implicit concern with social mores and failure to include women. Some of these are frighteningly erudite, written with the specialist in mind, but it is refreshing to see a chapter by T. C. Smout and A. Gibson, about 'Food and Hierarchy in Scotland', examining the food chain at the court of James VI. Had it not been for the onward march of female (if not feminist) history in Scotland, it is hard to believe that an essay of such scope would have been written.

Another unlikely essay is 'Geographical Mobility of Women in Early Modern Scotland' by Ian D. and Kathleen Whyte. It is an established fact that the spread of women throughout society cannot simply be examined by looking at where their husbands happen to be. The Whytes begin by acknowledging the bias towards documenting the activities and concerns of men. Their essay examines the migration of women through marriage, chiefly through the marriage register. It notes a regular influx of women, especially into the lowlands, from south of the border, perhaps due to the homecoming of the daughters of ex-patriots. This essay, however, leaves much unsaid – nothing, for example, is said about the seasonal migration of the herring-gutters. Literature comes to the rescue here if you think of Neil Gunn's *Butcher's Broom*, in which Elie, to escape her shame as a pregnant 'single person' leaves her community to seek work in the south. Her experience was not happy. Gunn, indeed, is an early champion of the woman's view of Scottish history in his novels spanning a thousand years and more.

The essay in Houston and Whyte's *Scottish Society, 1580–1800*, (1989) on 'Women in the Economy of Society of Scotland 1500–1800' begins with the observation that women are treated as peripheral and unimportant, and that attempts to render them more visible have only concentrated on royal and aristocratic women who, as representatives of their gender, are untypical. This is true, of course, but their subsequent claim to 'seek to add women to Scottish history, to look at their experience in a predominantly masculine rendering of historical discourse' strikes me as rather extravagant, as if you could add women to the mix as one would a pinch of salt. Undoubtedly, the essay achieves something, pointing to the lack of documentation, diaries, autobiographies, surviving from women, making a genuine attempt to deal with all aspects of women's lives: economic, marriage and the family, education and cultural life, politics, social relationships and witchcraft.

Economically, Houston emphasizes the importance of women in early agrarian Scotland, and shows how they were gradually marginalized, even from this sector, by the advent, for example, of the scythe. Opportunities for the economic independence of women were indeed few. Weaving, spinning, being fishwives, buying and selling certain goods, and wet-nursing were some of the few avenues open, and most employers operated on the basis that a woman's wage wasn't intended to keep an entire family, so pay was low. They reiterate the important point made by Engels, that the status of women depends on their participation in the public sphere, and indeed that is my thesis here, but I would add that it also depends on society's evaluation of the private sphere and the mechanisms it is prepared to create to allow women into the public sphere.

In the legal sphere Houston covers the area of women's rights to property, dowries, etc. over the period in view. Male primogeniture was preferred, but women could inherit property in the event that there were no male heirs. At least in Scotland the paternal control over daughters was not extensive, so they conclude that there was 'no lifelong subjugation of women' – a psychologically dubious conclusion.

Whereas other historians fail to discriminate effectively enough, Houston deals fairly thoroughly with the education of women – for the higher classes a restricted and polite affair, with a curriculum more intended to cultivate the women as a status symbol than an intelligent individual. He points to the salient fact that during the eighteenth century, when Scotland was supposed to be literate, there was 70 per cent female illiteracy, as opposed to only 35 per cent in males. Even the enlightened Scottish Enlightenment advocated the identification of men with reason (culture) and women with instinct, emotion, and frivolity (nature). The theological background to Scottish 'Enlightened' thought has fortunately begun to be explored.

The section on social relationships pointed to women's prominent role as purveyors of culture, that 'conversation and song were a central part of the cultural experience of women and girls'. The spirited liveliness of Scots women, much documented elsewhere, is visible – the women drank along with the men in alehouses – in fact, three Stirling women were observed drinking in the open air on a Sunday afternoon, an activity which they continued until 4 o'clock next morning. Houston concludes that Scots and English experiences were broadly similar. Sexual equality before God was not generally a principle practised. This essay is generally good but one chapter does not make a history.

For effective coverage of the witchcraft subject, the aspect of women's history most rigorously covered by historians, the definitive text is Christina Larner's *Enemies of God*. As Norman Cohn demonstrates in his *Europe's Inner Demons*, Scotland's was one of the major witchhunts of Europe. Larner makes many key points: that the witch was the mirror image of the stereotype of the saint, and that the lore of satanic witchcraft has no origin save in the minds of the persecuting witch hunters. This gives real insight into the intensity of the hunts in Scotland which were exacerbated by the aforementioned ambivalent status of women under Federal Calvinism. The hunts were also a timely pretext for an attack on the traditional female healers by an emergent male medical profession whose pretences were, at least, exposed by the Scottish Enlightenment. Yet witchhunting can largely, if not entirely, be equated with woman hunting; more properly it was the hunting of women who did not conform to the male view of how they ought to conduct themselves. But most importantly, it was as enemies of God that they were hunted. Larner establishes that it was an idea before it was a phenomenon, that it was fostered by the ruling classes and was not a natural peasant pastime. The witchhunts also criminalized women for the first time and affected women at the bottom of the social heap most. This is a thorough and authoritative account. Not the least important point is the extent of brainwashing which occurred, so that the women actually believed their accuser's fantasies.

Recent generations of historians, especially the women, have rescued ordinary sex as a historical topic worthy of discussion, and not merely a motive for persecution or the method of getting Kings. Mitchison and Leneman in *Sexuality and Social Control* investigate their subject with enthusiasm and rigour and, what's more, without a sense of fun. They point out the differential treatment meted out by the Kirk to men and women respectively. A man who refused to bow to the Kirk was let alone, a stubborn woman was further punished. Their chapter, 'Where, When and Why', is full of rich illustration that sex was by no means confined to the marriage bed. They conclude that via the Book of Discipline Scotland made a genuine effort to contain the sexual impulse out of a genuine acceptance of religious doctrine, but that this code of behaviour didn't survive the industrial revolution. They confirm the social observation of Helen B. Cruickshank in her poem 'Shy Geordie' that to people in the North East there was no stigma attached to illegitimacy.

In *Class Conflict and Collective Action*, Louise A. Tilly makes a definitive statement about women's role in political protest, concluding that 'Women were by no means passive bystanders but actors in economic and popular struggles. Their patterns of participation were different from those of men because women's interests often were more defined by a combination of individual socioeconomic structural position and family position and their action shaped by household divisions of labour'. Tilly is not especially concerned with Scotland, but with England and France where women joined in food riots and other protests. Like the rest of Scottish history, the fact that women played a part in political protest in Scotland has been ignored. Margaret Bain, now Ewing, writing in *Chapman* draws attention to the participation of women in, for example, the Suffragette movement, something regarded as an English phenomenon. James D. Young, in his book *Women and*

Popular Struggles (1985) charts women's participation in work and strife throughout the ages. Fairly consistently, more of the female population, pro rata with men, were in employment than was the case in England, and Young argues very hard throughout to show a special Scottish, female radicalism. His book, full of valuable information, is marred by the forcing of too much socialist dogma and class clichés. I would like to believe him when he says 'The often riotous militancy of Scottish working-class women in the 19th and 20th centuries can be seen as a continuation of the self-assertion, independent identity and long tradition of women's "riots" in the 17th and 18th centuries,' but that seems an oversimplification. For a start, throughout he underestimates the vigour of women of the middle and upper classes and he seems unable to countenance the thought that anything can be accomplished by a Tory. Young's book certainly aroused the ire of James J. McMillan (*Cencrastus* No 22, 1936) who recommended that the book should be pulped, which I can't quite go along with, while sharing his irritation at the narrowing of thought down to a single doctrine.

Things are improving, as I have said. Women are popping up with increasing frequency where before there was assumed to be a desert. Rosalind Marshall's *Virgins and Viragos* (1983) gives a thorough account of the last millennium for Scottish women of the aristocracy, illustrating beyond any shadow of a doubt the talented and spirited enterprise of so many Scotswomen. Marshall, wrongly, criticises Simon Somerville Laurie's words to the Edinburgh Merchant Company in 1861: 'The truth is that the intellect of a woman is a very difficult growth and that it is interwoven with her imagination, her affection and her moral emotions much more intimately than in man. What the world wants is not two men, a big one in trousers and a little one in petticoats, but a man and a woman'. David Fraser's *The Christian Watt Papers* (1983) reveals an important Scottish character and observer of fisher life in the north east. Sian Reynolds' excellent book *Britannica's Typesetters: Women Compositors in Edinburgh*, shows women attempting to compete in a male world and gradually being marginalized by unions who wished to preserve the exclusive rights of the 'wage-earner'. 'The women's story is one of exclusion and loss', but thanks to Reynolds, their story has been told, and repeated in her essay in the recent collection of essays, *The World is Ill Divided*. This book examines many different aspects of women's experience in Scotland: medical graduates, homeworkers, sexuality and an important piece 'In Bondage: The Female Farm Worker in South-East Scotland' by Barbara W. Robertson, drawing attention to the system of female agriculture work chiefly in the Lothians during the 19th century.

This strange system was also the subject of a recent successful play, *Bondagers* by Sue Glover. The ambitious three-volume *People and Society in Scotland*, setting out the results of recent research to transform past misconceptions of Scottish life and society, gives considerable space to the 'woman's sphere'. Most welcome of all are the six volumes recently published by Aberdeen University Press: *A Guid Cause*, a study of the suffragette movement in Scotland by Leah Leneman, *Upstairs to Downstairs*, by James Drummond, a compilation of advice given to women on various subjects from making rhubarb water to how to live a healthy life. Elizabeth Craik's *Marriage and Property* examines women and marital customs in history, Elisabeth Gerver and Lesley Hart's *Strategic Women* looks at women in senior positions in Scotland, and, of course, at the lack of them; *Katharine Atholl, 1874–1960* by Sheila Hetherington examines the career of Scotland's first woman MP and *Bajanellas and Semilinas* by Lindy Moore views the education of women in Aberdeen University.

Perhaps most welcome of all is the least obviously significant, essays like 'The View from the Workplace: Women's Memories of Work in Stirling' by Jayne D. Stephenson and Callum Brown in *The World is Ill-Divided*, which interviews women about their work experiences and their response to life in general, and *Voices from the Hunger Marches* compiled by Ian MacDougall, which asks women as well as men for their recollections. Even the *Old Town and South-side News* discovered this pervasive neglect in a recent article 'The Missing Women of Old Town History'. What must be recognized is that the 'Woman's sphere' is as big as the men's sphere, their world as much a universe, but one with different priorities, and, like the Indian women in search of their heritage, we must now gather as much first hand information as is available to us. The world has been ill-divided, but at least now the divisions are almost universally rejected as unacceptable. There is little snug asylum in taciturnity. Future generations of women and men must know as much as can be uncovered about the contribution of Scottish women to history, and the future.

9

The Historical Creation of The Scottish Highlands

CHARLES WITHERS

Perhaps more than any other region, the Highlands have played a crucial role in the manufacture of Scottish history and in the making of Scottish national identity. The Highlands are both real – an area of upland geologically largely distinct from the rest of Scotland – and they are a myth, a set of ideologically laden signs and images. As one commentator has remarked 'We know that the Highlands of Scotland are romantic. Bens and glens, the lone sheiling in the misty island, purple heather, kilted clansmen, battles long ago, an ancient and beautiful language, claymores and bagpipes and Bonny Prince Charlie – we know all that, and we also know that it's not real' (Womack, 1989, 1). In short, the Highlands have been created.

What follows explores the origins of these images and the reasons for their enduring historiographical significance. Attention is paid to the several forms, past and present, visual, written, theatrical, military, nostalgic, through which the Highlands have been represented and to the ideological bases to those representations. It is suggested in conclusion that an understanding of the historiographical Highlands can help explain the symbolic fascination of 'Tartanry' and other elements of what may be called 'Highlandism' as part of Scottish national identity. This is not to separate out the historiographical chaff from the factual grain of Highland history. Quite the reverse. It is to claim that the creation of the Highlands as a set of myths is now (and has been, in the past, more so), part of the very 'facts' of history itself.

The entry of the Highlands into Scottish history

The historical creation of the Scottish Highlands is often regarded as an eighteenth-century phenomenon. Certainly, this is a claim made by Trevor-Roper (1983) in his discussion of 'the invention of Highland tradition' and it is a perspective perpetuated by other studies.

More precise understanding of the historiographical significance of the Highlands rests with two related earlier factors: the geographical 'emergence' of the region in the Scotland of the middle ages and, as importantly but neglected in most accounts, the reaction of the Highlanders themselves to the creation, from 'outside and above', of Highland regional identity.

The origin of the Highlands as a distinct cultural region defined in the eyes of most commentators as the area in which the Gaelic language was prevalent stems from the linguistic retreat of Gaelic from the Scottish lowlands in the medieval period (Withers, 1984, 16–27). The commonly reiterated division within Scotland between Highlands and Lowlands is not an immutable fact of geography. It is a cultural creation with precise chronology and known causes: 'Neither in the chronicle nor in the record of the twelfth and thirteenth centuries do we hear of anything equivalent to the "Highland Line" of later time. Indeed, the very terms "Highlands" and "Lowlands" have no place in the considerable body of written evidence surviving from before 1300. "Ye hielans and ye lawlans, oh whaur hae ye been?" The plain answer is that they do not seem to have been anywhere: in those terms, they had simply not entered the minds of men. We commonly think of this highland-lowland dichotomy as being rooted deep in the history of Scotland, as being, indeed, imposed upon that history by the mere facts of physical geography. Yet it seems to have left no trace in the reasonably plentiful record of two formative centuries' (Barrow, 1973, 362 and see Barrow, 1989).

To this appearance of the Highlands as a culture region – the Highlands become synonymous with the *Gaidhealtachd* or Gaelic-speaking area (Withers, 1984; 1988) – we should add the perception of the Highlander. To the Gael, now or in the past, the term Gaidhealtachd does not directly translate into 'Highlands' nor does the Gaelic term 'Galldachd' find equivalence in 'Lowlands' (MacInnes, 1981, 1989). The principal reason for this is that parts of Scotland, now Scots-English-speaking, were once Gaelic. The folk memory of the Gael has firmly distinguished between *Goill* ('lowlanders') and *Sasannaich* (the 'English'), at the same time as it has expressed a sense of grief at the earlier linguistic retreat of Gaelic and the consequent loss of the greater Gaelic Scotland. As MacInnes argues, the Gaelic perception of the Lowlands is one of lament. ' ... We the Gaels are the disinherited, the dispossessed' (MacInnes, 1989, 99). By the seventeenth century, by virtue of the continued use of Gaelic (both a symbol and a means to the supposed cultural isolation of the Highlands), because of the perceived irreligion and lawlessness of the inhabitants, the Highlands had become the focus for administrative policies designed to unite Scotland into what contemporaries understood as a single 'Commonwealth'. The Gaelic language was seen by outside authority as, in the words of one act of 1616, ' ... one of the cheif and principal causes of the continewance of barbaritie and incivilitie amongis the inhabitantis of the Illis and Heylandis' (Withers, 1988, 113). By direct association, the Highlands and Highlanders respectively were deemed a region and a people beyond direct political control and cultural improvement, but demanding of it.

The point of this brief background survey is two-fold. Firstly, just as Barrow is right to claim that the Highlands, in a sense, did not exist before about 1300, so, too, we should be careful not to argue (as some have) that the Highlands enter Scottish history from some sort of standing start in the middle years of the eighteenth century. It is true, of course, that the 1745 rebellion was important in directing attention to the Highlands and it is undeniable that the region is ideologically burdened with its images of romance, valour, and aesthetic reward from this period. But the region had entered the minds of men as deserving 'Improvement' well before 1745. Indeed, it could be argued that the Highlands were such a focus of attention from the mid-eighteenth century onwards precisely because they had earlier been 'set up' in opposition to the values of outsiders: as wild, tribal, and speaking a barbarous language. Secondly, the historiographical creation of the Highlands from the eighteenth century – shown in what follows to be the formative period for the several Highland myths – has either misrepresented Highlander's views or it has omitted them altogether (Hunter, 1976).

The cultural creation of the Highlands, 1745–1822

The creation of the Highlands is the result of several agencies in combination: the geographical 'discovery' of the region; the idea of the Highlander as 'noble savage' in the context of enlightenment theories on the stages of societal development; and a Romantic interest in primitive virtue alongside interests in the aesthetic pleasures to be gained in contemplation of picturesque scenery.

The sense in which the Highlands were seen as geographically wild, even by the 1600s, was reinforced during the later seventeenth and early eighteenth centuries by memories of clan feuds, cattle raids on the Lowlands, and the Jacobite risings. Thus, the commentator who wrote in 1724 that 'Their [Highlanders] notions of virtue and vice, are very different, from the more Civiliz'd part of Mankind', not only echoes many later claims but would also have argued that the social qualities of Highlanders were a result of their physical environment. As a 1747 proposal 'for civilising that Barbarous people' noted, '... the numbers of woods, mountains, and Secret Glens ... are great allurements to incite that perverse Disposition that reigns amongst all Ranks of them, stimulated by the rudeness of their Nature'. In one sense, then, the 1745 Rebellion served more to reinforce existing prejudices about the 'wildness' of the Highlands than it did to form those views.

Smout (1983) has identified several trends in the 'discovery' of the Highlands: the representation from the early eighteenth century of the region as a sort of natural or anthropological curiosity; the later eighteenth-century and early nineteenth-century emphasis on the sublime and picturesque; the opening-up of the Highlands through the 'vulgar tourism' of the later nineteenth century; and twentieth-century mass tourism (Smout, 1983). The Highlands have always attracted visitors (Hume Brown, 1978). But what drew people to the region after the political and military threat of the Jacobite rebellions had been removed was the very wildness that the Highlander, in culture, language, and social system was despised for. By some, the Highlands were seen as a laboratory of natural knowledge (Bray, 1986; Cooper, 1979). More widely, the Highlands were invested with qualities of wildness, scenic grandeur, and sublime horror because of contemporary aesthetic attitudes towards a recreational and adversarial nature and a related rejection of the regularity of improved and cultivated landscapes (Thomas, 1983).

In geography, as in other ways, the Highlands were created as a combination of opposites: a cultural interest in uncultivated nature occurred alongside but in opposition to economic demands for cultivation, delight in the geometry of enclosed fields and persistent moral reproof towards unproductive land. Moral, aesthetic and economic judgements about Highland landscape were then (and are now) inseparable (Andrews, 1989).

Beattie's 1762 essay saw connections between his country's character and the environment. He wrote, 'The highlands of Scotland are a picturesque, but in general a melancholy country. Long tracts of mountainous desert, covered with dark heath, and often obscured by misty weather; narrow valleys, thinly inhabited, and bounded by precipices resounding with the fall of torrents; a soil so rugged, and a climate so dreary; as in many parts to admit neither the amusements of pasturage, nor the labours of agriculture' (in Andrews, 1989). These views and similar claims made by others find clear expression in several painted representations of the Highlands. (see Figure 1). The visual image of the Highlands is discussed more fully below.

Several points may be made about the geographical presentation of the region. First, these views are largely confined to bourgeois sensibilities. As MacCulloch noted in 1824, 'If a Highlander would show you a fine prospect, he does not lead you to the torrent and the romantic rocky glen, to the storm-beaten precipice or the cloud-capt mountain. It is to the strath covered with hamlets and cultivation, or to the extended tract of fertile lowlands, where the luxuriance of vegetation and wood depends on the exertions of human labour' (MacCulloch, 1824, III, 88). Second, it is not the Highlands as a whole that are 'discovered' in this way, but rather the south west and central Highlands. Only those districts south of the Great Glen or even south of Loch Tay were really known to the eighteenth-century tourist: the north-west Highlands figure in the later rise of tourism (Smout, 1983). Third, the accurate cartographic delineation of the region – first under William Roy and then in later surveys – was itself part of eighteenth-century intentions to establish order on the land, yet these mapped perspectives are persistently over shadowed by the geographical portrayal of 'philosophic light and gothic gloom' (Baridon, 1987; Whittington and Gibson, 1986).

What lent these ideas particular weight in the European and Scottish mind in the eighteenth century was the idea of the Highlander as a 'noble savage'. Many contemporary writers and philosophers couched their enlightenment investigations into 'the Science of Man' in terms of stages of socio-economic development. Adam Smith, for example, made a major contribution to these notions of social progress in his claim that 'There are four distinct states which mankind passes through. 1st, the age of Hunters; 2nd, the age of Shepherds; 3rd, the age of Agriculture; 4th, the age of Commerce' (Smith, 1776, I, 3). John Millar likewise concluded, 'There is thus, in human society, a natural progress from ignorance to knowledge, and from rude to civilized manners, the several stages of which are usually accompanied with peculiar laws and customs' (Millar, 1779, 6). These ideas not only represented a model of the stages of societal development through which, it was argued, all peoples and nations would progress. They also provided a means by which the history of civil society could be understood and simultaneously provided ideological support for such processes of 'Improvement' as might be brought to bear in bringing a society to a higher stage of development.

Highlanders fitted this notion of the primitive, a rude savage in an uncultivated landscape, very well. To the urbane *philosophe* of the late eighteenth century, the Highlander was a contemporary ancestor, the Highlands the Scottish past on the doorstep. As Chapman has noted, 'The Scottish Gael fulfilled this role of the 'primitive', albeit one quickly and savagely tamed, at a time when every thinking man was turning towards such subjects. The Highlands of Scotland provided a location for this role that was distant enough to be exotic (in customs and language) but close enough to be noticed; that was near enough to visit, but had not been drawn so far into the calm waters of civilisation to lose all its interest' (Chapman, 1978, 19). The incorporation of the Highlands into these eighteenth-century theoretical histories additionally de-manded that the object of interest and the subject of improvement – the Highlander, his region and the Gaelic language and customs – were portrayed in images and in language diametrically opposed to the values of civilized culture.

It is possible to see this geographical and cultural 'discovery' of the Highlands as a reflection of the wider administrative interest taken in the region from the later 1700s as institutions with one or a combination of educational, agricultural, or industrial motives were established. In another sense, however, the attention given by some historians to measures like the 1746 Disarming Act, the 1752 Annexing Act, the establishment of schools or small-scale industrial developments on the annexed estates and to the general material transformation of Highland life after the '45 rebellion, has neglected the facts attaching to the symbolic appropriation of the Highlands (see, for example, the works of Grant, 1967; Gray 1957; Haldane, 1962).

Only more recently has there been more critical attention paid either to the ways in which the Highlands were ideologically 'made' in order to legitimize their improvement, or to the Highlander's reaction to that improvement (Chapman, 1978; Hunter, 1976, 1986; MacLean and Carrell, 1986; Richards, 1982, 1985; Withers, 1988; Womack, 1989). This shift in focus, (which should neither be overplayed nor used to reduce the importance of those earlier more 'factually-based' works), may be considered a reflection in the Highland context of wider and deeper historiographical shifts in the last twenty years towards the place of theory in history, the perspectives afforded by the critique of Marxist ideas on historical materialism, and an emphasis on what may broadly be termed 'cultural' topics in contrast to study of economic and social matters (Anderson, 1980, 1983; Hirst, 1985; Thompson, 1974).

Womack's discussion of the process of 'converting the Uncouth Savage' shows how the Highlander was represented as fool, rogue, and beggar in order to sustain the legitimacy of outside authority in bringing a new order to the Highland mind and landscape. The Highlander as rustic fool appears in the ballad-opera The Highland Fair; or the Union of the Clans, performed at Drury Lane in 1731. In O'Keefe's 1788 comedy The Highland Reel, the Highland chieftain with his presentiments of loyalty and clannish pride.is likewise a source of comic fun. In the 1790 *Harlequin in Hebrides* by contrast, the emphasis was on stylized versions of Highland scenery in the stage sets (Andrews, 1989, 206; Womack, 1989, 7, 51). This portrayal of the Highlander as disingenuous oaf is evident in the later nineteenth century in the 'Hielan' picture postcard. In this form of visual representation, we can trace a continued belittlement of the moral worth and physical form of Highlanders: 'Generally ... the Highlander is not depicted as a sex symbol and remains more oatcake than cheesecake. Most frequently, males and females appear as dummies in speckled drapery to which bits of flora and fauna have been stuck .... Highlanders, as they emerge from this welter of popular images, seem to have all the sartorial, physical, emotional and intellectual qualities (and the oomph) of garden gnomes' (MacLean and Carrell, 1986, 88).

However persistent this representation as fool, rogue, or beggar is as one strand of Highlandism, it is also denied by the articulation of the Highlander as warrior. Indeed, ideas of the Highlander as 'primitive' and his depiction as canny peasant on stage, screen, or postcard stand in direct opposition to the image of the Highlander as martial figure and to the sense of worth attached to that image. The ideological weight given the Highlander as soldier does not alone explain the place of the Highlands in Scottish historiography, but it is a major element of Highlandism.

The recurring pattern of Jacobite unrest that ended on Culloden Moor in 1746 made the Highlander impossible to ignore as a military figure. In concert with contemporary ideas on the progress of civil society from barbarism to commerce, the Highland soldier was not only seen as part of a whole society geared to war, but also portrayed as a 'natural' soldier whose upland environment and physical qualities as well as his clan system predisposed him to be warlike (Womack, 1989, 28). Highland regiments were recruited before 1745, but from the later eighteenth century the recruitment of Highlanders into the British army established a persistent tradition of employment for many Highland men and secured an enduring symbolic liaison between the region and militarism. But, as in other strands of Highlandism, it is a symbolism made at a precise moment and in close relation to other, seemingly contradictory claims: clan battles (once used to justify the view of the region as lawless) are re-presented as what Womack terms 'the expression of an essence: in a romantic realisation of the neo-classical placing of the barbarian, the Highland zone produces warfare from its own dark interior' (Womack, 1989, 38). Qualities once despised are now virtuous. The Highland regiment mirrors in its bonding sense of fealty the clan system at the same time as the clan system is made out to be neither actual threat nor a real future for Highland society but rather exotic survival and 'loyal' commodity, a source of men to fight Britain's battles. By 1881, the association between militarism and Highlandism was so strong that the War Office ordered all Lowland regiments, even those whose past battle honours were gained in opposition to Highlanders, to wear tartan 'trews' and Highland-style doublets. Pipes, drums, and the Edinburgh Tattoo affirm the created facts: 'The military victory of Highlandism is now complete' (Rosie, 1989, 13).

Trevor-Roper's assessment of the invention of Highland tradition places a great deal of importance on the kilt, tartan and Ossian. His analysis is by turns mischievous and enlightening. His claim, for example that 'Before the later years of the seventeenth century, the Highlanders of Scotland did not form a distinct people. They were merely the overflow of Ireland' (Trevor-Roper, 1983, 15), would be tenable if one were to argue of the English that they too were not a distinct people but 'merely the overflow' of Jutes and Saxons. But his discussion of the 'invention' of the kilt is important in the light of the other creations of Highlandism.

The kilt, known also as the 'philibeg' from the Gaelic '*Feileadh-beag*' (not *felie beg* as Trevor-Roper dramatically misrepresents it), is that part of the plaided tartan cloth worn from waist to knee. It is only part of the 'feileadh-bhreacain', the lengthy plaid which was usually wrapped round the upper body as well as hanging down to the knees. The modern version of this, the kilt, was largely the work of one Thomas Rawlinson who shortened the lengthy plaids of his workmen in the Furnace iron foundry, had tailor-made an already pleated version for himself and his business associate, MacDonell of Glengarry, and thus set in train what has become the sartorial badge of Highlandism and Scottishness both ever since. For Trevor-Roper, ' ... the kilt is a purely modern costume ... bestowed ... on Highlanders in order not to preserve their traditional way of life but to ease its transformation: to bring them out of the heather and into the factory' (Trevor Roper, 1983, 22).

Here the factual warp and historiographical weft of Highland history are inextricably bonded for, as most commentators on this theme note, the kilt and 'any Part whatsoever of what peculiarly belongs to the Highland Garb' as the Act put it, was banned under the 1746 Disarming Act (Telfer Dunbar, 1962). But proscription of the kilt as a cultural artefact in just that period when the Highlands were being culturally created in the other ways we have seen was perhaps doomed to failure. The Disarming Act was repealed in 1782 largely through the efforts of the Highland Society of London, itself founded in July 1777 and known at first as the Gaelic Society of

London. By early 1778, the initial basis for membership – fluency in Gaelic – had been found too restrictive and only 'Highland descent' was deemed suitable. For Sir John Sinclair ' … the true qualification is not so much the distinction of "Highland Birth" … but the possession of a "Highland Spirit"' (Sinclair, 1813, 5). In 1789, the Prince of Wales donned tartan in the character of 'the Royal Highland Laddie' at a masquerade in London (Womack, 1989, 46), and when, in 1822, George IV landed in Scotland in a kilt, the royal imprimatur effectively sealed the future significance of an historical fake and added those connotations of Royalty to things Highland that attained full expression in the nineteenth-century (Nairn, 1988; Prebble, 1988, and below).

Most historians are agreed on the central place in the creation of Highlandism of 'the Ossianic controversy' and the topic has been well served in a number of recent studies (e.g., Chapman, 1978; Gaskill, 1986; Sims-Williams, 1986). Put simply, the facts of the Ossian case are these: in 1760, James Macpherson published a work entitled *Fragments of Ancient Poetry, collected in the Highlands of Scotland, and translated from the the Gaelic or Erse Language.* The following year saw publication of his *Fingal, an Ancient Epic Poem in Six Books,* and this was followed in 1763 by *Temora, an Ancient Epic Poem in Eight Books.* Macpherson claimed these texts as, in translation, the works of Ossian, an ancient Caledonian bard. In context with those other trends operating to make the Highlands fashionable, the widespread impact of Ossian (throughout Europe where Macpherson's works were translated into at least 12 different languages as well as in Britain) reinforced the image of the Highlands as both the desolate refuge of a primitive people and an example, *par excellence*, of a sublime landscape. In this sense, we are back where we started: with the central significance of geographical 'ways of seeing' in the historical creation of the Highlands. Leneman's observation that 'Ossian provided a new way of looking at wild and desolate scenery (Leneman, 1987, 358) is indisputable. But we should be cautious about attributing too much weight to Ossianic influences alone and be careful, too, of chronology. Macpherson's works and Hugh Blair's laudatory analysis of them in his 1765 *Critical Dissertation on the Poems of Ossian* came after Edmund Burke's 1757 *Philosophical Enquiry into the Origins of our Ideas of the Sublime and Beautiful.* That work was itself part of wider shifts in contemporary attitudes to landscape (see above and Thomas, 1983), and was exactly contemporary with the beginnings of scenic tourism by tourists preconditioned as to what it was they saw. Ossian certainly figured largely in some Scottish art of the late eighteenth century, notably in the work of Alexander Runciman, and Ossianic scenes even figured in interior decor (Okun, 1967). But Runciman's Ossianic paintings may also be seen as the reflection in one particular way of persistent interest in Homeric and classical themes in European art of the time (MacMillan, 1986, 42–62). In contrast, the work of Jacob More and, more importantly, Alexander Nasmyth, has been considered to show more 'realistic' Highland landscapes – 'landscapes of association' as MacMillan calls them (1986, 143). But even their work may be considered part of that misleading iconography in then British art in which visions of rustic simplicity are presented as the 'natural' order in society (Barrell, 1982; Howard, 1985).

Modern forms of Highlandism have their origins, then, in the later eighteenth and early nineteenth centuries and within a range of cultural processes affecting much of Europe, and not Scotland alone.

The region is created as a combination of opposites: the cultivated classes place value on uncultivated nature whilst demanding its 'Improvement' according to bourgeois codes of social development; genuine Gaelic culture is ignored whilst largely fake Ossianic myths are feted by urbane society; Highland scenery, laden with notions of the sublime and the picturesque, becomes an aesthetic commodity at just the moment agricultural change and over-population prompts the clearance and emigration of the native inhabitants. From the second quarter of the nineteenth century, these myths are reinforced and additional meanings accrue to the created image.

Royalty, 'Balmorality', and the Highland myth from 1822

In August 1822, King George IV landed in Scotland to a massive reception glorified by its participants as a Highland occasion set within Edinburgh's civic grandeur. Prebble has assessed the King's welcome and its context in his *The King's Jaunt* (1988). Prebble documents in great detail the degree to which the visit was a sham manifestation in an urban setting of all the elements of Highlandism – 'a Plaided Panorama': Lowlanders pretending to be Highlanders, the faked antiquity of 'the Highland garb' sported by his Majesty, his legs covered in flesh-coloured hose, and the creation of myths of Highland custom and celebration which alluded (falsely) to ancient traditions within the Highlands.

The book shows, too, how in this context as in others the painted image mirrored the false creation: J. M. W. Turner's 'March of the Highlanders', which purported to show the King's procession from Leith, is a wild flight of artistic imagination much removed from the actual passage of the King to Edinburgh Castle yet quite in keeping with prevalent Romanticized notions of display and Highland grandeur. It is surpassed only as a piece of inaccurate fakery by David Wilkie's 'George IV entering the Palace of Holyrood House'. Prebble shows how important Sir Walter Scott was to this creation of Highlandism. Scott was Master of Ceremonies for the King's visit and together with one William Murray and David Stewart of Garth organized a Highland Ball at which kilts and full Highland dress was worn. David Stewart of Garth had published that year his *Sketches of the Character, Institutions and Customs of the Highlanders of Scotland* and it is clear that he saw himself and his work as underwriting the historical legitimacy of the occasion. Prebble notes that this Ball, 'determined the kilt as the national dress of all Scotsmen', if any single historical moment can be said to have done so.

Royalty was wearing the kilt and the Highlands were invented before 1822, of course, but Prebble is probably correct in placing the emphasis he does upon 'the King's Jaunt'. 'Scotland could not be the same again once it was over. A bogus tartan caricature of itself had been drawn and accepted, even by those who mocked it, and it would develop in perspective and colour. With the ardent encouragement of an Anglo-Scottish establishment, and under the patronage of successive monarchs who took to kilt and cromach with Germanic thoroughness, Walter Scott's Celtification continued to seduce his countrymen, and thereby prepared them for political and industrial exploitation' (Prebble, 1988, 364).

The significance of Sir Walter Scott in the creation of a Highland myth that, when enlarged, suited Scotland as a whole, has also been discussed by Harvie (1989). Both Harvie and Prebble show that Scott's invented Highlands (in his novels and in his stage management of the 1822 visit) flew in the face of the evictions and other changes then being forced on real Highlanders. If, as Harvie notes, 'Scott makes the Highland predicament a metaphor for Scotland as a whole' (Harvie, 1989, 190) in the sense that national fortunes are mirrored and even foretold in the breakup of Highland society, it is also true that the creators of the Highland image and the forms taken in the image itself studiously avoided reference to, what were then, facts of Highland history. 'No laments were heard – or none beyond the bounds of the *Gaidhealtachd* – for the evictions, the burnings and the white-sailed ships that were emptying the glens while the men who profited from this Diaspora formed their Highland societies and solemnly debated the correct hang of a kilt and the exact drape of a plaid' (Prebble, 1988, 365).

Further affirmation of Royalty's role in Highlandism came in 1848 when Queen Victoria and Prince Albert bought Balmoral Castle as a summer residence on 'Royal' Deeside. The Castle was furnished with 'Balmoral' tartan, designed by Albert. Portraits by the artist MacLeay depict estate retainers as loyal, sturdy men often with countenances as rugged as the scenery in which they stand. Many such pictures show Highlanders as 'gillies' (a sportsman's attendant, from the Gaelic *gille*, a lad or man-servant), armed with rod or rifle. The Highlands become a hunting ground – populated by a people in part made out to conform to prevailing ethnological theories as physiologically suited to labour in the open air and not to the rigours of regular indoor work (itself a carry over from eighteenth-century ideas of the 'fittedness' of native Highlanders for battle given their environment), and in part represented as servants to their own landscape.

The Highlands became a recreational commodity from the 1830s and 1840s for the sportsman and, with the coming of the railways, were much more accessible than earlier. The sport, the scenery, patronage by Royalty but perhaps above all the by then deeply rooted historical associations of things Highland meant that the land itself was valued beyond its economic returns. As Devine has noted, 'It [land] became a form of conspicuous consumption, a means by which material success could be demonstrated, status and place in society assured and family line established. In this sense buying a Highland estate and 'improving' it gratified the same passion for possession as the collection of fine art or the acquisition of expensive and elaborate furniture' (Devine, 1989, 129). For those who could not get to the Highlands, purchase of the stylized paintings of Highland life by Landseer brought the Highlands to them: in Landseer's art especially, the transformation of social relations then characterizing Highland and Scottish society are simply denied (Pringle, 1986).

Many of the symbolic elements characterizing Highlandism in the nineteenth century were, then, rooted in earlier myths. What is also true is that they were a reflection in a certain way of more prevalent ideological constructions concerning the past and national identity, in England especially. English nationality during the 1800s is typified as essentially rural at just the same time that England was becoming massively urbanized and industrialized (Dodd, 1986). Wiener's notion of the 'Janus face' of English culture is directly applicable to nineteenth century Scotland where, in literature at least, the experience by most Scots of urban life is passed over by writers who focus more on rural themes (Noble, 1985). Without denying the importance of 'Kailyardism' to these cultural representations (see Michael Fry's chapter in this volume), what is also undeniable is that the Highlands, particularly but not only the historical Highlands, had become during the nineteenth century a major element in Scotland's national identity.

Highlandism and Scottish National Identity

In *The Eclipse of Scottish Culture*, Beveridge and Turnbull (1989) consider that much of Scotland's history has been characterized by an 'inferiorist historiography'. Scotland has, they argue, suffered from being uncritically compared with England, the more 'advanced' and 'developed' neighbour and has had her history written in ways which see 'progress' and 'development' as conforming to colonial models in which 'backward' societies are 'Improved'. Considerable attention is given in their analysis to the 1707 Act of Union, a date and an event given undue attention as a watershed in Scottish history between earlier 'gloom' and later Enlightenment. Scottish rural history in particular, they suggest, has been subject to persistent historiographical misrepresentation.

Their claims find support in the way the Highlands have been represented both by some historians now and in the past. The function of the 1707 Act of Union is, for the Highlands, fulfilled by the 1745 Rebellion and the 'Improvements' that came in its wake. However 'backward' and 'outdated' was Lowland society and its rural economy, the Highlands were far worse. As Carter (1971) shows, the work of historians like Graham (1900), Hamilton (1932) and Mitchell (1900) is cast in this way and there are others more recently who see the 1745 Jacobite Rebellion either as a turning point or almost a 'new beginning' to Highland history as the region emerges from its 'traditional' barbarism under the guiding hand of external influences (e.g., Youngson, 1974). And it is certainly true that the eighteenth- and nineteenth-century improvers' view of their own mission in the Highlands – whether focussed on language, education, agriculture, or industry – was underlain by a legitimating belief in the propriety of their actions.

What is important about those recent historiographical analyses of the Highlands discussed here is their attention to the origins and forms of the Highland myth. The Highlands do not figure in the Scottish consciousness in the way they do because of historical and current interest in the material transformation of Highland society. The region has national associations precisely because it has been made in the minds of outsiders and because the historiographical creation of how we have *believed* the Highlands to be has been both more enduring and more fascinating (and enduring because it has been fascinating) than our knowledge of changes in Highland life and economy.

For the Highlands, it is not a question of 'false perceptions' in opposition to a 'real' history for the region for the simple reason that many of the generally understood images of the Highlands were held to be 'real' by people at the time. Highland societies today, in

Scotland and throughout the many clan associations across the world, perpetuate in their gatherings what they believe to be their own past (Jarvie, 1989). Many of these cultural productions relating to the Highlands were made in the past and are renewed today by Lowlanders. 'Lowlanders may not have known anything about the Gaelic tradition, but it was their idealization of Highland virtues and their appropriation of Highland accoutrements such as bagpipes, kilts, and tartans – not to mention the Stewart line of kings – which helped to create a new Scottish identity' (Leneman, 1988, 120). For Womack, there is an unbroken connection between modern Highlandism and the created myths on which it is based: 'That all Scots wear tartan, are devoted to bagpipe music, are moved by the spirit of clanship, and supported Bonny Prince Charlie to a man – all these libels of 1762 live on as items in the Scottish tourist package of the twentieth century' (Womack, 1989, 20). And not just in tourist advertising. There is a persistent representation of images of Highlandness in denoting a sort of primitive wildness (in adverts for the film *Highlander*, for example), or in depicting Highlanders as kilted warriors to help sell other essentially Highland and Scottish products like whisky (Figure 2).

The Highlands figure as a major part of Scottish national identity because of the attention given to the mythic creation of the region in the eighteenth and nineteenth centuries. The created Highlands served to justify a self-sustaining larger myth about the cultural and national development of Scotland itself. The Highlands then (in the eighteenth century especially) were what all Scots once were: 'before and after' readings dominate the reading of every Highland phenomenon (Womack, 1989, 175). The Highlands enjoy the historiographic vigour they do because of the ways in which Scottish nationality has been too commonly perceived as backward: 'Wha's like us? Damn few an' they're a' deid'.

A number of authors have considered how the search for a truly 'Scottish' culture has too often been retrospective and romantic, a celebration of the past (Ash, 1980; Foster, 1989; McCrone, 1989; Mitchison, 1980). Highlandism has both conformed to and directed this broader search for a national identity. That it has in the way it has and that it continues to do so says a great deal about the present state of our own past and about the significance of a certain set of myths to the making and re-making of Scotland's image of itself.

10

Museumry and the Heritage Industry

GEORGE ROSIE

For more than thirty years my father served on the North Carr lightship, first as a deckhand, then as mate and finally as the skipper. The ungainly old ship was his pride and joy. Every two or three years the red-painted vessel would be towed into Leith docks to have her generators overhauled, her anchor chains inspected and her hull cleared of barnacles. The docking of the North Carr was a great event in the family calendar. My young brother and I never failed to make the pilgrimage down to the old dry dock to marvel at the North Carr's immaculate paintwork, scrubbed decks, whirring instruments and gleaming brass.

But for me the greatest treat was to climb – under close supervision – up into the light tower to inspect the lamp and the lens. This was a wonderland. The polished facets of the big Fresnel lens broke up the light into a million fragments. I can still remember the way the colours played on my father's face as he explained how the whole system worked. To us, the North Carr lightship was a thing of wonder. A creation engineered with no other purpose than to save lives.

The North Carr is now a museum. People pay to step on her deck. Her skipper is the Curator, North East Fife District Council, Department of Recreation. She lies awkwardly in the shallow water of Anstruther harbour, her lamp and lens stripped out, her engines silent, her big foghorn mute. The North Carr has been preserved, true. But she's been preserved in the way an embalmed corpse is preserved. All the innards and working parts gone. She's a creature drained of all life. 'Not the same ship at all' was my father's sour comment the last time he saw his old charge. 'They should have just scrapped her altogether.'

But should they? I could understand his affront. But the old ship had played her part in making safe the sea lanes of the Firth of Forth. Wasn't she, therefore, a part of Scotland's maritime 'heritage'?

Didn't she deserve to be remembered? And wasn't it possible – likely even – that some ten-year-old day tripper from Grangemouth or Dundee would run an eye over the graceless lines and top-heavy superstructure and wonder what such vessels were for? And how many of them there were? And who had designed them? And ask why they were no longer needed?

The plight of the North Carr seems to encapsulate the conundrum presented by Museumry and what has come to be called the Heritage Industry. Important artefacts should be, perhaps must be, preserved for posterity. But the loss of use and purpose can be painful to see. And the process can render them as irrelevant as the North Carr's blind and empty light tower. And the waxwork 'crew' will never replace the squads of ex-trawler hands and Caithness fishermen who used to man the ship.

The North Carr is now part of a kind of 'maritime experience' created by the nearby Scottish Fisheries Museum which moors its 'Fifie' and 'Zulu' fishing boats not far from the lightship. Very few working fishermen now use Anstruther Harbour. The illusion has largely replaced the reality. The past has banished the present. The North Carr has paid the price of joining Britain's burgeoning museum culture.

Museumry and Tourism

In fact, the North Carr light vessel is now one of the hundreds or so museums which bedeck Scotland. They fall into a variety of categories. There are the great institutions like the Royal Museum of Scotland in Edinburgh which is completely funded by Her Majesty's Government. There are establishments like the Royal Observatory in Scotland which is funded by the Science Research Council (a central government quango). There are municipal museums in Dundee, Edinburgh, Glasgow, Aberdeen, and all over Scotland which are paid for by the appropriate district councils.

There are regimental museums underwritten partly by the Ministry of Defence and partly by regimental associations. There are the various properties owned and operated by the National Trust for Scotland. There are scores of 'independent' museums run by a wide assortment of museum trusts, heritage societies, arts societies, preservation societies etc., most of which are propped up by grants from the Scottish Museums Council. And there are dozens of 'private' museums owned and run by individuals or private limited companies. Many of these are the properties of the landed gentry or aristocracy.

The variety on offer is dazzling. Scotland now has museums dedicated to a quite astonishing range of subjects. There are museums about coal mining, highland clans, fisheries, the Scottish rugby team, railways, slate quarrying, bicycles, motor cars, wirelesses, gaol conditions, aeroplanes, shipping, fossils, gem rocks, textiles, the Roman occupation, the savings bank movement, and the Loch Ness Monster. There is even a museum called The Cornice (in Peebles) which is all about the arts of decorative plasterwork.

The figures are startling. There are now more than 2 000 museums throughout Britain which is more than twice the number which existed in the mid 1970s. In Scotland the syndrome is even stronger. There are around 400 museums north of the border which, according to the Scottish Museums Council (who should know), gives Scotland more museums per head than any other part of the United Kingdom. And that figure does not include many of the stately homes, ancient monuments, and commercially run 'visitor centres' with which Scotland is decked.

Misgivings about Britain's burgeoning museum culture and heritage industry are now widespread. They were probably best expressed by Robert Hewison in his book *The Heritage Industry* which was sparked off by a government minister's claim that somewhere in Britain a new museum 'unfolds its treasures to the public gaze' every two weeks. 'When it turned out to be more or less accurate' Hewison writes 'it seemed appalling. How long would it be before the United Kingdom became one vast museum?'

The reasons for this explosive growth in museums and Museumry are not hard to find. They can be found in the statistics produced by the Scottish Tourist Board (STB). From these it is plain that there are now huge swarms of people drifting around Scotland every year looking for something to look at. The STB does not count heads, it counts 'trips', and what those trips spend. At the last count (1989) there were 11.5 million trips into Scotland, generating a handy £1.8 billion.

The huge majority of them, 10 million in fact, came from elsewhere in the UK and spent around £1.3 billion, or £130 per head. But by far the biggest spenders were the 1.5 million foreign trips who dropped £420 million, or £280 a head. Which makes a busload of Americans and Canadians seeking their Scottish heritage worth more than twice as much as, say, a coach full of pensioners from Halesowen.

In trying to exploit this huge drift of foreign and home grown visitors, Scottish (and English) entrepreneurs have been throwing up museum after visitor centre, heritage trail after highland experience, until the land is groaning under the cultural weight. The historymongers seem to be the most effective shakers and movers in Britain. But the intelligentsia fear that historical illusion is replacing modern reality, and that the trippers are leaving Scotland with a thin, paltry and bowdlerised view of Scottish culture and history.

Museums and the Industrial Graveyard

Robert Hewison sees even graver dangers in the museum boom. 'The urge to preserve as much as we can of the past is understandable' he writes 'but in the end our current obsessions are entropic; that is to say, as the past solidifies around us, all creative energies are lost. Through entropy all things become equally inert; in thermodynamics it means the end of heat and light, form, matter and motion. In culture, entropy will leave us frozen in a dead moment or stopped time'.

Well, maybe Hewison has a point but he is inclined to overstate it. His message seems to be that if Britain was not lavishing so much *nous* (and cash) on the heritage trail, there would be more energy and creativity to spend on saving the steel industry, resurrecting heavy engineering, bailing out the shipyards, or creating a consumer electronics sector all of our own. Heritage and 'real' industry are seen to be, somehow, mutually exclusive.

This is a dubious proposition, and one which the Germans disprove at every turn. Take the Bavarian town of Ingolstadt, on the Danube. Ingolstadt is a stunningly well preserved little city with a population of around 200 000. It has ancient university buildings (where Victor Frankenstein was supposed to have been educated), some of the finest Baroque churches in southern Europe, a venerable *schloss* which is used as the city library, and another which serves as the Bavarian army museum. Long stretches of the old town walls survive intact, two of the town gates (the *Kreuz Tor* and the *Feldkirchner Tor*) date back to the thirteenth century and are still in place. The old medical school has been converted into a fine anatomical and medical museum and part of the nineteenth-century fortifications have been made into a spacious and well-organized municipal museum.

The burghers of Ingolstadt like to boast that they have lavished more cash restoring their city than any municipality in Bavaria. 'It has spent more money – in total figures and not just in relation to the number of inhabitants – than the other towns, not even excepting the capital Munich, a town with over a million inhabitants' (Gerd Treffer *Ingolstadt International*). In short, Ingolstadt reeks of history and heritage. On a sunny day its spires, onion-shaped domes, bell towers, and pitched roofs are straight out of a picture book.

But Ingolstadt is equally proud of its industrial *persona*. The concentration of heritage has not prevented the Audi car firm from employing around 28 000 people in their huge plant just to the north of the city. Nor has it deterred the hugely successful textile machinery firm of Schubert & Salzer from carving out a large chunk of the European market from its base in Ingolstadt. Nor did it stop Ingolstadt becoming the petrochemical capital of southern Germany; there are four large, burgeoning oil refineries to the east of the city. Ingolstadt is living proof that heavy heritage and heavy industry are not incompatible. The two can rub along together quite nicely.

Similarly, no European city plays host to more bureaucracies than Geneva. The north side of the city bristles with national and international organisations. The banks of the Rhone are lined with Swiss and foreign financial institutions. Geneva is one of the bureaucracy capitals of the world. It is a hugely successful economy. It is also groaning with galleries and assorted museums. And the old *haute ville* which runs from Saint Peter's Cathedral down to the River Rhone is a lot better preserved than the Old Town of Edinburgh. Again, big money and big history go together.

Museums and Industrial Decline

Which suggests that there is nothing wrong with Museumry if the underlying economy is healthy. When the worship of heritage coincides with a burgeoning commerce there is no problem. In fact, well funded and well run museums and galleries can be seen as part of the reward of prosperity – one of the treats that money can buy such as theatres, libraries and botanical gardens. A bit like a well-heeled family decorating the living room by putting old snapshots of the family into silver frames.

Britain's problem, however, is that popular enthusiasm for the past has coincided with industrial decline. The country's dismal failure to keep up with the industrialized world is reflected in our museums. Evidence of our wretched industrial performance can be found in almost every local museum. Over the past fifty years, local museums up and down the land (and not just in Scotland) found themselves surrounded by dead or dying industries, all begging to be acknowledged.

But nothing alarms critics like Hewison more than these 'industrial' museums and heritage centres. These are seen as Museumry at its worst. These establishments are often used as handy metaphors for the death and fossilization of industrial Britain. 'If the only new thing we have to offer is an improved version of the past' Hewison writes 'then today can only be inferior to yesterday. Hypnotized by images of the past we risk losing all capacity for creative change.' Particularly, he implies, industrial change.

On the other hand, few industries last forever. They come and go

with the demand for the goods and services they produce. Should
they be allowed to sink without trace? Is there anything intrinsically
wrong in marking the achievements of the people who worked in
them? As the Scottish coalfield is closed down pit by pit, is the two-
site Scottish Mining Museum at Prestonpans and Newtongrange
not better than nothing at all? Or should the site of the Lady
Victoria mine have been sold for yet another B&Q warehouse and
the winding gear broken up for scrap?

Without the Museum of Scottish Leadmining at Wanlockhead,
who, apart from a few historians, would have been aware that
generations of border folk struggled under the Lanarkshire hills in
dire conditions for the enrichment of His Grace the Duke of
Buccleuch. Or that the fifth duke expressed his gratitude by refusing
the leadminers and their families a scrap of land on which to build a
Free Church after the Disruption of 1843?

When British Rail Engineering Ltd (BREL) closed the locomotive
building works at Springburn in Glasgow, all that the Springburn
Museum Trust could do was mark the former glories of the St
Rollox, Hyde Park and Atlas engine-building sheds. This was the
illusion of industry and not the reality. But plenty of local people
were pleased to see some tribute to their skill and years of hard work

There's no doubt that the turners, welders, riveters and pattern-
makers of Springburn would have preferred a thriving engineering
works to an award-winning museum. But that choice was not on
offer. Nor is it likely to be on offer in the Midlothian coalfield, the
fishing ports of Fife, or in the steeltowns of Lanarkshire.

Industrial Memorabilia

But if Hewison is right to fret, and that Museumry equates with
industrial ruin, then Scots should worry. Scotland abounds with
industrial museums and heritage centres, some of them in the most
unlikely places. The old gasworks at Biggar, for example, is now the
property of the National Museums of Scotland, and is used to
display coal-gas technology. There is an eighteenth-century char-
coal-fuelled ironworks at Bonawe, near Taynuilt in Argyll. The
Scottish Maritime Museum at Irvine in Ayrshire has an outlier at the
old 'ship model tank' at Denny near Dumbarton. The old slate
quarries on the tiny island of Easdale in Argyll (which were wiped
out by a wave in 1881) are celebrated at the Easdale Island Folk
Museum.

The various sites at the Bo'ness Heritage Area ('an underground
experience at Birkhill Clay Mine') are linked by the steam trains of
the Bo'ness and Kinneil Railway which itself 'illustrates the history
of the Scottish railways'. There is a lot more transport (steam

wagons, ancient tractors, fire engines, buses, and vintage motor cars) to be found at the Grampian Transport & Railway Museum at Alford in Aberdeenshire.

Professions are harder for Museumry to cope with but are not immune. The Royal College of Surgeons of Edinburgh has long had a permanent show of exhibits (some of which are unnervingly pathological). And anyone anxious to see how their ancestors dosed themselves with laudanum, smelling salts, and purgatives should locate the Royal Pharmaceutical Society's version of a Late Victorian Pharmacy at York Place in Edinburgh.

The latest industrial venture is the Scottish Shale Oil Museum at the Almond Valley Heritage Centre in West Lothian. This museum, according to *The Scotsman* of May 6th 1991 '... provides a fascinating illustration of the nature of a unique industry which in its heyday employed more than 6 000 men in Scotland'. Waxwork models of miners and their families inhabit 'replica', (company) cottages, while other waxwork miners hew phantom shale from a latex-rubber and glassfibre reinforced plastics shale mine. Large tribute is paid to the shale oil industry's sole begetter, James 'Paraffin' Young (1851–1883).

The shale oil industry was notoriously unpleasant to work for – at every stage of the process. The fumes from the smelting process were almost as dangerous as the mines themselves. The shale miner's life tended to be nasty, brutish and short. But none of that has prevented British Petroleum – the inheritors of Young's Paraffin, Light & Mineral Oil Company – from donating a 'major sum' to this sanitized version of West Lothian history. Or declaring that 'BP is proud to support the shale oil museum at Livingston'. Heritage is good PR.

The Historymongers

Also high on the intelligentsia's hate list are the newish breed of 'visitor centre', or 'heritage centre'. These establishments are generating all kinds of angst and, it should be said, some unease among museum professionals. These are (usually) commercial operations which specialize in 'edutainment', i.e. amusing and informing the public at once, while at the same time relieving them of their cash. These historical emporia usually involve a great deal of 'audio visual' technology, plus piped sound effects and even smells.

A nifty example of the *genre* is the Scotch Whisky Heritage Centre in the old Castlehill School in Edinburgh. For an admission price of a few pounds, visitors are trundled in mobile whisky barrels around a series of *tableaux* which illustrate how whisky is made. They are then shepherded into a well-stocked shop which sells almost every variety of whisky made in Scotland, at prices which do no one any favours.

This scheme was devised by a York-based company called Heritage Projects Ltd which created the famous 'Jorvik Viking Centre' in York plus similar projects in Oxford and Canterbury. Heritage Properties were behind the plan to convert the old Highland Tollbooth Church in Edinburgh into a Jorvik-type history of Edinburgh and/or Scotland. But at the time of writing (May 1991) that plan appears to have collapsed. The cost of transforming Pugin's impressive but damp-ridden Gothic pile into a (literally) sanitized version of medieval Edinburgh proved too much for the heritage-industry capitalists.

The cultural weakness of projects such as the 'Jorvik Viking Centre' or the similar 'Pilgrim Way' at Canterbury is that they are unashamedly commercial. Unappealing history does not appeal to them. Seamy facts chase away the paying customers. Anthony Gaynor, one-time managing director of Heritage Projects Ltd, made that very plain at a museums conference in Edinburgh in 1988. He'd been approached, he said, to build a 'Museum of Slavery' but refused point blank on the grounds that it would be unacceptable to the public. 'We are a commercial company' he told the delegates. 'Let's not get away from that' (Timothy Ambrose ed. *Presenting Scotland's Story* 1989).

Now, it might be that a well-designed museum which laid bare the anatomy of the slave trade could be very useful. It could very well shed some interesting light on a vile trade which is little understood, which is still partly concealed, and in which the British, including some Scots, played a big part. Many fortunes were made from peddling black flesh. Such a museum might still embarrass some very influential families. Bristol would be its natural home. But judging from what Gaynor says, the facts which would make a museum of slavery intriguing are the very ones which would discourage the commercial historymongers.

But there seems to be no stopping the big-money heritage industry. In May 1991 a brand new heritage wheeze was unveiled for the Old Town of Edinburgh. It is to be built on the site of the old Holyrood Brewery, a site from which Edinburgh folk have been brewing beer since the medieval times. But not any more. Scottish & Newcastle have cleared the site, and are to build the 'Younger Universe' (after the brewery firm).

It will take the form of a tent-like structure which will house the story of '... the creation of the earth, its decay, renewal and the reshaping of continents coupled with the evolution of the essential ingredients for life'. Which is nothing if not ambitious. But it comes

as no surprise to hear that this exalted exhibit is art and part of a
£100 million development which will also include offices, housing,
a three star hotel, commercial workshops and of course 'quality
shopping'. Cynics might construe the Younger Universe as Heritage
as Planning Gain.

But the techniques dreamed up by the commercial operators are
seeping through to the 'straight' museums. Audio visuals – slide
shows, videotapes, computer graphics etc. – are now common. Wax
models arranged in helpful *tableaux* are no longer unusual. The
recently-opened People's Story Museum in Edinburgh (proprietors
the Edinburgh District Council) features piped eighteenth-century
street sounds (shouting, horses hooves, handbells etc). What distin-
guishes it from the usual historical 'experience' is that it costs
nothing to walk around.

Royalism and Highlandism

What is intriguing about Scotland's museum network is the light it
sheds on popular perceptions of Scottish history. There is the usual
fascination with Royalty, however inept and discredited. Thousands of visitors to Holyrood Palace gaze in horror at the very spot
where David Riccio was butchered in 1566 and stare solemnly up at
the totally bogus seventeenth-century pictures of 'ancient' Scottish
kings dating back, it seems, to Noah's Flood. Roxburgh District
Council run a handsome century 'bastel house' in Jedburgh as
'Mary Queen of Scots' House' on the tenuous grounds that the
Stuart queen once visited the town (also in 1566).

Most of Scotland's 'great' houses and 'stately homes' can be
viewed as a subtext of Royalism. They are the homes and former
homes of the Scottish aristocracy, many of whom were kinglets. The
Duke of Atholl still has his own little army. And his establishment at
Blair Castle is as splendid as Falkland Palace. Inverary Castle is just
as grand as Holyrood House. The policies of Glamis Castle are as
lush as Balmoral's. The Countess of Sutherland's turreted castle at
Dunrobin looks more exalted than any of them.

It is interesting to see these quasi-Royal piles 'back to back', as it
were, with the scores of 'folk' museums which pepper Scotland. The
latter shows how people lived and worked; the former shows how
their masters lived and didn't. There could hardly be a greater
contrast than the Macleod seat of Dunvegan Castle on Skye ('this
historic castle by the sea') and the Colbost Folk Museum which
consists of the kind of cramped and wretched 'Black House' that
was home to most of the Macleod's loyal clanspeople.

Gaelic sentimentalists like to bang on about the 'egalitarian'
nature of Celtic polity. But the evidence of the Highland museums

and stately homes seems to suggest that the living arrangements were as unequal as those anywhere else in Britain. More perhaps, if only because clan society seemed woefully short of a middle class. The Highland bourgeoisie appears to have been pitifully small.

If the museums are anything to go by, there were dirks and targes aplenty but precious little in the way of ledgers, medical texts and statute books. Which raises the question of how accurate the pictures drawn by our museums are? Does the inevitable selection of artefacts bend the historic reality? Basket-hilted broadswords are more glamorous than estate ledgers, but were they more important?

Of course Highlandism and tartanry loom large. The Scottish Tartans Museum at Comrie in Perthshire has acquired a reputation as a quasi-official authority on the Garb of Old Gaul. The Piping Heritage Centre at Dunvegan in Skye (prop. Hugh Ross MacCrimmon) peddles the myth of the MacCrimmon musical dynasty beside which the Bachs pale into insignificance. The Highland Tryst Museum in Crieff portrays that douce little burgh as a sort of Dodge City in the rain, the 'capital of royal Strathearn, wild frontier town where Highlands met Lowlands ...'

Naturally, Bonnie Prince Charlie has a substantial museum presence. There are traces of him all around Scotland. As well as the portraits and artefacts curated by Her Majesty's Government in Edinburgh, the Bonnie Prince pops up at the Glenfinnan Monument, the Culloden Visitor Centre, various 'clan' museums, and in the West Highland Museum at Fort William. The whole first floor of this establishment is given over to the Bonnie Prince: Jacobite medals, snuff mills, wine glasses, tartan dress, cannonballs from Culloden, French bagpipes, and the famous 'secret portrait' which becomes a portrait of the Pretender when reflected in a cylinder.

And it is interesting that while there are five clan museums and heritage centres – lan Gunn, Clan Macpherson, Clan Cameron, Clan Donnachaidh, and Clan Donald – there are no museums charting the history of fearsome border tribes like the Armstrongs, the Kerrs or the Elliots. They may have borne the brunt of English hostility and played a crucial role in Scottish history, but they lack the glamour of their Gaelic counterparts. (The trinket shops, do, however sell Armstrong etc. 'clan' crests on a background of appropriate tartans.)

Great Manism

Scotland is peppered with museums and monuments to the memory of Great Men. Thomas Carlyle is remembered at Ecclefechan, David Livingstone at Blantyre, Robert Louis Stevenson (and Walter Scott) in Lady Stair's House in Edinburgh, J. M. Barrie at Kirriemuir, John

Buchan at Broughton, Andrew Carnegie in Dunfermline, the painter William Lamb in Montrose, John Knox in the High Street in Edinburgh. Sir Walter Scott's estate at Abbotsford is a pilgrimage centre for *aficionados* from all over the world. And the Edinburgh District Council are currently (in 1991) spending huge sums of money dusting off George Meikle Kemp's monument to Scott in Princes Street.

(The monument to Scott is also a monument to the baleful face of hero worship. When George Meikle Kemp drowned in the Union Canal off Lothian Road his friends arranged to have him interred in the vault under Sir Walter's statue. At the very last minute – on the morning of the funeral in fact – Sir Walter's followers objected to the arrangement. They claimed that the dead architect was not eminent enough to share the space with the image of the Great Man. Kemp's funeral was cancelled and his bones were buried elsewhere.)

The Great Man museum *genre* has one or two surprises There is a little museum at Duns commemorating the achievements of the Scots grand prix racing driver Jim Clark. And the Giant Macaskill Museum at Dunvegan on Skye celebrates (if that's the word) a local man who disappeared into North America at an early age. His claim to greatness was that he was extremely large (an estimated 7'9") and extremely strong. And apart from a museum to Jane Welsh Carlyle at Haddington and Mary Queen of Scots' House in Jedburgh, women hardly rate a mention.

Scotland's great men of science, however, come off just as badly as the ladies. Literary chaps abound, but very few scientists. Which is odd given the contribution of Scots to world science. There is no museum of the life and work of, say, Sir David Brewster, or Lord Kelvin, or Joseph Black, or John Logie Baird, or Sir Charles Lyell, or Alexander Graham Bell, or even early photographers like David Hill and Robert Adamson. No man did more to create the modern world than James Clerk Maxwell, but Scotland has ignored him. The geologist and palaeontologist Hugh Miller does rate a museum (at his birthplace in Cromarty) but that's probably because he was also a crusading journalist and Free Church polemicist.

But what the Great Man museums of Scotland do reflect is Scotland's obsession with Robert Burns. The Ayrshire poet has more museums dedicated to him than anyone else. Apart from the Burns Cottage and Museum at Alloway there is also the Burns Monument and Gardens, Alloway, the Land O' Burns Centre, Alloway, the Robert Burns Centre, Dumfries, Ellisland Farm, Dumfries, the Glasgow Vennel Museum and Burns Heckling Shop, Irvine, the Irvine Burns Club Museum, Souter Johnnie's Cottage, Kirkoswald, Burns House Museum, Mauchline, the Bachelors Club,

Tarbolton, and of course the Burns memorabilia in Lady Stair's House, Edinburgh.

Some of these locations have fairly tentative connections with the bard. The Bachelor's Club at Tarbolton, for example, happens to be the venue where Burns was initiated into Freemasonry and attended a few dancing classes. Not much, perhaps, but enough to open yet another Burns museum. The museum is operated by the National Trust for Scotland. This preoccupation with Burns and all his doings is a phenomenon almost unique in Britain. Only the Stratford-based William Shakespeare industry comes close.

Burnsmania is a Scottish cultural quirk which has left many commentators (particularly English commentators) baffled. 'That he should be held up for a model by Scottish writers and Scottish preachers is a crying scandal' was the view of that engaging Scotophobe T. W. H. Crosland (*The Unspeakable Scot*, 1906) 'That his memory should stand for so much in Scotland constitutes the very gravest reflection upon the Scottish character and the Scottish point of view'.

Popular Militarism

Predictably perhaps, Scotland's taste for militarism is fairly well catered for. The slaughter of the English at Bannockburn is chronicled in great (and some would argue unfortunate) detail by the National Trust for Scotland at their Bannockburn Heritage Centre. The display comes close to the kind of military triumphalism we could do without. The Jacobite rebellions are 'topped and tailed' (also by the National Trust for Scotland) at the Pass of Killiecrankie and at the Culloden Visitor Centre near Inverness.

The selection of Scottish battles taken into the heritage fold appears to be random. Bannockburn (1314) and Culloden (1746) were both decisive, of course, but Killiecrankie (1690) was not. Graham of Claverhouse's Highland/Irish army did rout a Williamite force under Hugh McKay of Scourie. But the Jacobite victors were thrashed a few weeks later at Dunkeld by a small force of Lowland psalm-singers. (Their descendants – The Cameronians – have long since marched into history).

The decisive battle at Harlaw in Aberdeenshire, which put an end to the claims of Clan Donald to the Scottish throne once and for all is unmarked. And the crucial battle at Dunnichen near Forfar in the late seventh century where the southern Picts destroyed the invading Angles might never have happened. But Dunnichen (also called Nechtansmere) was probably as important as Bannockburn in shaping Scotland.

And nobody is planning to build 'heritage trails' or 'visitor centres' at Solway Moss, Dunbar, or Pinkie where Scottish armies were crushed and routed by the English. But, whether we like it or not, these historic confrontations are as much a part of our military 'heritage' as the bloody victories at Bannockburn and Stirling Bridge.

Museumry & God

Even odder, perhaps, is Museumry's apparent reluctance to mark Scottish enthusiasm for religion. Edinburgh may have been the second most important Reformation city in Europe, but there is very little sign of it. The Magdalen Chapel in the Cowgate may have been as important to Reformation thinking as the 'Auditoire' in Calvin's Geneva, but it languishes neglected and is in disrepair. Apart from John Knox's House in the High Street of Edinburgh, and a few monuments and plaques scattered around the countryside (particularly in the south-west) God is hardly to be found in the Scottish museums.

Which is a pity. A museum of church history which disentangled the kirk/state struggles of the Reformation, the Covenanting times, the eighteenth-century Secessions and the Disruption of 1843 would be a substantial addition to Scots history. It could chart the Irish immigration of the nineteenth and twentieth centuries, the rise of the State-funded Catholic schools, the sectarianism of the 1920s, the acrimonious 'Bishops in the Kirk' rows of the 1950s, even the Kirk's role in the post-war Home Rule debates.

Scotland's ecclesiastical history is, after all, full of strange and potent figures; John Knox himself; the masked moorland preacher Alexander Peden; William Carstares, one of the architects of the Union; Ebenezer Erskine, the original secessionist; William Robertson the great historian; Johnnie Witherspoon, the only clergyman to sign the American Declaration of Independence; Thomas Chalmers, the great Evangelical organizer; George Macleod, the spirit behind the Scoto-Catholic movement of the twentieth century

And it is hard to believe that a permanent collection of Scottish football – and not just Rangers and Celtic – memorabilia would go unviewed. If they can do it for golf at St Andrews, they can do it for the Great Game. Scots are traditionally the footballing mercenaries of Britain. The socio-religious history of teams like Hearts and Hibs, Dundee and Dundee United could shed a lot of light on urban Scotland.

Conclusion

All of which raises the question; what does the burgeoning museum and heritage industry tell us about ourselves? That we like to go in for historical English bashing, certainly. That we are mildly enthusiastic royalists, probably. That our perception of our history shades to the Jacobite end of the spectrum. That clans and clansmen are still celebrated beyond their historical importance. That we disdain our turbulent ecclesiastical past. That we favour our poets, novelists, playwrights, and explorers over our world-class scientists and engineers. That the mildly disreputable poet Robert Burns (née Burness) is our national hero.

And, perhaps above all, it tells us that our days as diggers of shale oil, coal, and lead and makers of steel, ships, railway engines, and heavy equipment are in the past. Which is where they are likely to remain. As reminders of our failure to hang on to the markets we once dominated. A truly healthy relationship between museum culture and Scottish (indeed British) society awaits the revival of Britain's industrial economy. Which seems to be a long time coming.

Meanwhile, plans for the first Museum of Scottish Computing are probably already well advanced. No doubt it will present a shimmering vision of Scotland the Electronic that never existed. And no doubt it will be erected on the site of a foreign-owned plant that once supplied microprocessors to the world.

Bibliography

Adam Smith, J. (1965) *John Buchan*

Alison, A. (1883) *Some Account of my Life and Writings*

Ambrose, T. (1989) *Presenting Scotland's Story*

Anderson, P. (1980) *Arguments within English Marxism*
(1985) *In the Tracks of Historical Materialism*

Anderson, R. D. (1983) *Education and Opportunity in Victorian Scotland. Schools and Universities*

Andrews, M. (1989) *The Search for the Picturesque*

Ash, M. (1980) *The Strange Death of Scottish History*

Baridon, M. (1987) 'Philosophic light and Gothic gloom: landscape and history in eighteenth-century Scotland' in Carter, Pittock (1987)

Barrell, J. (1982) *Dark Side of the Landscape: the rural poor in English painting*

Barrow, G. W. S. (1973) *The Kingdom of the Scots*
(1989) 'The lost Gaidhealtachd of medieval Scotland' in Gillies (1989)

Bell, T. (1941) *Pioneering Days* Lawrence & W. Shark

Bercé, Y. M. (1990) *History of Peasant Revolts*

Beveridge, C. and Turnbull, R. (1989) *The Eclipse of Scottish Culture: Inferiorism and the Intellectuals*

Beveridge, W. (1953) *Power and Influence*

Bohstedt, J. (1983) *Riots and Community Politics in England and Wales 1790–1810*

Bray, E. (1986) *The Discovery of the Hebrides*

Broadie, A. (1990) *The Tradition of Scottish Philosophy*

Brock, W. R. (1982) *Scotus Americanus. A Survey of the Sources for the Links between Scotland and America in the eighteenth century*

Brodie, G. (1823) *A Constitutional History of the British Empire*

Brown, C. (1987) *The Social History of Religion in Scotland Since 1730*
(1990) 'Protest in the Pews. Interpreting Presbyterianism and Society in Fracture During the Scottish Economic Revolution, in Devine (1990)

Brown, P. H. (1911) *History of Scotland*

Buchan, J. (1919) *Mr Standfast*

Buckle, H. T. (1861) *History of Civilisation in England*

Buckle, H. T. (1870) *On Scotland and the Scotch Intellect*

Buckroyd, J. (1980) *Church and State in Scotland*

Burnet, G. (1979) *History of his own Time* (Everyman edition)

Burns, J. H. (1985) 'Stands Scotland where it did?' *History*

Butt, J. (ed.) (1971) *Robert Owen. Prince of Cotton Spinners*

Butterfield, Sir H. (1932) *The Whig Interpretation of History*

Cage, R. A. (ed.) (1985) *The Scots Abroad. Labour, Capital, Enterprise, 1750–1914*

Calder, J. (1986) *The Enterprising Scot. Scottish Adventure and Achievement*

Calderwood, D. (1843) *History of the Kirk of Scotland*

Campbell, A. B. (1979) *The Lanarkshire Miners. A Social History of their Trade Unions, 1775–1874*

Campbell, R. H. (1980), *The Rise and Fall of Scottish Industry*
(1990) 'Scottish Economic and Social History: Past Developments and Future Prospects' *Scottish Economic and Social History*

Carter, I. (1971) 'Economic models and the recent history of the Highlands' *Scottish Studies*

Carter, J. J. and Pittock, J. H. (eds.) (1987) *Aberdeen and the Enlightenment*

Chapman, M. (1978) *The Gaelic Vision in Scottish Culture*

Charlton, D. G. (1984) *New Images of the Natural in France*

Checkland, S. G. (1975), *Scottish Banking. A History, 1695–1973*

Checkland, S. G. and O. (1984), *Industry and Ethos. Scotland 1832–1914*

Chitnis, A. C. (1976) *The Scottish Enlightenment: A Social History*
(1986), *The Scottish Enlightenment and Early Victorian English Society*

Church, R. (ed.) (1980) *The Dynamics of Victorian Business. Business Problems and Perspectives to the 1870s*
(1986), *The History of the British Coal Industry 1830–1914: Victorian Pre-eminence*

Churchill, W. (1932) *The World Crisis*

Clarke, T. and Dickson, T. (1988) 'The Birth of Class?' in Devine and Mitchison (1988)

Clive, J. and Bailyn, B., (1954) 'England's Cultural Provinces: Scotland and America' *William and Mary Quarterly XI:2*

Cockburn, H. Lord. (1852) *Life of Francis Jeffrey*
(1856) *Memorials of his Time*
(1874) *Letters on the Affairs of Scotland*

Cole, G. D. H., (1927) *Short History of the British working class movement*

Colls, R. and Dodd, P. (eds) (1987) *Englishness: Politics and Culture 1880–1920*

Communist Party of Great Britain (1927) *Communist Party Training*

Connolly, S. (1988) 'Albion's Fatal Twigs: Justice and Law in the Eighteenth Century', in Houston and Whyte (1989)

Cooper, D. (1979) *Road to the Isles: travellers in the Hebrides 1770–1914*

Cowan, E. J. (1980) *The People's Past*

Cowan, I. B., (1976) *The Scottish Covenanters 1976*
(1981a) *The Scottish Reformation 1981*
(1981b) 'The Inevitability of Union – A Historical Fallacy' *Scotia*

(1983) (ed), with Shaw, D. *The Renaissance and Reformation in Scotland*

Crawford, T. (1979) *Society and the Lyric...the Song Culture of Eighteenth Century Scotland*

Cronin, J. (1979) *Industrial Conflict in Modern Britain*

Crouzet, F. (1985) *The First Industrialists. The Problems of Origins*

Cumming, A. D. (1910) *Olden Times in Scotland*

Daiches, D., Jones, P and Jones, J. (1986) *A Hotbed of Genius: The Scottish Enlightenment 1730–1790*

Damer, S. (1980) 'State, Class and Housing in Glasgow 1885–1919' in *Housing, Social Policy and the State*, ed. J. Melling

(1985) 'The State, local State & local struggle: the Clydebank Rent Struggle of the 1920s', Paper 22, Centre for Urban and Regional Research, Glasgow University

Davie, G. E. (1991) *The Scottish Enlightenment and other essays*

Devine, T. M. (1975) *The Tobacco Lords*

(1978), 'Social stability and agrarian change in the eastern Lowlands of Scotland, 1810–1840', *Social History*, Vol. 3

(editor) (1984) *Farm Servants and Labour in Lowland Scotland, 1770–1914*

(1988) 'Unrest and Stability in Rural Ireland, 1760–1840', in Mitchison and Roebuck (eds) 'Economy and Society in Scotland and Ireland' 1500–1939

(editor) (1988) with Mitchison, R. *People and Society in Scotland Vol 1, 1760–1830*

(1989) 'Social Responses to agrarian "improvement": the Highland and Lowland clearances in Scotland', in *Scottish Society, 1500–1800* Houston, R. and Whyte, T. D

(1989) *Improvement and Enlightenment* 'The emergence of the new elite in the western Highlands and Islands, 1800–1860'

(editor) (1990) *Conflict and Stability in Scottish Society*

Dicey, A. V. & Rait, Sir R. (1920) *Thoughts on the Union between England and Scotland*

Dickinson, W. C. & Pryde, G. S. (1961–2) *New History of Scotland 2 Vols*

Dickson, T. (ed.) (1980) *Scottish Capitalism*

(ed.) (1982), *Capital and Class in Scotland*

Dodd, P. (1987) 'Englishness and the national culture' in Colls and Dodd, (1987)

Donaldson, G. (1949) (ed.) *The Accounts of the Collectors of Thirds of Benefices*

(1960) *The Scottish Reformation*

Donaldson, G. (1961) and Dickinson, W. C. *A Source Book of Scottish History III*

Donaldson, G. (1963) with Dickinson W. C. & Milne, I. *A Source Book of Scottish History II*

Donaldson, G. (1965) *James V – James VII*

(1966), *The Scots Overseas*

(1974, 1980 ed.) *Scotland: the Shaping of a Nation*

Donaldson, W. (1976) '"Bonny Highland Laddie": the making of a myth'
  Scottish Literary Journal
Donaldson, W. (1988) *The Jacobite Song: political myth and national
  identity*
Donnachie, I. (1979), *A History of the Brewing Industry in Scotland*
Dow, F. (1979) *Cromwellian Scotland 1651–60*
Drummond, A. C. and Bulloch J. (1973) *The Scottish Church, 1688–1843*
Duckham, B. F. (1970) *History of the Scottish Coal Industry 1700–1838*
Ferguson, W. (1968) *1689 to the Present*
  (1977) *Scotland's Relations with England*
Fewster, J. M. (1957) 'The Keelmen of Tyneside in the Eighteenth
  Century', *Durham University Journal*
Foster, J. (1989) 'Nationality, social change and class: transformations of
  national identity in Scotland' in McCrone, (1989)
  (1990) 'Strike Action and Working Class Politics on Clydeside, 1914–
  1919' *International Review of Social History*
Foster, W. R. (1959) *Bishops and Presbytery*
  (1975) *The Church before the Covenants*
Fraser, W. H. (1988a) *Conflict and Class: Scottish Workers 1700–1838*
  'Patterns of Protest', in Devine and Mitchison, (1988b) (1988)
Fry, M., (1987) *Patronage and Principle: a political history of modern
  Scotland*
Gallacher, W. (1936) *Revolt on the Clyde*
Gaskill, H. (1986) '"Ossian" Macpherson: towards a rehabilitation'
  Comparative Criticism
Gillies, W. (ed.) (1989) *Gaelic and Scotland*
Gilpin, W. (1789) *Observations relative to Picturesque Beauty Made in
  the Year 1776, on Several Parts of Great Britain; particularly the
  Highlands of Scotland*
Gordon, E. and Breitenbach, E. (eds.) (1990) '*The World Is Ill Divided*'.
  Women's Work in Scotland in the 19th and Early 20th Centuries
Graham, H. G. (1901) *Scottish Men of Letters in the Eighteenth Century*
  (1909) *The Social Life of Scotland in the Eighteenth Century*
Grant, I. F. (1967) *Highland Folk Ways*
Gray, M. (1957) *The Highland Economy, 1750–1850*
  (1984) 'Farm Workers in North-East Scotland', in Devine (1984)
  (1990) *Scots on the Move, Scots Migrants 1750–1914*
Haldane, A. R. B. (1962) *New ways through the Glens*
Hamilton, H. (1932) *The Industrial Revolution in Scotland*
  (1945) *Selections from the Monymusk Papers, 1713–55*
  (1963) *An Economic History of Scotland in the Eighteenth Century*
Hanham, H. (1969) *Scottish Nationalism*
Harvie, C. T. (1977) *Scotland and Nationalism. Scottish Society and
  Politics, 1707–1977*
  (1981) *No Gods and Precious Few Heroes. Scotland 1914–1980*
  (1989) 'Scott and the image of Scotland' in Samuel, R. (ed.), *Patriot-
  ism: the making and unmaking of British national identity: volume II –
  Minorities and outsiders*

Haws, C. (1972) *Scottish Parish Clergy at the Reformation*
Hewison, R. (1987) *The Heritage Industry. Britain in a Climate of Decline*
Hewitt, G. R. (1982) *Scotland under Morton*
Hinton, J. (1973) *The First Shop-stewards Movement*
Hirst, P. (1985) *Marxism and Historical Writing*
Houston, G. (1957) 'Labour Relations in Scottish Agriculture before
    1870' *Agricultural History Review*
Houston, R. (1983) 'Coal, class and culture: labour relations in a Scottish
    mining community, 1650–1750', *Social History*
    (1989), with Whyte, I. D. (eds.) *Scottish Society, 1500–1800*
    (1985) *Scottish Literacy and the Scottish Identity, Illiteracy and
    Society in Scotland and Northern England 1600–1800*
Howard, P. (1985) 'Painters' preferred places' *Journal of Historical
    Geography*
Hume Brown, P. (1911) *History of Scotland to the Present Time*
Hume Brown, P. (ed.) (1978) *Early Travellers in Scotland*
Hume, D. (1973) *History of England*
Hume, J. R. and Moss, M. (1979), *Beardmore. The History of a Scottish
    Industrial Giant*
Hunter, J. (1976) *The Making of the Crofting Community*
    (1986) *For the People's Cause*
Hutt, A. (1937) *A Post-War History of The British Working Class*
Jackson, W. T. (1968) *The Enterprising Scot. Investors in the American
    West after 1873*
Jarvie, G. (1989) 'Culture, social development and the Scottish Highland
    gatherings' in McCrone, (1989)
Johnston, T. (1952) *Memories*
Jones, P. (ed.) (1989) *The Science of Man In The Scottish Enlightenment:
    Hume, Reid and Their Contemporaries*
Jones, T. (1969) *Whitehall Diaries*
Kirk, J. (ed.) (1978) *The Second book of Discipline*
    (1980) 'The Politics of the Best Reformed Kirks', *Scottish Historical
    Review*
Kirkwood, D. (1935) *My Life of Revolt*
Larner, Christina (1981) *Enemies of God: The Witch-hunt in Scotland*
Lee, M. (1953) *James Stewart, earl of Moray*
    (1981) *Government by Pen*
Leneman, L. (1987) 'The effects of Ossian in Lowland Scotland' in
    Carter, and Pittock, (1987)
    (1988) 'A new role for a lost cause: Lowland romanticisation of the
    Jacobite Highlander' in Leneman, L. (ed.) *Perspectives in Scottish
    Social History*
Lenin, V. (1920/1966) *Collected Works XXXI*
Lenman, B. (1973) 'The Teaching of Scottish History in the Scottish
    Universities' *Scottish Historical Review*
    (1977) *An Economic History of Modern Scotland 1660–1976*
    (1981) *Integration, Enlightenment and Industrialisation: Scotland
    1746–1832*

Lindsay, Maurice (1977) *The History of Scottish Literature*

Leopold, J. (1980) 'The Levellers Revolt in Galloway in 1724' in the *Scottish Labour History Society Journal*

Lloyd George, D. (1938) *War Memoirs*

Lockhart, J. G. (1839) *Memoirs of the Life of Sir Walter Scott*

Lynch, M. (1981) *Edinburgh and the Reformation*

Lythe, S. G. E. and Butt, J. (1975) *An Economic History of Scotland 1100–1939*

Macaulay, T. B. Lord. (1828) *History,* Edinburgh Review, xvii (1849) *History of England*

McCrie, T. (1899) *Life of Andrew Melville, 2 vols*

McCrone, D. (1989) 'Representing Scotland: culture and nationalism' in McCrone, D., Kendrick, S., and Straw, P. (eds.) *The Making of Scotland: nation, culture and social change*

MacCulloch, J. (1824) *The Highlands and Western Isles of Scotland*

Macdougall, N. (ed.) (1984) (ed.) *Church, Politics, and Society, Scotland 1408–1929*

MacInnes, J. (1981) 'Gaelic poetry and historical tradition; in MacLean, L. (ed.), *The Middle Ages in the Highlands*
(1989) 'The Gaelic perception of the Lowlands' in Gillies (1989)

MacKenzie, Agnes M. (1949) *Scottish Pageant*

McKinlay, A. (1991) '"Doubtful wisdom or uncertain promise": strategy, ideology & organisation, 1918–1922' in *The ILP on Clydeside 1893–1932,* eds McKinlay, A. & Morris, R

Mackie, J. D. (1964) *A History of Scotland*

Mackintosh, J. (1895) *The History of Civilisation in Scotland Vol IV*

McLean, I. (1983) *The Legend of Red Clydeside*

MacLean, M., and Carrell, C. (eds.) (1986) *As an Fhearann: From the land*

MacMillan, D. (1967) *Scotland and Australia 1788–1850. Emigration, Commerce and Investment*

MacMillan, D. (1986) *Painting in Scotland: the Golden Age*

McRoberts, D. (ed.) (1962) *Essays on the Scottish Reformation*

Makey, W. (1979) *The Church of the Covenant*

Marshall, G. (1980), *Presbyteries and Profits. Calvinism and the Development of Capitalism in Scotland, 1560–1707*

Marshall, R. (1983) *Virgins and Viragos*

Marwick, A. (1970) *The Nature of History*

Marwick, W. H. (1936) *Economic Developments in Victorian Scotland*
(1967) *A Short History of Labour in Scotland*

Mathieson, W. L. (1916) *Church and Reform in Scotland*

Meikle, H. W. (1912) *Scotland and the French Revolution*

Melling, J. (1990) 'Whatever Happened to Red Clydeside?' *International Review of Social History*
(1991) 'Work, Culture & Politics on "Red Clydeside"' in *The ILP on Clydesdale 1893–1932,* eds. McKinlay, A & Morris, R

Middlemass, K. (1963) *The Clydesiders*
(1979) *The Politics of Industrial Society*
Millar, J. (1803) *Historical View of the English Government*
Miller, K. (1975) *Cockburn's Millennium*
Milton, N. (1978) *John Maclean*
Mingay, G. E. (1989) *The Unquiet Countryside*
Ministry of Munitions (1920) *Official History* HMSO Copy in Public
Records Office, Kew
Mitchell, D. (1900) *History of the Highlands and Gaelic Scotland*
Mitchison, R. (1970) *A History of Scotland*
(1980) 'Nineteenth century Scottish Nationalism: the cultural back-
ground' in Mitchison, R. (ed.) *The Roots of Nationalism studies in
northern Europe*
(1983) *Lordship to Patronage*
Mitchison, R. M. and Roebuck, P. (eds.) (1988) *Economy and Society in
Scotland and Ireland 1500–1939*
(1989), with Leneman, L. *Sexuality and Social Control: Scotland,
1600–1780*
Morton, A. L. (1938) *A People's History of England*
Moss, M. and Hume, J. R. (1981) *The Making of Scotch Whisky. A
History of the Scotch Distilling Industry*
Mossner, E. C. (1980) *The Life of David Hume*
Munro, R. W. *Taming the Rough Bounds: Knoydart 1745–1784*
Murdoch, A. (1980) *The People Above*
Mure Mackenzie, A. (1941) *Scotland in Modern Times*
Nairn, T. (1988) *The Enchanted Glass: Britain and its Monarchy*
Nicolson, R. (1974) *The Later Middle Ages*
Noble, A. (1985) 'Urbane silence: Scottish writing and the nineteenth
century city' in Gordon, G. (ed.), *Perspectives of the Scottish City*
Okun, H. (1967) 'Ossian in Painting' *Journal of the Warburg and
Courtauld Institutes*
Payne, P. L. (1979) *Colvilles and the Scottish Steel Industry*
(1980) *The Early Scottish Limited Companies 1856–1895. An
Historical and Analytical Survey*
Pelling, H. (1963) *History of British Trade Unionism*
Percy, E. (1937) *John Knox*
Phillipson, N. T. (1973) 'Towards a Definition of the Scottish Enlighten-
ment' *City and Society in the 18th Century*, eds P. Fritz and D.
Williams
Prebble, J. (1988) *The King's Jaunt: George IV in Scotland, 1822*
Prentis, M. (1983) *The Scots in Australia. A Study of New South Wales,
Victoria and Queensland, 1788–1900*, Sydney University Press
(1987) *The Scottish in Australia* (Australian Ethnic Heritage Series)
Pringle, T. R. (1988) 'The privation of history: Landseer, Victoria and the
Highland myth' in Cosgrove, D. and Daniels, S. (eds.), *The Iconogra-
phy of Landscape*

Pryde, G. S. (1962) *Scotland from 1603 to the Present Day*

Ramsay, D. (1873) *Reminiscences of Scottish Life and Character*

Reid, A. (1985) 'Trade Unionism and the State in Britain during the First World War' in Tolliday, S. and Zeitlin, J. (eds.), *Shop Floor Bargaining and the State*

Reid, W. S. (1974) *Trumpeter of God*

Reynolds, S. (1989) *Brittanica's Typesetters. Women Compositors in Edinburgh*

Richards, E. (1982) *A History of the Highland Clearances Volume 1: agrarian transformation and the evictions*
(1985) *A History of the Highland Clearances Volume 2: emigration, protest, reasons*

Ridley, J. (1968) *John Knox*

Riley, P. W. J. (1964) *The English Ministers and Scotland*

Robertson, W. (1759) *History of Scotland*

Rosie, G. (1981) *Hugh Miller: Outrage and Order*
(1989) 'How rampant Highlandism created a new history' *Observer Scotland* (8 January)

Rudé, G. (1964) *The Crowd in History, 1730–1848*

Sanderson, M. (1982) *Scottish Rural Society in the Sixteenth Century*

Scott, J. and Hughes, M. (1980) *The Anatomy of Scottish Capital. Scottish Companies and Scottish Capital, 1900–1979*

Scott, W. R. (1932) *Economic Survey of South West Scotland*

Shaw, D. (1964) *The General Assemblies of the Church of Scotland, 1560–1600*

Shaw, J. S. (1983) *The Management of Scottish Society 1707–1764. Power, Nobles, Lawyers, Edinburgh Agents and English Influences*

Shinwell, E. (1973) *I've Lived through it all*

Sims-Williams, P. (1986) 'The Visionary Celt: the construction of an ethnic preoccupation', *Cambridge Medieval Celtic Studies*

Skelley, J. (1976) *The General Strike*

Slaven, A. (1975) *The Development of the West of Scotland: 1750–1960*

Slaven, A. and Checkland, S. (eds) (1986) *Dictionary of Scottish Business Biography 1860–1960. Vol. 1. The Staple Industries*
(1990), *Vol. 2. Processing, Distribution, Services*

Smith, A. G. R. (ed.) (1973) (ed.) *The Reign of James VI and I*

Smout, T. C. (1969) *A History of the Scottish People 1560–1830*
(1983) 'Tours in the Scottish Highlands from the eighteenth to the twentieth centuries' *Northern Scotland*
(1986) *A Century of the Scottish People 1830–1950*

Spottiswoode, J. (1851) *History of the Church of Scotland*

Stafford, F. (1988) *The Sublime Savage: A Study of James MacPherson and The Poems of Ossian*

Starr, M. (1927) *A Worker Looks at History*

Stevenson, D. *The Scottish Revolution, 1637–44, 1973*
(1977) *Revolution and Counter-Revolution in Scotland 1644–51*

(1981) *Scottish Covenanters and Irish Confederates*
(1982) (ed.) *The Government of Scotland under the Covenanters*
(1988) *The Origins of Freemasonry: Scotland's Century 1590–(1710)*
Stevenson, J. (1979) *Popular Disturbances in England, 1700–1870*
Strawhorn, J. (1985) *The History of Irvine*
Telfer Dunbar, J. (1962) *History of Highland Dress*
Thomas, K. (1983) *Man and the Natural World: changing attitudes in England 1500–1800*
Thompson, E. P. (1974) *The Poverty of Theory*
(1974) 'Patrician Society, Plebeian Culture', *Journal of Social History*
Tilly, L. A. and C. (1981) *Class, Conflict and Collective Action*
Trevor Roper, H. (1967) 'The Scottish Enlightenment' *Studies in Voltaire and the Eighteenth Century LVIII*
(1983) 'The invention of tradition: the Highland tradition of Scotland' in Hobsbawm, E., and Trevor-Roper, H. (eds.) *The Invention of Tradition*
Whatley, C. A. (1987a) 'A governable people? A preliminary survey of popular attitudes to authority and change in eighteenth century Scotland', in *Dissent, Protest and Rebellion in Pre-Industrial Scotland*
(1987b) '"The Fettering Bonds of Brotherhood": combination and labour relations in the Scottish coal mining industry, c. 1693–1775', *Social History*
(1989) 'Economic Causes and Consequences of the Union of 1707: A Survey', *Scottish Historical Review*
(1990) 'How tame were the Scottish Lowlanders during the Eighteenth Century?', in Devine (1990)
Whittington, G. and Gibson, A. J. S. (1986) *The Military Survey of Scotland 1747–1755: a critique* Historical Geography Research Series 18, Lancaster
Whyte, I. D. (1977) *Agriculture and Society in Seventeenth Century Scotland*
Wiener, M. (1982) *English culture and the decline of the industrial spirit 1850–1980*
Winslow, C. (1975) 'Sussex Smugglers', in D. Hay (et. al., eds.) *Albion's Fatal Tree*
Withers, C. W. J. (1984) *Gaelic in Scotland 1698–1981: the geographical history of a language*
(1988) *Gaelic Scotland: the transformation of a culture region*
Womack, P. (1989) *Improvement and Romance: constructing the myth of the Highlands*
Wormald, J. (1981) *Court, King and Community*
Wright, P. (1985) *On Living in an Old Country: the national past in contemporary Britain*
Wrightson, K. (1988) 'Kindred adjoining kingdoms: an English perspective on the social and economic history of early modern Scotland;' in Houston and Whyte, (1989)

Young, J. D. (1979) *The Rousing of the Scottish Working Class*
   (1985) *Women and Popular Struggles*
Youngson, A. J. (1973) *After the Forty-Five*
   (1974) *Beyond the Highland Line*
   (1985) *The Prince and the Pretender: A Study in the Writing of History*

Notes on Contributors

Angus Calder is Reader in Literature and Cultural Studies at The Open University in Scotland. He has recently edited (with William Donnelly) a new Penguin Edition of the poems of Robert Burns and his latest book, *The Myth of the Blitz,* continues his long-standing interest in the Second World War.

Ian Donnachie is Senior Lecturer in History at The Open University in Scotland and is co-editor (with Christopher Harvie and Ian S. Wood) of *Forward! Labour Politics in Scotland 1888–1988,* also in the Determinations Series. He is currently working (with George Hewitt) on a history of New Lanark.

John Foster is Professor of Applied Social Studies at Paisley College of Technology and author of the acclaimed book, *Class Struggle and the Industrial Revolution,* as well as numerous other works on the history of class and politics.

Michael Fry, the well-known journalist, broadcaster and historian, is author of *Patronage and Principle: a Political History of Modern Scotland.* He has recently completed a major new biography of Henry Dundas.

Joy Hendry, poet, writer and broadcaster, is editor of *Chapman,* one of Scotland's leading literary journals. She is currently Writer in Residence in Stirling.

George Hewitt lectures in History at Langside College, Glasgow, and is author of *Scotland Under Morton*, a major study of the Regency, and also (with Ian Donnachie) of *A Companion to Scottish History*.

George Rosie, the distinguished journalist, writer and broadcaster, has a long-standing interest in Scottish historical controversies. He is author of a major study of Hugh Miller.

Christopher A. Whatley is a Lecturer in Scottish History at the University of St Andrews. Author of a book on *The Scottish Salt Industry*, he is currently working on a study of Scottish social history in the eighteenth century.

Charles W. J. Withers is Principal Lecturer in Geography at Cheltenham and Gloucester College of Higher Education, who has made a special study of the Scottish Highlands. His many publications include *Gaelic Scotland: The Transformation of a Culture Region*.

Index